Excel

Revise in a Month

Year 7
NAPLAN*-style Tests

PASCAL
PRESS

* This is not an officially endorsed publication of the NAPLAN program and is produced by Pascal Press independently of Australian governments.

Alan Horsfield & Allyn Jones

© 2010 Alan Horsfield, Allyn Jones and Pascal Press
Reprinted 2011
Revised for NAPLAN Test changes 2011
New NAPLAN Test question formats added 2012
Reprinted 2015
Conventions of Language questions updated 2016
Reprinted 2017, 2018, 2019

Revised in 2020 for the NAPLAN Online tests

Reprinted 2020, 2021 (twice), 2022, 2023, 2024

ISBN 978 1 74125 209 5

Pascal Press
PO Box 250
Glebe NSW 2037
(02) 9198 1748
www.pascalpress.com.au

Publisher: Vivienne Joannou
Project Editor: Mark Dixon
Edited by Rema Gnanadickam, Mark Dixon and Rosemary Peers
Proofread by Peter Little and Dale Little
Answers checked by Peter Little, Dale Little and Maya Puiu
Typeset by Precision Typesetting (Barbara Nilsson) and Grizzly Graphics (Leanne Richters)
Cover and page design by DiZign Pty Ltd
Printed by Vivar Printing/Green Giant Press

Acknowledgements
Perfect Timing by Jeremy Fisher, HBJ, 1992
Through the web and other stories by Ian Steep, HBJ, 1992
The Sylvia Mystery by Penny Hall, HBJ, 1992

NAPLAN is a trademark of Australian Curriculum, Assessment and Reporting Authority (ACARA).

Disclaimer
While information in this book is correct at the time of going to press, students should
check the official NAPLAN website and ask their teachers about the exact requirements or
content of the tests for which they are sitting, as this may change from year to year.

All efforts have been made to obtain permission for the copyright material reproduced in this book. In the event of any oversight,
the publisher welcomes any information that will enable rectification of any reference or credit in subsequent editions.

The publisher thanks the Royal Australian Mint for granting permission to use Australian currency coin designs in this book.

Notice of liability
The information contained in this book is distributed without warranty. While precautions have been taken in the preparation
of this material, neither the authors nor Pascal Press shall have any liability to any person or entity with respect to any liability,
loss or damage caused or alleged to be caused directly or indirectly by the instructions and content contained in the book.

Contents

WHAT IS NAPLAN?

- NAPLAN stands for National Assessment Program—Literacy and Numeracy.
- It is conducted every year in March and the tests are taken by students in Years 3, 5, 7 and 9.
- The tests cover Literacy—Reading, Writing, Conventions of Language (spelling, grammar and punctuation)—and Numeracy.

WHAT IS NAPLAN ONLINE?

Introduction

- In the past all NAPLAN tests were paper tests.
- From 2022 all students have taken the NAPLAN tests online.
- This means students complete the NAPLAN tests on a computer or tablet.

Tailored test design

- With NAPLAN paper tests, all students in each year level took exactly the same tests.
- In the NAPLAN Online tests this isn't the case; instead, every student takes a tailor-made test based on their ability.
- Please visit the official ACARA site for a detailed explanation of the tailored test process used in NAPLAN Online and also for general information about the tests: https://nap.edu.au/online-assessment.
- These tailor-made tests mean broadly, therefore, that a student who is at a standard level of achievement takes a test mostly comprised of questions of a standard level; a student who is at an intermediate level of achievement takes a test mostly comprised of questions of an intermediate level; and a student who is at an advanced level of achievement takes a test mostly comprised of questions of an advanced level.

Different question types

- Because of the digital format, NAPLAN Online contains more question types than in the paper tests. In the paper tests there are only multiple-choice and short-answer question types. In NAPLAN Online, however, there are also other question types. For example, students might be asked to drag text across a screen, measure a figure with an online ruler or listen to an audio recording of a sentence and then spell a word they hear.
- Please refer to the next page to see some examples of these additional question types that are found in NAPLAN Online and how they compare to questions in this book. As you will see, the content tested is exactly the same but the questions are presented differently.

NAPLAN Online question types

Additional NAPLAN Online question types	Equivalent questions in this book
Drag and drop Danielle wrote numbers on five different cards. 1^5 3^2 2^3 4^2 2^2 Rearrange the cards from smallest to largest. ☐ ☐ ☐ ☐ ☐ smallest largest	Arrange the following from smallest to largest: 1^5 3^2 2^3 4^2 2^2 A B C D E ☐ ☐ ☐ ☐ ☐ smallest largest
Online ruler The diagram shows an angle. Use the online protractor to measure the size of the angle. The size of the angle is ☐ degrees.	What is the size of the angle marked by the arrow? A 40° B 70° C 110° D 140°
Text entry Time at the _____ centre is time well spent! Click on the play button to listen to the missing word. ▌▌ ◀)) ——●———— 0.08 / 0.09 Type the correct spelling of the word in the box. ☐	Please ask your parent or teacher to read to you the spelling words on page 247. Write the correct spelling of each word in the box. <table><tr><th>Word</th><th>Example</th></tr><tr><td>1. leisure</td><td>Time at the leisure centre is time well spent!</td></tr></table> ☐
Drag and drop Drag these events to show the order in which they happened in the text. Use the tab to read the text. 1 ☐ 2 ☐ 3 ☐ 4 ☐ Bosley is discovered under a table. Bosley passes by the Indian Curry Palace. Bosley rejects the thought of eating a hamburger. Bosley ventures into a restaurant with French cuisine.	Write the numbers 1, 2, 3 and 4 in the boxes to show the order in which action occurs. ☐ Bosley is discovered under a table. ☐ Bosley passes by the Indian Curry Palace. ☐ Bosley rejects the thought of eating a hamburger. ☐ Bosley ventures into a restaurant with French cuisine.

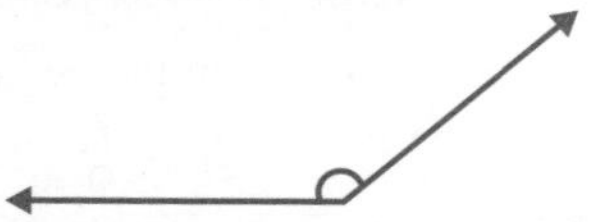

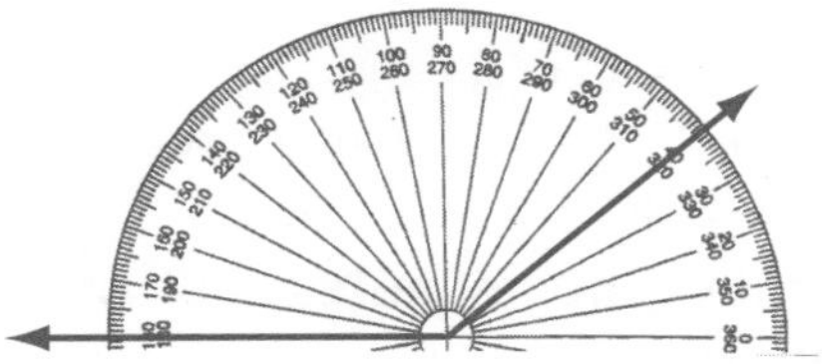

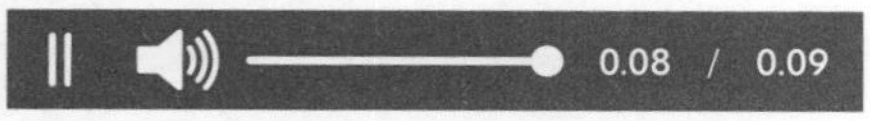

Maximise your results in NAPLAN Online

STEP 1: USE THIS BOOK

How *Excel* has updated this book to help you revise

Tailored test design

- We can't replicate the digital experience in book form and offer you tailored tests, but with this series we do provide Intermediate and Advanced NAPLAN Online–style Literacy and Numeracy tests

- This means that a student using these tests will be able to prepare with confidence for tests at different ability levels.

- This makes it excellent preparation for the tailored NAPLAN Online Literacy and Numeracy tests.

Remember the advantages of revising in book form

There are many benefits to a child revising using books for the online test:

- One of the most important benefits is that writing on paper will help your child retain information. It can be a very effective way to memorise. High-quality educational research shows that using a keyboard is not as good as note-taking for learning.

- Students will be able to prepare thoroughly for topic revision using books and then practise computer skills easily. They will only succeed with sound knowledge of topics; this requires study and focus. Students will not succeed in tests simply because they know how to answer questions digitally.

- Also, some students find it easier to concentrate when reading a page in a book than when reading on a screen.

- Furthermore it can be more convenient to use a book, especially when a child doesn't have ready access to a digital device.

- You can be confident that *Excel* books will help students acquire the topic knowledge they need, as we have over 30 years experience in helping students prepare for tests. All our writers are experienced educators.

STEP 2: PRACTISE ON *Excel Test Zone*

How *Excel Test Zone* can help you practise online

We recommend you go to www.exceltestzone. com.au and register for practice in NAPLAN Online–style tests once you have completed this book. The reasons include:

- for optimal performance in the NAPLAN Online tests we recommend students gain practice at completing online tests as well as completing revision in book form

- students should practise answering questions on a digital device to become confident with this process

- students will be able to practise tailored tests like those in NAPLAN Online, as well as other types of tests

- students will also be able to gain valuable practice in onscreen skills such as dragging and dropping answers, using an online ruler to measure figures and using an online protractor to measure angles.

Remember that *Excel Test Zone* has been helping students prepare for NAPLAN since 2009; in fact we had NAPLAN online questions even before NAPLAN tests went online!

We also have updated our website along with our book range to ensure your preparation for NAPLAN Online is 100% up to date.

About the NAPLAN tests and this book

ABOUT THE TESTS

Test results

- The test results are used by teachers as a diagnostic tool. The results provide students, parents and teachers with information that can be used to improve student learning.

- The student report provides information about what students know and can do in the areas of Reading, Writing, Conventions of Language (spelling, grammar and punctuation) and the various strands of Numeracy. It also provides information on how each student has performed in relation to other students in their year group and against the national average and the national minimum standard.

- NAPLAN tests are not aptitude or intelligence tests. They focus on what has been achieved, especially on the knowledge and skills taught in the syllabus. These are often called KLAs (key learning areas).

- Official tests are trialled on selected groups to test the reliability of the questions. The questions in this book are representative of questions that you can expect to find in an official test. They have been prepared by professionals who have an understanding of teaching and of testing procedures.

- The NAPLAN results present an objective view of student performance and form the basis from which schools can make informed educational decisions about further school learning programs.

- Because NAPLAN tests are national tests they provide authorities with sufficient information to track student educational development from primary to high school, or when transferring from one Australian school to another.

TYPES OF TESTS

- There are four different types of tests in Year 7 NAPLAN Online.
  1 The Numeracy test (65 minutes)
  2 The Conventions of Language test (45 minutes)
  3 The Reading test (65 minutes)
  4 The Writing test (42 minutes)
  Tests 2–4 form the Literacy component of the test.

- The Writing test is held first, followed by the Reading test, the Conventions of Language test and finally the Numeracy test.

USING THIS BOOK

- This book is designed to be used over four weeks, with weekly exercises in various aspects of literacy and numeracy.

- Each session gives students an opportunity to Test their Skills, revise Key Points and practise a Real Test on a specific aspect of the curriculum.

- In a month the student will have covered much of the material that could be included in a NAPLAN Online test.

- Finally there are two Sample Test Papers based on the content used in past Year 7 NAPLAN test papers.

- Because NAPLAN tests are timed tests, times have been suggested for completing the various units in this book.

Week

1

This is what we cover this week:

Day 1   **Number and Algebra:** ◎ Whole numbers
                                ◎ Addition and subtraction
                                ◎ Multiplication and division

Day 2   **Spelling:** ◎ Making plurals from nouns
                    ◎ Common misspellings

            Grammar and punctuation: ◎ Types of sentences and articles

Day 3   **Reading:** ◎ Understanding narratives

Day 4   **Writing:** ◎ Persuasive texts
                  ◎ Recounts

Test Your Skills

NUMBER AND ALGEBRA
Whole numbers

20 MIN

1 What is the place value of the 3 in 4307?
A 3 ones   B 3 tens
C 3 hundreds   D 3 thousands

2 What number is three hundred and seven thousand and forty?
A 307 040   B 307 400
C 374 000   D 30 740

3 Which of the following is the smallest?
A 907   B 3416
C 2001   D 99

4 Which of these numbers is between 3^2 and 5^2?
A 4   B 8   C 10   D 27

5 Which of these is **not** true?
A 40 > 16   B 32 < 321
C 16 ≤ 32   D 18 > 19

6 What is 753 rounded off to the nearest ten?
A 70   B 80
C 750   D 760

7 2873 to the nearest hundred is
A 29.   B 290.
C 2800.   D 2900.

8 191 + 326 + 708 is closest to
A 100 + 300 + 700.
B 200 + 300 + 700.
C 200 + 400 + 800.
D 200 + 400 + 700.

9 What number is the arrow pointing to?

```
  ┼───┼───┼───┼───┼───┼───┼
          0   1   2   3
```

A 3   B −1
C −2   D −3

10 What number is the arrow pointing to?

```
  ┼───┼───┼───┼───┼───┼───┼
 −8  −6  −4  −2   0   2   4   6   8
```

A −9   B −7
C −5   D −3

11 Which of these is a multiple of 8?
A 4   B 16
C 18   D 81

12 Which of these is the lowest common multiple (LCM) of 8 and 10?
A 18   B 20
C 24   D 40

13 Which of these numbers is **not** a factor of 20?
A 4   B 5
C 8   D 10

14 How many factors does the number 30 have?
A 3   B 15
C 6   D 8

15 Which of the following is a prime number?
A 4   B 25
C 31   D 39

16 Which of these is the highest common factor (HCF) of 10 and 16?
A 2   B 4
C 5   D 8

17 Which of the following is a composite number?
A 13   B 15
C 23   D 29

18 Which of the following is not a square number?
A 16   B 36
C 63   D 81

19 How many zeros are there in one hundred million?
A 2   B 6
C 7   D 8

☞ **Explanations on page 183**

Key Points

NUMBER AND ALGEBRA
Whole numbers

1 **Place value** is the value of a digit depending on its position in the numeral, whether in the millions, hundred thousands, ten thousands, thousands, hundreds, tens or units (ones) place.
Example: What is the place value of 4 in 34 906?
The 4 is 4000 or four thousands.

2 **Expanded notation** is the manner of writing numerals in an expanded form showing the place value of each digit.
Example: Rewrite 32 070 in expanded form.
$$32\ 070 = 3 \times 10\,000 + 2 \times 1000$$
$$+ 0 \times 100 + 7 \times 10 + 0 \times 1$$

3 Numbers can be written in order of size: either in **ascending** (increasing) **or descending** (decreasing) **order**
Example: Rewrite 67, 7, 640, 604 in ascending order. The order is 7, 67, 604, 640.

4 **Signs** used in mathematics include:
= is equal to   < is less than
> is greater than   ≤ is less than or equal to
≥ is greater than or equal to
Examples: Write true or false:
a 324 > 299   true as 324 is greater than 299
b 32 ≥ 91   false as 32 is not greater than or equal to 91

5 When numbers are to be **rounded off** or estimated we use this process:
• less than 5 (0, 1, 2, 3, 4) round down
• 5 or more (5, 6, 7, 8, 9) round up
Examples:
a Round off 246 to the nearest ten.
The 6 in 246 means the answer is 250.
b Estimate 68 324 to the nearest thousand.
The 3 in 68 324 means the answer is 68 000.
[Note 68 000 is sometimes written as 68K.]

6 **Negative numbers** are used when describing very cold temperatures (–10 °C), in golf (–2), etc. The number line is extended to the left.

–4 –3 –2 –1 0 1 2 3

Example: Locate –6 on a number line.

–8 –7 –6 –5 –4 –3 –2 –1

7 If a number is multiplied by a second number, then a **multiple** is formed. When multiples of two or more numbers are listed, a **lowest common multiple (LCM)** can be found.
Examples:
a Write the first five multiples of 3:
3: 3, 6, 9, 12, 15
b What is the LCM of 4 and 6?
4: 4, 8, **12**, 16, 20, …
6: 6, **12**, 18, …   The LCM is 12.

8 **Factors** are numbers that divide evenly into a given number. This means there is no remainder. If two or more numbers have the same factor it is called a common factor and we often find the **highest common factor (HCF)** of two or more numbers.
Examples:
a Write the factors of 12.
12: 1, 2, 3, 4, 6, 12
b What is the HCF of 18 and 24?
Factors of 18: 1, 2, 3, **6**, 9, 18
Factors of 24: 1, 2, 3 ,4 ,**6**, 8, 12, 24
The HCF is 6.

9 A **prime number** has only 2 factors: 1 and itself. A **composite number** has more than 2 factors. 0 and 1 are not considered prime or composite.
Examples:
a Is 21 a prime or composite number?
Factors of 21 are 1, 3, 7, 21.
This means 21 is a composite number.
b Write the first ten prime numbers.
2, 3, 5, 7, 11, 13, 17, 19, 23, 29

10 **Square numbers** are
$1^2 = 1 \times 1 = 1$ $2^2 = 2 \times 2 = 4$
$3^2 = 3 \times 3 = 9$ $4^2 = 4 \times 4 = 16$
Here are the first 10 square numbers:
1, 4, 9, 16, 25, 36, 49, 64, 81, 100
Example: What is 7^2? $7^2 = 7 \times 7 = 49$

11 Large numbers that are multiples of 10 are referred to as **powers of 10**.
$10^2 = 10 \times 10 = 100$ (hundred)
$10^3 = 10 \times 10 \times 10 = 1000$ (thousand)
$10^6 = 10 \times 10 \times 10 \times 10 \times 10 \times 10$
= 1 000 000 (million)
$10^9 = 1\ 000\ 000\ 000$ (billion)
$10^{12} = 1\ 000\ 000\ 000\ 000$ (trillion)
The number of zeros indicates the number in the 'power'.
Example: Write 10^5?
$10^5 = 100\ 000$ (5 zeros)

Real Test

NUMBER AND ALGEBRA
Whole numbers

1 What is the number one hundred and sixty million in numbers? *Hint 1*
- **A** 1 600 000
- **B** 1 060 000
- **C** 160 000 000
- **D** 1 060 000 000

2 Another way of writing 3^2 is
- **A** 3×3.
- **B** 3×2.
- **C** $3 + 3$.
- **D** $2 \times 2 \times 2$.

3 What number is greater than 602?
- **A** 63
- **B** 601
- **C** 73
- **D** 610

4 The population of a town is six thousand four hundred and eight.

Which number shows this population?
- **A** 6480
- **B** 6408
- **C** 6048
- **D** 60 408

5 Simpson's Butchery made a profit of $237 509 last year. How much is this amount to the nearest ten thousand dollars? *Hint 2*
- **A** $230 000
- **B** $237 000
- **C** $238 000
- **D** $240 000

6 Arrange the following from smallest to largest:

1^5	3^2	2^3	4^2	2^2

smallest   **largest**

7

Phillip used the cards to make a four-digit number. What was the smallest even number that Phillip could make?

Write the number in the box: ☐

8 Which arrow is pointing to the number –5? *Hint 3*

```
  -8  -6  -4  -2   0   2   4   6   8
          A  B          C  D
```

9 Which of these is **not** a factor of 18? Select **all** the correct answers.

1	4	8	9	18
A	**B**	**C**	**D**	**E**

10 What number is the arrow pointing to?

```
   30  34  38  42 ↑ 46  50  54  58
```
- **A** 43
- **B** 44
- **C** 48
- **D** 49

11 Which number is 36 709?
- **A** thirty thousand, six hundred and seventy nine
- **B** thirty-six thousand, seven hundred and ninety
- **C** thirty-six thousand, seven hundred and nine
- **D** thirty thousand, seven hundred and nine

12

326	276	830	545

Jarrod placed the cards in ascending order.

What number goes here? *Hint 4*

		↑	

- **A** 326
- **B** 276
- **C** 830
- **D** 545

13 Which of these is the closest estimate to 38×73?
- **A** 40×70
- **B** 30×70
- **C** 30×80
- **D** 40×80

14 Between what two numbers is 9^2?
- **A** 2 and 4
- **B** 8 and 10
- **C** 70 and 80
- **D** 80 and 90

15 Sahil wrote the number 452. If he placed a zero after the 2, the new number is
- **A** 10 more than 452.
- **B** 10 less than 452.
- **C** 10 times larger than 452.
- **D** 10 times smaller than 452.

16 Which of these is a multiple of 9? Select **all t**he correct answers.

19	45	108	378	993
A	**B**	**C**	**D**	**E**

Hint 1: Remember place value.
Hint 2: Rounding off rules: less than 5 round down; 5 or more round up.
Hint 3: The number line extends to the left for the negative numbers.
Hint 4: Ascending order runs from smallest to largest.

☞**Answers and explanations on page 183**

NUMBER AND ALGEBRA
Addition and subtraction

1 What is the sum of 57 and 4?
A 60   B 61   C 62   D 97

2 From 95, count forward by 12. What is the answer?
A 97   B 103   C 107   D 117

3 Increase 620 by 68. What is the answer?
A 668   B 688
C 698   D 708

4 What is the difference between 42 and 16?
A 24   B 26   C 32   D 36

5 By how much does 100 exceed 45?
A 45   B 55
C 65   D 145

6 What is 53 + 83 + 175?
A 208   C 301
C 311   D 313

7 What is the answer?

$$
\begin{array}{r}
129 \\
209 \\
21 \\
+ \ 100 \\
\hline
\end{array}
$$

A 449   B 458
C 459   D 1550

8 What number is subtracted from 20 to give 13?
A 5   B 6   C 7   D 8

9 A DVD costs $19. How much change is received from $50?
A $31   B $41   C $59   D $69

10 Find the answer:

$$
\begin{array}{r}
7639 \\
1386 \\
+ \ 3910 \\
\hline
\end{array}
$$

A 12 195   B 12 935
C 13 035   D 13 145

11 Complete:

$$
\begin{array}{r}
340 \\
- \ 129 \\
\hline
\end{array}
$$

A 211   B 221
C 229   D 231

12 100 − 78 =
A 12   B 32
C 23   D 22

13 Subtract 32 from 88. The answer is
A 46.   B 50.
C 55.   D 56.

14 Take 440 from 1000. The answer is
A 450.   B 560.
C 660.   D 1440.

15 What is added to 73 to make 100?
A 13   B 17
C 23   D 27

16 Find:

$$
\begin{array}{r}
1000 \\
- \ 327 \\
\hline
\end{array}
$$

A 573   B 583
C 673   D 683

17 Subtract 811 from 1000. The answer is
A 89.   B 189.
C 199.   D 209.

18 From 48 Liam counted backwards to 17. How many did Liam count back?
A 21   B 29
C 31   D 39

19 Find:

$$
\begin{array}{r}
3000 \\
- \ 1283 \\
\hline
\end{array}
$$

A 1717   B 1817   C 2817   D 2827

20 25 − 3 − 5 − 2 − 6 − 2 =
A 7   B 8   C 9   D 10

☞**Explanations on page 184**

Key Points

NUMBER AND ALGEBRA
Addition and subtraction

❶ We use special words and symbols to represent **mathematical operations**:

+ : **add**, sum, total, increase

− : **subtract**, minus, difference, decrease

Example: Write in symbols 'The sum of five and eight is less than the difference between eighteen and two': $5 + 8 < 18 − 2$

❷ When adding numbers look for shortcuts by **grouping numbers** that add to 10.

Example: $7 + 8 + 2 + 6 + 3$
$$= \underline{7 + 3} + \underline{8 + 2} + 6$$
$$= 10 + 10 + 6$$
$$= 26$$

❸ When adding two-digit numbers look for a strategy that **adds the tens and the units separately**.

Examples: a $\quad 32 + 43 = 32 + 40 + 3$
$$= 72 + 3$$
$$= 75$$
b $\quad 25 + 19 = 25 + 20 − 1$
$$= 45 − 1$$
$$= 44$$

❹ When **adding numbers written in columns** make sure to **add them in the correct place values**.

Example: $326 + 284 + 35$

$$\begin{array}{r} {}^1 3\, {}^1 2\ 6 \\ 2\ 8\ 4 \\ +\quad 3\ 5 \\ \hline 6\ 4\ 5 \end{array}$$

Write numbers in columns with the correct place value under each other. Starting with the units, $6 + 4 + 5$ is 15. Put down the 5, and then the 1 is included in the tens column: $1 + 2 + 8 + 3 = 14$. Put down the 4, and then the 1 is included in the hundreds column: $1 + 3 + 2 = 6$. The final answer is 645.

❺ When **subtracting numbers** look for any shortcuts.

Examples: a $\quad 48 − 15 = 48 − 10 − 5$
$$= 38 − 5$$
$$= 33$$
b $\quad 65 − 19 = 65 − 20 + 1$
$$= 45 + 1$$
$$= 46$$

❻ When **subtracting large numbers** rewrite them in columns. There are different subtraction methods—the examples below are of the **decomposition method**.

Examples:

a $\quad 75 − 39$

$$\begin{array}{r} {}^6\cancel{7}\ {}^1 5 \\ −\ 3\ 9 \\ \hline 3\ 6 \end{array}$$

Write numbers in columns with the correct place value under each other. Start with units: 5 minus 9 means the 5 becomes a 15 and the 7 tens becomes 6 tens. So 15 minus 9 is 6. Now the tens: 6 minus 3 is 3. The answer is 36.

b $\quad 4792 − 1857$

$$\begin{array}{r} {}^3\cancel{4}\ {}^1 7\, {}^8\cancel{9}\ {}^1 2 \\ −\ 1\ 8\ 5\ 7 \\ \hline 2\ 9\ 3\ 5 \end{array}$$

Write numbers in columns with the correct place value under each other. Start with units: 2 minus 7 means the 2 becomes a 12 and the 9 tens becomes 8 tens. So 12 minus 7 is 5. Now the tens: 8 minus 5 is 3. Now the hundreds: 7 minus 8 means the 7 becomes 17 and the 4 thousands becomes 3 thousands. So 17 minus 8 is 9. Finally 3 minus 1 is 2. The answer is 2935.

c $\quad 1000 − 674$

$$\begin{array}{r} \cancel{1}\ {}^9\cancel{0}\ {}^9\cancel{0}\ {}^1 0 \\ −\quad 6\ 7\ 4 \\ \hline 3\ 2\ 6 \end{array}$$

Write numbers in columns with the correct place value under each other. [Firstly the 1000 will be rewritten as 9 hundreds, 9 tens and 10 units.] Start with units: 0 minus 4 means the 0 becomes a 10, and so on. So 10 minus 4 is 6. Now the tens: 9 minus 7 is 2. Now the hundreds: 9 minus 6 is 3. The answer is 326.

❼ The **inverse operation of addition is subtraction and vice versa**.

Examples:

a What must be added to 16 to get 42?
This question is $16 + \_\_\_ = 42$?
We can rewrite the number sentence using a subtraction: $42 − 16 = \_\_\_$.
This means the answer is 26.

b What number minus 18 gives an answer of 51?
As $\_\_\_ − 18 = 51$, we can change the question to $51 + 18 = \_\_\_$. This means the answer is 69.

Real Test

NUMBER AND ALGEBRA
Addition and subtraction

1 James bought a scooter for $79. How much change will he receive from $100?

A $11   B $21   C $29   D $31

2 In the box write the number which is 15 more than 67: ☐

3

| 24 | 15 | 33 | 48 | 60 |

Brendan notices that two of the numbers on the cards are odd. What is the sum of the odd numbers?

A 39   B 48   C 58   D 75

4 Lee's father is 18 years older than he is. If his father is 47 years old, how old is Lee?

A 19   B 21   C 29   D 31

5 53 add 20 minus 17. What is the answer?

A 50   B 56   C 63   D 67

6 What is 53 + 83 + 175? *Hint 1*

A 208   B 301   C 311   D 313

7 Which group of numbers gives a total which is between 60 and 70? *Hint 2*

A 7, 7, 7, 7, 7, 7   B 8, 8, 8, 8, 8, 8
C 9, 9, 9, 9, 9, 9   D 11, 11, 11, 11, 11, 11

8

Nicole bought a DVD for $19 and a magazine for $7. How much change did she receive from $40?

A $14   B $16   C $24   D $26

9 $1^2 + 2^2 + 3^2 + 4^2 =$

A 10   B 20   C 30   D 100

10 Graeme used the four cards to make the largest possible four-digit number and the smallest possible four-digit number. What is the difference between these numbers?

| 4 | 2 | 8 | 1 | *Hint 3*

A 7173   B 6499   C 8121   D 1999

11 Subtract 123 from 987.

Write your answer in the box: ☐

12 What is the sum of the square numbers less than 10?

A 13   B 14   C 15   D 16

13 In 1995 the population of Cooper's River was 6278. After 25 years the population increased by 3709. What was the population in 2020?

A 2573   B 9897   C 9978   D 9987

14 Renato bought a gelato for $5.20. She paid $10 and received the correct change. What is the least number of coins Renato could receive as change?

A 4   B 5   C 6   D 7

15 The table shows the distance Joseph cycled each day for 5 days. *Hint 4*

Day 1	13 km
Day 2	21 km
Day 3	18 km
Day 4	18 km
Day 5	21 km

What was the total distance cycled over the five days? Write your answer in this box:

☐ km

16 Start with 5420. Subtract 2000.

Add 1000. Subtract 3000. What is the new number?
Hint 5

☐

Hint 1: Rewrite the numbers in columns.
Hint 2: Try each of the choices.
Hint 3: The largest number has digits in descending order; the smallest number has digits in ascending order.
Hint 4: Always read carefully the titles of the rows and columns of a table so that you understand what the different rows and columns represent.
Hint 5: Look for shortcuts when adding or subtracting.

☞**Answers and explanations on pages 184–185**

NUMBER AND ALGEBRA
Multiplication and division

1 What is the product of 40 and 8?
  A 5   B 32   C 48   D 320

2 16 × 3 =
  A 38   B 48   C 54   D 56

3 Which of these does not give the same answer as 4 × 6?
  A 12 × 2   B 3 × 8   C 1 × 24   D 4 × 8

4 What is 8 lots of 6?
  A 48   B 54   C 60   D 64

5 What is 63 × 200?
  A 6300   B 1230
  C 12 600   D 13 200

6   275
       ×   8
  ───────────
  A 1660   B 1760
  C 1770   D 2200

7 What is the fourth multiple of 11?
  A 33   B 44
  C 55   D 66

8 Which of these is not a multiple of 9?
  A 90   B 108
  C 900   D 901

9 Find the value of 725 × 30.
  A 2175   B 2280
  C 21 750   D 23 200

10 What is 20 × 30 × 10?
  A 600   B 6000
  C 60 000   D 600 000

11   327
        ×   35
  ───────────
  A 11 445   B 12 445
  C 12 555   D 12 645

12 What is the remainder when 30 is divided by 4?
  A 0   B 1   C 2   D 3

13 Half of 24 times twice 3. What is the answer?
  A 64   B 72
  C 84   D 96

14 What is 755 ÷ 5?
  A 151   B 155
  C 161   D 165

15 Find $4\overline{)353}$

  A $80\frac{1}{4}$ B $80\frac{3}{4}$

  C $88\frac{1}{4}$ D $88\frac{3}{4}$

16 How many hundreds are in 23 900?
  A 23   B 239
  C 2390   D 2 390 000

17 What is a third of 423?
  A 41   B 108
  C 121   D 141

18 What is the average of 14, 15, 22 and 21?
  A 16   B 17   C 18   D 19

19 $5\overline{)647}$
  A 121.2   B 128.4
  C 129.2   D 129.4

20 Find the value of 20 ÷ 5 + 5 × 2.
  A 14   B 4   C 5   D 12

21 Find the value of 5 + 6 × 2.
  A 11   B 16   C 17   D 18

☞**Explanations on pages 184-185**

Answers: 1D 2B 3D 4A 5C 6D 7D 8D 9C 10B 11A 12C 13B 14A 15C 16B 17D 18C 19D 20A 21C

Key Points

NUMBER AND ALGEBRA
Multiplication and division

1 We use words and symbols to represent mathematical operations:

× : **multiply**, product

÷ : **divide**, quotient

Example: Write in symbols 'The product of six and three is greater than the quotient of twenty and ten'.

$6 × 3 > 20 ÷ 10$

2 We need to know our **times tables**:

×	1	2	3	4	5	6	7	8	9	10	11	12
1	1	2	3	4	5	6	7	8	9	10	11	12
2	2	4	6	8	10	12	14	16	18	20	22	24
3	3	6	9	12	15	18	21	24	27	30	33	36
4	4	8	12	16	20	24	28	32	36	40	44	48
5	5	10	15	20	25	30	35	40	45	50	55	60
6	6	12	18	24	30	36	42	48	54	60	66	72
7	7	14	21	28	35	42	49	56	63	70	77	84
8	8	16	24	32	40	48	56	64	72	80	88	96
9	9	18	27	36	45	54	63	72	81	90	99	108
10	10	20	30	40	50	60	70	80	90	100	110	120
11	11	22	33	44	55	66	77	88	99	110	121	132
12	12	24	36	48	60	72	84	96	108	120	132	144

3 The **multiples of a number** can be found by multiplying it by 1, 2, 3, 4, and so on.

Example: Write the first six multiples of 7.

7, 14, 21, 28, 35, 42

4 When we multiply whole numbers by **multiples of 10** we just place zeros at the end of the number.

Example: Evaluate $183 × 100$.

As 100 has 2 zeros, we place 2 zeros at the end.

This means $183 × 100 = 18\,300$.

5 We can **rewrite a multiplication using columns**.

Example: $136 × 4$

$$\begin{array}{r} 136 \\ \times _{12}4 \\ \hline 544 \end{array}$$

Write numbers in columns with the correct place value under each other. 4 times 6 is 24, put down the 4 units and the 2 tens will be added after we multiply 4 times 3, etc.

6 If a **number sentence involves mixed operations**, we **multiply or divide before we add or subtract**. When grouping symbols are involved they are calculated first.

Examples:

a Find the value: $7 + 2 × 3$

$$\begin{aligned} 7 + 2 × 3 &= 7 + 6 \\ &= 13 \end{aligned}$$

b Find the value: $12 + 2 × (30 ÷ 6)$

$$\begin{aligned} 12 + 2 × (30 ÷ 6) &= 12 + 2 × 5 \\ &= 12 + 10 \\ &= 22 \end{aligned}$$

7 When we multiply by a two-digit number we use **long multiplication**.

Example: $743 × 26$

$$\begin{array}{r} 743 \\ \times 26 \\ \hline 4458 \\ 14860 \\ \hline 19318 \end{array}$$

As $26 = 6 + 20$, in this question we will multiply by 6, then multiply by 20 and then add the answers together.

6 times 743 is 4458.

20 times 743 means put down a 0 and then multiply by 2. This answer is 14 860.

Now add the two answers (products) together.

8 When we divide whole numbers by **multiples of 10** we just remove any zeros at the end of the number.

Example:

Evaluate $20\,670 ÷ 10$.

As 10 has 1 zero, we take a zero off the end. This means $20\,670 ÷ 10 = 2067$.

9 A **division question** can be written in a number of ways: $25 ÷ 4$ or $\dfrac{25}{4}$ or $4\overline{)25}$.

Examples:

a $25 ÷ 4 = 6$ and remainder $1 = 6\frac{1}{4}$

b $263 ÷ 3$

3 goes into 26: 8 times with 2 left over. This 2 means we now have 3 going into 23 which is 7 with 2 left over. This means the

$$87\frac{2}{3}$$
$$3\overline{)26^23}$$

answer is 87 with remainder 2, or $87\frac{2}{3}$.

c $457 ÷ 2$

2 goes into 4: 2 times. Now 2 goes into 5 two times with 1 left over. This means we now have 2 going into 17 eight times with 1 left over. Putting down a decimal point and a zero we then have 2 going into 10 five times. This means the answer is 228.5.

$$228.5$$
$$2\overline{)45^17.^10}$$

10 The average is found by adding the quantities and dividing by the number of quantities.

Example: Find the average of 15, 8 and 7.

$$\text{Average} = \frac{15 + 8 + 7}{3} = \frac{30}{3} = 10$$

Real Test

NUMBER AND ALGEBRA
Multiplication and division

1 Ramnah puts 6 cakes on each of 4 plates. She has 2 left over. She wants to put 7 cakes on each of the plates. How many more cakes does she need?

2	5	7	8	9
A	**B**	**C**	**D**	**E**

2 The table shows the number of sit-ups five students could do.

Student	Number of sit-ups
Mark	14
Garry	9
Tony	22
Billy	16
Craig	14

What is the average number of sit-ups the students can do? *Hint 1*

A 12   **B** 15   **C** 18   **D** 22

3 Nick had six bags each containing a dozen golf balls. What was the total number of golf balls?

Write your answer in the box: ☐

4 Julia bought 3 oranges at 65 cents each, 2 bananas at 75 cents each and 5 apples at 85 cents each. Which number sentence would calculate the total number of dollars the fruit would cost Julia? *Hint 2*

A $3 \times 65 + 2 \times 75 + 5 \times 85$
B $3 \times 0.65 + 2 \times 7.5 + 5 \times 8.5$
C $3 \times 6.5 + 2 \times 7.5 + 5 \times 8.5$
D $3 \times 0.65 + 2 \times 0.75 + 5 \times 0.85$

5 $6405 \div 5 =$ ☐

What is the number to put in the box?

A 1201   **B** 1281   **C** 1481   **D** 1581

6 Sandy multiplies 34 by 200. What is her answer?

A 36   **B** 3600   **C** 234   **D** 6800

7 A high school has an enrolment of 600. All the students are to travel by bus to the local theatre. What is the least number of buses that will be needed if each bus can transport 50 students?

A 10   **B** 11   **C** 12   **D** 13

8 What is 20×76?

A 760   **B** 1420   **C** 1520   **D** 1540

9 The average of 3 numbers is 10. If 2 of the numbers are 4 and 14, what is the other number?

A 10   **B** 12   **C** 15   **D** 30

10 Jane starts with a number. She multiplies it by 5, then divides it by 4. The answer is 10. What number did Jane start with?

A 8   **B** 40   **C** 20   **D** 28

11 When a box of apples is shared evenly between 8 people, each person receives 12 apples and there are 4 left over. How many apples were originally in the box?

A 92   **B** 100   **C** 112   **D** 116

12 At a school fete, cupcakes are being sold in two different-sized packs. A pack of 6 sells for $3.50 while a pack of 8 sells for $4.50. Carmel needs to buy 20 cupcakes. What is the least amount Carmel can pay?

A $8.00   **B** $11.50
C $13.50   **D** $16.00

13 Three pizzas are cut into eight slices and shared between six people. How many pieces are there for each person?

A 4   **B** 5   **C** 6   **D** 7

14 $79 \times 3 =$

Write your answer in the box: ☐

15 $399 \div 21 =$ *Hint 3*

A 0.19   **B** 1.9   **C** 19   **D** 190

16 $16 - 4 \times 2 = 4 + 20 \div$ ☐   *Hint 4*

What number is placed in the box to make the number sentence true?

A 1   **B** 4   **C** 5   **D** 8

Hint 1: The average is found by adding quantities and dividing by the number of quantities.
Hint 2: Check the question to find the correct units to be used in the answer,
Hint 3: Use estimation to exclude some of the 4 choices.
Hint 4: Remember the rules for order of operations.

☞ **Answers and explanations on pages 184–185**

 With most spelling rules there are exceptions. English words have many different origins (e.g. 'café' comes from French and 'kindergarten' comes from German).

Key Points

1 You simply add 's' to most words to make a plural. (These rules can apply to singular verbs.)
Examples: dollars, displays, paintings, teachers, elephants, stages

2 To make plurals with words that end with a consonant + 'y', change the 'y' to 'i' and add 'es'.
Examples: try → tries, jelly → jellies, berry → berries, canary → canaries, pony → ponies

3 To make plurals of words that end with 's', 'ss', 'x', 'zz', 'ch' and 'sh', add 'es'.
Examples: gas → gases, glass → glasses, box → boxes, buzz → buzzes, church → churches, bush → bushes

4 For quite a few words ending in 'f' or 'fe', change the 'f' to a 'v' and add 's' or 'es'.
Examples: life → lives, shelf → shelves, hoof → hooves

5 For quite a few words that end with a single 'o', add 'es'.
Examples: potato → potatoes, tomato → tomatoes, volcano → volcanoes
Note, however, there are quite a few common exceptions to this rule: radios, solos, trios.

6 A few words have unusual spellings. You will just have to know them.
Examples: child → children, foot → feet, man → men, goose → geese, mouse → mice

7 A few words refer simply to the substance's mass. *Examples:* water, rice, flour

8 A few common words don't change at all. *Examples:* deer, fish, sheep, tuna

Test Your Skills

Learn the words below. A common method of learning and self-testing is the **LOOK, SAY, COVER, WRITE, CHECK** method. If you make any mistakes, you should rewrite the word three times correctly, immediately. In this way you will become familiar with the correct spelling. If the word is particularly troublesome, rewrite it several more times or keep a list of words that you can check regularly.

This week's theme word: BUSINESS

business	_____	businesses	_____
manager	_____	managers	_____
delivery	_____	deliveries	_____
customer	_____	customers	_____
advertisement	_____	advertisements	_____
success	_____	successes	_____
bookshelf	_____	bookshelves	_____
research	_____	researches	_____

Write any troublesome word three times: _____ _____ _____

_____ _____ _____

Real Test

Please ask your parent or teacher to read to you the spelling words on page 247.
Write the correct spelling of each word in the box.

1 Time at the _____ centre is time well spent!

2 With those _____ you should see a doctor.

3 I can't _____ tickets to the rock concert.

4 Jo is quite _____ about what she drinks.

5 If _____ your leg is difficult then let me help.

6 The _____ came in through a window.

7 Mandy was _____ her shoes when the storm struck.

8 A low fence _____ the crowd from the players.

9 We had to _____ four floors before finding the office.

10 How _____ has the weather been this week!

11 The vandals _____ the front garden.

12 The _____ was snagged in an old, discarded fishing net.

13 The boys were _____ their hair for the city's celebrations.

14 Shoppers were _____ over bargains at the opening sale.

15 Does the _____ of the sheets dazzle your eyes?

Each sentence has one word that is incorrect.
Write the correct spelling of the underlined word in the box.

16 Keep a <u>ballance</u> between your savings and commitments.

17 The manager <u>wellcomes</u> his staff each morning.

18 Has it ever occurred to you that I might <u>perchase</u> a poodle?

19 The <u>begining</u> was imaginative but the ending was crude.

20 He slammed the <u>cuborad</u> door. All shelves were bare!

☞ **Answers on pages 186-187**

Each sentence has one word that is incorrect.
Write the correct spelling of the word in the box.

㉑ By the forth day of travelling everyone was cranky.

㉒ Mark's surprize party was postponed due to the cyclone.

㉓ I play sport regulerly but I missed this week's competition.

㉔ I could have won the marathon exsept I tripped at the start.

㉕ They say jaeleousy is a curse. I say it's a disaster!

☞ **Answers on pages 186-187**

Key Points

1 All sentences start with a capital letter. There are four main types of sentences.

a **Statements** end with a full stop. A simple statement contains one verb and makes sense on its own. *Example:* The dog <u>ran</u> across the road.

More complex sentences can contain two or more verbs and two or more ideas.
Example: The dog <u>ran</u> across the road when it <u>saw</u> the dogcatcher arrive.

b **Questions** end with a question mark. Questions usually need answers.
Example: Where <u>are</u> you going? (Answer: I am going home.)

c **Exclamations** end with an exclamation mark. Exclamation sentences are often quite short.
Example: <u>Look</u> at the strange bird!

d **Commands** end with a full stop (unless they are particularly sharp; then use an exclamation mark). *Example:* <u>Bring</u> your work over here.

e In **narratives**, the way the author intends the words to be understood is indicated by the type of stop. Consider the difference between: Your name is Jack?, Your name is Jack! and Your name is Jack. The narrative **context** often indicates the type of sentence.

2 The small words 'a', 'an' and 'the' are called articles.

a We use the word '**the**' before specific objects or people. It is called a **definite article** because it refers to a definite object or person.
Examples: Dad put his coat on <u>the sofa</u> in the study. (By this we mean that Dad put his coat on one special sofa, not any old sofa.)
<u>The 8:30 bus</u> is always on time. (In this sentence the writer is referring to one special bus at one special time, not just any bus.)

b The word '**a**' is an **indefinite article**. It is used when you are referring not to a particular object or person, but to things in general.
Examples: Dad put his coat on <u>a chair</u> in the kitchen. (We are not told if it was a particular chair.)
<u>A bus</u> should come along soon. (In this sentence the writer is not referring to any particular bus—he doesn't know which one will come.)

c The word '**an**' is also an **indefinite article**. It is used before words that start with vowels:
<u>an</u> umbrella, <u>an</u> ice-cream, <u>an ol</u>d lady. It is also used with silent 'h': <u>an hour</u>
Example: Dianne took an apple from the bowl. (The writer means that Dianne took no particular apple from the bowl, she just took any apple in general.)

Test Your Skills

1 Put the correct stop in brackets at the end of each sentence.

a Has anyone seen my pen ( )

b Stop, thief ( )

c Put a cross on your lunch box ( )

d I sometimes wonder if you read the questions carefully ( )

2 Write 'a', 'an' or 'the' in the spaces.

Yesterday I caught _____ usual school bus but Ian took _____ cab to work. _____ school is ___ short distance from _____ nearest bus stop. Ian's trip took half ___ hour. My trip took _ few short minutes. When I get ___ job I hope it is close to _____ efficient transport service.

GRAMMAR AND PUNCTUATION
Types of sentences and articles

1 Which of the following correctly completes this sentence?

The referee made ▢ honest mistake when he awarded the first goal.

a	an	the	and
A	**B**	**C**	**D**

2 Which of the following correctly completes this sentence?

The sun was sinking ▢ in the west.

fast	fastly	quick	quicker
A	**B**	**C**	**D**

3 Write the word in the box that best completes this sentence.

Either you do your homework now ▢ you miss the cricket on TV.

4 Which of the following correctly completes this sentence?

The mountain was so ▢ the peak was hidden by clouds.

tall	long	large	high
A	**B**	**C**	**D**

5 Which of the following correctly completes this sentence?

We didn't recognise the anglers even though we were looking right ▢ them.

by	at	to	on	into
A	**B**	**C**	**D**	**E**

6 Choose the words that complete this sentence.

I know they are ▢ pens, but are ▢ sure ▢ being fair?

you're you your	your you're your	your you you're	yours your you
A	**B**	**C**	**D**

7 Which sentence has the correct punctuation?
A The speaker quietly asked us to sit, so we did.
B The speaker quietly asked us to sit, so we did?
C the speaker quietly asked us to sit, so we did.
D The speaker quietly asked us to sit, so we did!

8 Which sentence has the correct punctuation?
A When buying breakfast Cereal I always buy Farmer's Choice brand.
B When buying breakfast cereal I always buy farmer's choice brand.
C When buying Breakfast Cereal I always buy Farmer's Choice brand.
D When buying breakfast cereal I always buy Farmer's Choice brand.

9 Which of the following correctly completes the sentence?

Pam has a rose bush ▢ is covered in bugs!

what	which	who	when
A	**B**	**C**	**D**

☞ **Answers and explanations on pages 187-189**

10 Which of the following correctly completes the sentence?

Our teacher _____ the room as soon as the bell rang.

leave	leaves	left	leaved
A	**B**	**C**	**D**

11 Which phrase correctly begins this sentence?

Draw a line from the correct option to the sentence beginning.

_____ were last to arrive.

The twins and I	The twins and me	Me and the twins	I and the twins

12 Which sentence is correct?
- **A** The team and the coach was on the bus before the driver had arrived.
- **B** The team and the coach were on the bus before the driver arrive.
- **C** The team and the coach is on the bus before the driver had arrived.
- **D** The team and the coach are on the bus before the driver arrives.

13 Which sentence has the correct punctuation?
- **A** Dad shouted! At the top of his voice, get out now.'
- **B** Dad shouted! 'At the top of his voice, Get out now!'
- **C** Dad shouted at the top of his voice, 'Get out now!'
- **D** 'Dad shouted at the top of his voice, Get out now!'

14 Using as many boxes as you need list all the **adjectives** used in this sentence.

We chose the house painter with an honest face and a friendly smile.

15 Which of the following correctly completes the sentence?

Zara was late for the races, _____ she saw two heats and the final.

and	so	if	however	furthermore
A	**B**	**C**	**D**	**E**

16 Shade a bubble to show where the missing apostrophe (') should go.

Ⓐ   Ⓑ   Ⓒ   Ⓓ

Marcu▾s left his glasse▾s on the stair▾s at his friend▾s place.

17 Which sentence has the correct punctuation?
- **A** The liner, at Pier Seven, won't be leaving before next Wednesday.
- **B** The liner, at Pier Seven won't be leaving before next Wednesday.
- **C** The liner, at Pier Seven, won't be leaving, before next Wednesday.
- **D** The liner at Pier Seven won't be leaving, before next Wednesday.

☞**Answers and explanations on pages 187-189**

Real Test

GRAMMAR AND PUNCTUATION
Types of sentences and articles

18 Which sentence uses brackets properly?

  A The Lakes Way from Buladellah (to Forster) see Map 4 winds up and over two small ranges before connecting with the turn-off to Seal Rock.

  B The Lakes Way from Buladellah to Forster (see Map 4) winds up and over two small ranges before connecting with the turn-off to Seal Rock.

  C The Lakes Way from Buladellah to Forster see Map 4 winds up (and over) two small ranges before connecting with the turn-off to Seal Rock.

  D The Lakes Way from Buladellah to Forster see Map 4 winds up and over two small ranges before (connecting with) the turn-off to Seal Rock.

19 Which sentence has the correct punctuation?

  A Mark my words, you won't see a view like that, for a while.

  B Mark my words, you won't see a view like that for a while.

  C Mark my words, you won't see a view, like that for a while.

  D Mark my words, you won't see a view, like that, for a while.

20 Which sentence has the correct punctuation?

  A Every town north of Port Allen has a town mayor except for Ibis Lake.

  B Every town north of Port Allen has a town Mayor except for Ibis Lake.

  C Every town north of Port Allen has a town Mayor except for Ibis lake.

  D Every town north of port Allen has a town mayor except for Ibis lake.

21 Write the article in the box that best completes this sentence.

Jerry demanded ☐ clean towel after each swim!

22 Which sentence has the correct punctuation?

  A During June, we began weekly walks, camping by creeks along the way.

  B During June, we began, weekly walks, camping by creeks along the way.

  C During June we began, weekly walks camping by creeks, along the way.

  D During June, we began weekly walks camping by creeks, along the way.

23 Shade a bubble to show where the missing question mark (?) should go.

'How is your knee,' my friend asked Ⓐ 'If it is improving Ⓑ you should start walking Ⓒ' Ⓓ

24 Choose the underlined word that is a noun in this statement.

It was their <u>belief</u> that <u>everyone</u> should be <u>willing</u> to be involved and to <u>participate</u>.
              Ⓐ   Ⓑ   Ⓒ   Ⓓ

25 Which of the following correctly completes this sentence?

Tracy sat in the waiting room ▭ .

     most quiet   real quiet   very quiet   very quietly
       A   **B**   **C**   **D**

☞ **Answers and explanations on pages 187-189**

A narrative is a form of prose writing that tells a story. Its main purpose is to entertain.

Writers of narratives create experiences that are shared with the reader. To do this the writer uses literary techniques such as figurative language (similes and metaphors), variety in sentence length and type and variety in paragraph length and direct speech.

In many narratives, the **author** is the person who wrote the story. The **narrator** is the person (*I*) in the story who tells the story.

Read this passage and answer the questions.

Road across the Desert

Roger Hyfield looked up, then down the rutted road. The sun beat down from a bleached blue sky and a gusty wind blowing from the north-east was blow-torch hot and whipping sharp grains of sand at his face. A second good reason to keep his sunglasses on.

There was no shade—no let-up from the sun and sand. The boulders along the roadside radiated an <u>unforgiving</u> heat. His throat was parched and he was incredibly thirsty, but caution prevented him from drinking what was left in the one-litre bottle he had carried from the small town of Wentworth. He'd save the small amount left for when night fell, when it would do the most good. That would be several hours.

Mesmerised by the shimmering heat he stared southward towards Wentworth. The dirt road went straight up and over a sandy, rocky slope. To the north was Broken Hill—somewhere further ahead, much further ahead, the dirt was replaced by bitumen. No cars, no trucks, no clouds of dust were in sight. No rescue. The horizon wavered as he stared at it searching for some sign of hope. For a brief moment he thought he saw movement but it was only the heat haze playing games with his dry, scratchy eyes.

Roger turned to his stricken Holden ute and swore at it silently. He glared at the bonnet raised like a giant open mouth, as if it was facing an advancing predator. Then he cursed the wind and the heat and this stretch of road someone—surely in jest—had called the Silver City Highway!

The bonnet of the ute shuddered in a gust of stinging wind.

Then there were the flies, determined to get under his glasses and at his eyes. Swiping at them was energy wasting and heat producing. He had to ignore them as much as was humanly possible.

Roger had been stranded on the side of the road for two hours—regularly moving from the hot, narrow shade of the ute into the open to scan the road in both directions, before retreating. The nagging concern that the road might remain untravelled for days was becoming a real fear. He could last the night but the next day his situation could become dire.

In silent desperation he tried the ignition again, ignoring the burning sensation on the back of his legs from the seat. He willed the engine to burst into life. But nothing. No dash lights. No tell-tale click indicating a dying battery. Nothing. The inside of the car was like a steel mill furnace. He was sure the plastic fittings were starting to buckle.

Test Your Skills

READING
Understanding narratives

① Roger is finding his situation one of increasing

hope.	inconvenience.	prospects.	desperation.	contention.
A	**B**	**C**	**D**	**E**

② What was the problem with the ute? Write your answer on the line.

_____

③ What does Roger find most ludicrous about his situation?
A his water supply
B a lack of traffic
C the loneliness of the road
D the name of the road

④ What was the first good reason for Roger to keep his glasses on?
A the flies getting to his eyes
B the heat from the car's interior
C the glare from the desert sun
D the radiation from roadside boulders

⑤ Why was Roger looking for signs of dust? It could be
A another distant vehicle approaching.
B an indication of cooler temperatures.
C the threat of stronger winds to come.
D a possible change in wind direction.

⑥ As time passes Roger becomes
A increasingly anxious.
B resigned to his situation.
C practical and cautious.
D moody and reckless.
E optimistic and upbeat.
F confident and expectant.

⑦ The open bonnet of the ute is likened to
A a derelict vehicle.
B an animal being defensive.
C a person gasping for water.
D a roadside boulder.

⑧ The roadside boulders radiated unforgiving heat. 'Unforgiving' in this context means
A threatening and menacing.
B provided no shade.
C showed no mercy from the heat.
D hard and cruel.

Answers: 1 D 2 flat battery/electrical system failure 3 D 4 C 5 A 6 A 7 B 8 C

Read this extract from *Bosley—Cat Astray* by Alan Horsfield and answer the questions.

Bosley's French Cafe

The next cafe had open doorways. No security guard. Full of happy families. Children often tossed food to cats. But ...

No. Certainly not. Hamburgers weren't his scene. Commonplace, and so unrefined. He moved on. The Indian Curry Palace. Too spicy for a delicate stomach. Thai-Raid served half-cooked vegetables. Definitely not for a sophisticated cat.

He struggled on. Soon he could be too weak to eat and reduced to undignified begging. The thought mortified him.

Suddenly alert, his nose picked up something tempting. Thoughts of death by starvation slipped from his mind. Head up, he moved forward doggedly—well, probably not dog-gedly! He discovered a dimly lit place—The Truffle—Fine French Cuisine. The smells sent him into a spin.

No doorman, no receptionist, just relaxed diners at tables, enjoying flavoursome food in romantic candlelight. The place was luxurious. Ideal for a cat with cultured tastes.

Cats work on the principle it does no harm to go for what you want. Still he hesitated before entering. The carpet was a bonus. Later, he'd curl up in a shadowy corner and sleep contentedly.

Bosley explored the shadows until he found a smell that stopped him dead. Was it quail, or spatchcock, or possibly pheasant? He pressed under the tablecloth and brushed by a lady's legs. She gave a slight, 'Oo-ah!'

A nearby waiter said, 'Madame?'

'There's something under the table,' she replied demurely.

'Madame?'

'It brushed against my leg,' she added.

'Oui? I will look,' he said slowly lifting the tablecloth.

Bosley greeted him with a friendly smile.

'Oh! It's a cat,' the waiter exclaimed, dropping the cloth, much to Bosley's astonishment. Of course I'm a cat!

Chairs were suddenly pushed aside, feet disappeared. Someone in the dimness cried, 'A cat! A cat in here!'

The shuffling of chairs got suddenly louder. Tranquillity was gone, replaced with distraught pandemonium and lots of scuffing of feet.

Someone shouted some orders, in French.

The table under which Bosley had found sanctuary had unexpectedly become a pen. It was jolted violently by a diner escaping the mayhem. Crockery rattled and a glass toppled. Red wine dribbled onto the carpet.

Bosley wished he could sink into the carpet as he hunched lower and lower. Across the room a couple were looking quite pale. Then he saw three pairs of ominous black shoes surrounding the table. If only he could disappear.

Three waiters began removing the items on the table, one by one. Bosley's heart sank. Once the food and plates were gone they could move in for the capture—or the kill. He had to escape.

Real Test

1 Bosley has eating expectations that could be described as
  A commonplace **B** choosy. **C** indifferent. **D** modest.

2 The third place Bosley rejected as a possible place for a meal was
  A the French restaurant.
  B the Indian Curry Palace.
  C the family hamburger cafe.
  D the Thai-Raid cafe.

3 In the French restaurant, the discovery of Bosley was treated with
  A disbelief. **B** suspicion. **C** delight. **D** outrage.

4 Bosley's attitude could best be described as
  A assertive. **B** selfish. **C** disdainful. **D** shameful.

5 Why did Bosley reject the hamburger cafe as a possible place for food?
  A It was full of children.
  B Hamburgers were too spicy.
  C The food was not up to his expectations.
  D There was nowhere to curl up for a sleep.

6 The waiters in the French restaurant
  A were prepared for a visit from a cat.
  B responded firmly to an unwelcome cat.
  C treated cats as a normal occurrence.
  D took pity on hungry cats.

7 Write the numbers 1, 2, 3 and 4 in the boxes to show the order in which the actions occur.

  ☐ Bosley is discovered under a table.

  ☐ Bosley passes by the Indian Curry Palace.

  ☐ Bosley rejects the thought of eating a hamburger.

  ☐ Bosley ventures into a restaurant with French cuisine.

8 Bosley found a smell 'that stopped him dead'. This means he was
  A filled with fear.
  B knocked over by the sensation.
  C dying.
  D astonished beyond belief.

9 Choose **two** options. When Bosley was first discovered under the table he was
  A confused. **B** upset. **C** unruffled.
  D frightened. **E** complacent. **F** flustered.

☞ **Answers and explanations on page 189**

Read this extract from *Perfect Timing* by Jeremy Fisher and answer the questions.

It was a fine early summer evening. At quarter to six, the sun still shone low in the west, gilding everything with its luminescence. The air, even in the inner city, was rich with the odour of heat-baked eucalyptus. Cicadas drummed their final discord of the day.

<u>Andrew checked himself in the mirror one last time.</u> He hoped he looked all right. His tie was straight, his shoes were polished. Fortunately, a jacket wasn't required for this 'rock and roll formal'. Otherwise he'd be far too hot.

'Are you ready?' his mother called.

'Coming Mum.'

'You're looking really smart, Andrew,' his father said as Andrew made his way out of the house to the car where his mother was waiting for him. 'Amanda should be really pleased,' he shouted from the front door as Andrew clambered into the car.

His mother pulled up outside Amanda's house.

'I'll duck in and let her mother know we're here,' she said.

A few minutes later she and Amanda were walking towards the car. Amanda got into the back seat beside Andrew.

'This is like having a chauffeur, isn't it?' she whispered to him, as his mother got in and started the car.

When they arrived at school, they thanked his mother for the lift.

'I'll pick you up at 9.30,' she said. 'I'll wait here for you.'

Then she drove off, leaving them to walk towards the assembly hall with a straggle of other Year 7 students. None of them were their special friends, so mostly they just said hello.

Inside the hall, streamers and balloons were in profusion. Andrew recognised the streamers and decorations he had made among the many hanging from the ceiling and walls. He was pleased that the junk material they had gathered up and recycled had turned out looking so sharp.

Gaggles of kids stood about, talking excitedly and noisily about their clothes, their hair—for some boys had gone for the greased-back look, and several of the girls had teased their hair into towering beehives—and, of course, the band. At the end of the hall, on a small raised platform, stood the familiar drum kit. Guitars rested on their metal stands in front of it, and the keyboard system was arranged to one side. Large speakers had been placed on either side of the platform.

Real Test

1 The function Andrew and Amanda are attending is most likely a

A school disco.   **B** surprise party.   **C** major rock concert.

D parent-teacher night.   **E** dance lesson.   **F** band practice.

2 Andrew and Amanda arrive at the function

A after 9:30.   **B** before it has started.

C while the band is playing.   **D** during a break in proceedings.

3 'Andrew checked himself in the mirror one last time' suggests Andrew

A was full of self-importance.

B lacked confidence.

C had forgotten to do something.

D wanted to look his best.

4 According to the text **two** of the options from the text are correct and **two** are incorrect. Draw a line to connect each numbered box to the appropriate options.

The streamers for the function

	A were supplied by the band.
1 CORRECT	B were made from junk by Andrew.
	C were being put up as the students arrived.
2 INCORRECT	D were in plentiful supply.

5 The crowd at the function were

A orderly and excited.   **B** not very friendly.

C getting impatient.   **D** already seated.

6 Andrew did not wear his jacket because

A it was a night-time function.

B jackets were not necessary.

C it was in the back of the car.

D Amanda preferred he didn't wear one.

7 Draw a line to match the person with the fact.

1 Andrew	2 Amanda	3 Andrew's father	4 Andrew's mother

A sat in the back seat.	B drove the car.	C commented on Andrew's appearance.	D made streamers.

8 A good title for the extract would be

A The Chauffeur.   **B** Guitars and Drums.   **C** Amanda's Ride.   **D** Big Night Out.

☞**Answers and explanations on pages 189-190**

READING
Understanding narratives

Read this extract from *Through the web and other stories* by Ian Steep and answer the questions.

Dad, Mum, the Circus and me

That night, Carol and I did the washing-up as usual, while Mum organised Annette into getting ready for bed. Mum's voice came from inside, rereading Annette's favourite story. She could have read it herself but it was part of the ritual of going to bed. We'd always had someone read to us. Now there was only Mum to do it.

In the bathroom I brushed my teeth, watching myself in the mirror. 'He'll never be dead while Eddy's around.' That's what people used to say about my father. That was before he died. Now they looked at me and mumbled, in kind voices, about how much I looked like him. The toothbrush went round and round. I narrowed my eyes and squinted into the mirror. Was I like Dad? I had the same curly reddish hair, and our eyes were the same sort of bluey-green. And Mum had always said I'd inherited his frown and the way he walked. I peered into my reflection and tried to make it his, but all I could remember was Dad's laugh and the way his eyes slid and rolled whenever Mum presented him with a new problem. 'Don't worry my dear,' he would say, 'every cloud has a silver lining.' I shook myself away from the image and spat into the hand basin.

As usual the night was hot and still. I lay under the sheet, the family photograph album propped against my knees. Blurry black-and-white pictures of Mum and Dad before they were married, laughing together, Dad's motorbike, their first house. I'd seen them all before, the times when we would pore over our illustrated history, and Dad would link the images together with a commentary that would move us to laughter or tears. I knew them all—there was the day Grandad lost his teeth at the beach: here was Jigger, Dad's blue heeler that got hit (and killed) by Doctor Benson's new car … and you know what he was worried about? The car. (His voice going up and down.) Not Jiggers lying there in pain and dying, but his precious new car. And him a doctor … Then there were the baby photos, me, Carol, Annette, and the locations changing as we shifted from house to house and farm to farm. and Mum's face changing from a laughing girl to a thin-faced, irascible woman and Dad's shoulders growing lean and wiry with work and the burden of a family.

Real Test

① Which two responsibilities did the narrator's (Eddy's) mother undertake each night? Write your answers in the spaces.

1 _____

2 _____

② Why did the narrator spit into the basin?
A He was angry with himself.
B His memories put a bad taste in his mouth.
C He had just finished cleaning his teeth.
D He was trying to imitate his father's actions.

③ When the father suggests 'every cloud has a silver lining' he is saying
A that even when things are gloomy there is always some hope.
B that one day the family will be rich.
C don't worry about a thing: I will fix it.
D it is better to dream than face the difficulties of living.

④ What was lost at the beach?
A the family photo album   **B** a mirror   **C** the dog
D Grandad's teeth   **E** a storybook   **F** toothbrush

⑤ The family's feeling for the father is one of
A awe.
B respect.
C idolisation.
D tolerance.

⑥ What was life like for the family after the father's death? Write your answer on the lines.

_____

_____

⑦ What annoyed Eddy's father most about the death of the dog?
A Dr Benson being more concerned about his car than the dog
B the damage done to the doctor's new car
C the way in which the dog had died
D It was his father's dog.

⑧ What did people mean when they said 'He'll never be dead while Eddy's around'?
A Eddy would protect his father.
B Eddy was healthier than his father.
C Eddy was very much like his father.
D Eddy was most likely to die first.
E Eddy would be remembered by all.

☞ **Answers and explanations on page 190**

GENERAL WRITING TIPS

Each weekly writing plan provides four exercises. It is strongly suggested that you **attempt only three of the four exercises** in each practice period. This allows for three 40-minute writing sessions. The exercise not attempted in each unit can be used as additional practice at another time.

Writing tests are designed to test your ability to express ideas, feelings and points of view. You will be assessed on:

- the thought and content of your writing
- the structure and organisation of your ideas
- expression, style and appropriate use of language
- the amount you write in the given time.

To get the best test results, follow these steps.

Step 1 – Before you start writing

- **Read the question.** Be sure you understand the type of writing requested by the assessors. If you are expected to write an explanation, there is little point in writing a story. Read the instructions carefully. Ask yourself if you should be describing, explaining, entertaining, telling a story, expressing a point of view, expressing an emotion or persuading the reader.
- **Check the stimulus material carefully.** Make sure the stimulus material forms the basis of your writing. You will likely be given a topic, picture, words/phrases, short poem or prose extract as stimulus material.
- **What writing style?** If you are given a choice of writing styles (text types), pick the style you are most comfortable with.
- **Warning:** Don't try to make a pre-planned response, i.e. something you have already written, fit the stimulus material given.

Step 2 – Jot down points

Give yourself a few minutes before you start to **get your thoughts in order** and jot down points. You won't have time to write a draft. Depending on the style required, jot down points on:

- who (characters), why (reasons for action), where (setting), when (time)
- sequences of events/arguments/points
- any good ideas you suddenly have
- how to include the senses and your feelings.

Remember: You can discard ideas that don't fit into your final approach.

Step 3 – Make a brief outline

List the points or events in order. This will become your framework. It can be modified as you write.

GENERAL WRITING TIPS

Step 4 – Start writing

- Make your **paragraphing** work for you. New paragraphs are usually needed for
  - o new incidents in stories
  - o changes in time or place
  - o descriptions that move from one sense to another (e.g. from sight to sound)
  - o a change in the character using direct speech.
- The quality and extent of your **vocabulary** is being tested. Don't use unusual words or big words just to impress the assessor. A mistake here will expose your ignorance.
- It is important that you **complete your piece of writing**. Unfinished work will lose you marks, as will extremely short responses.
- Get as much of the **punctuation, spelling and grammar** right as you can, but allow yourself a couple of minutes after you finish to proofread your work. You won't have time for detailed editing.
- If you are writing a story, know the **ending** before you start. Your ending should not be trite or clichéd (e.g. *I woke up and found it was just a dream*).
- If you are asked to give a **point of view**, think through the evidence you can use to support your 'argument' so that you can build to a strong conclusion.
- If you are including **descriptions** in your writing, think about the importance and relevance of all the senses—sights, smells, tastes, sounds and physical feelings. You may also include an **emotional response**.
- Have a **concluding sentence** that 'rounds off' your work.
- Keep your **handwriting** reasonably neat (i.e. readable).

Step 5 – When you finish

When you finish, **re-read** your work and do a quick check for spelling, punctuation, capital letters and grammar.

Check the Writing section (www.nap.edu.au/naplan/writing) **of the official NAPLAN website for up-to-date and important information on the Writing Test**. Sample Writing Tests and marking guidelines that outline the criteria markers use when assessing your writing are also provided. Please note that, to date in NAPLAN, the types of texts that students have been tested on have been narrative and persuasive writing.

The Australian Curriculum for English requires students to be taught three main types of texts:

- imaginative writing (including narratives and descriptions)
- informative writing (including procedures and reports)
- persuasive writing (expositions).

Informative writing has not yet been tested by NAPLAN. The best preparation for writing is for students to read a range of texts and to get lots of practice in writing different types of texts. We have included information on all types of texts in this book.

TIPS FOR WRITING PERSUASIVE TEXTS

A **persuasive text** is sometimes known as an **exposition** or an **argument**. A persuasive text aims to argue a position and support it with evidence and reasons.

When writing persuasive texts it is best to keep the following points in mind. They will help you get the best possible mark.

Before you start writing

- Read the question carefully. You will probably be asked to **write your reaction** to a particular question or statement, such as *Excessive Internet usage is bad for teenagers.* Most of the topics that you will be asked to comment on are very general. This means you will probably be writing about something you know and can draw upon your experience.
- Give yourself a few minutes before you start writing to **get your thoughts in order** and jot down points.

Structure of persuasive texts

A persuasive text has a specific structure:

- The **introduction** is where you clearly state your ideas about the topic. You must ensure your position is clearly outlined. It is a good idea to list your main points in your introduction—three points is perfect.
- The **body** comprises a series of paragraphs where your opinions are developed. Evidence and/or reasons are given to support your opinions about the topic. Each paragraph usually opens with a sentence that previews what the paragraph will focus on.
- The **conclusion** is a paragraph where the main points of your argument are summarised and where you restate your opinion on the topic. Your conclusion should not include any new information.

Language features of persuasive texts

You can use some or all of the following features:

- **Emotive language:** use words or phrases that express emotion, e.g. *I find it shocking, terrible crime, terrific, heartless, desirable.*
- **Third-person narrative:** avoid using *I* in your argument. The third person is more formal and appropriate to a persuasive text of this kind.
- **Connectives:** these words link your points together, e.g. *firstly, secondly, finally, on the other hand, however, furthermore, moreover* and *in conclusion.*
- **Modality:** use modals to express different levels of certainty. High modal verbs, including *should, must, will not* and *ensure,* are strongly persuasive.
- **Repetition:** repeat key words or phrases to have a dramatic effect on the reader by drawing emphasis to a point or idea.
- **Rhetorical questions:** these questions are designed to make the reader think, e.g. *Have you ever lost a loved one?*
- **Statements of appeal:** these affect the emotions of your readers and encourage action, e.g. *We owe it to our children to act now on climate change.*

Don't forget to:

- plan your argument before you start
- write in correctly formed sentences and take care with paragraphing
- choose your words carefully and pay attention to your spelling and punctuation
- write neatly but don't waste time
- make no more than three different points
- quickly check your argument once you have finished.

You will find a sample annotated persuasive text **on the following page**. The question is from Sample Test 1 on page 130. Read the persuasive text and the notes before you begin your first Writing Test. This piece of writing has been analysed based on the marking criteria used by markers to assess the NAPLAN Writing Test. Remember: this sample was not written under exam conditions.

Language and ideas

Vocabulary
- A good variety of precise verb types are used to establish strong, informed arguments.
- Nouns are used to make generalised statements.
- Adverbs and adjectives are well selected to qualify statements.
- The pronoun *I* is used sparingly.

Sentence structure
- A good variety of sentence beginnings (e.g. *Skateboard, Finally*) are used.
- A variety of sentence types and lengths are included.
- Topic sentences are used to introduce each paragraph's main idea.
- Exclamations and questions are used to good effect.
- Metaphors are used effectively.

Ideas
- Ideas are well balanced to create a sense of rational, logical argument.
- A strong viewpoint is expressed through careful choice of words.
- Ideas are presented positively and forcefully.

Punctuation
- Punctuation, including apostrophes and full stops, is correctly applied.

Spelling
- There are no spelling mistakes of common or unusual words.

Skateboard facilities in the school car park

Dear School Council President

I am a student at Palmdale High School. I was shocked to learn that our School Council is planning to turn the staff car park into a skateboard park. I do not support this plan at all.

First of all it will mean that teachers and official visitors to the school will have to park in the nearby streets. This will increase congestion in those streets and increase the likelihood of accidents and injuries. Local residents could be inconvenienced and upset by the extra congestion and the lack of parking spaces for their visitors.

Secondly a skateboard park will only be used by a few students—mainly boys! This is a huge expense for a limited number of students. The money could be more usefully spent on library equipment, which would benefit all students. If the Council is thinking of students' physical wellbeing then it should spend the money on improving gym facilities!

As the skateboard facility will be in school grounds a teacher will be required to supervise the area. The car park is not supervised as it is an out-of-bounds area. This means that one more teacher will have less time for preparation, marking or to simply have a break.

Skateboard parks are ugly and can be dangerous. There are often accidents around skateboard parks. This will cause stress for the teacher on duty. The school will need staff with skills to cope quickly with serious accidents which don't normally happen in schools. Will special equipment have to be available for such emergencies?

Finally a skateboard park will attract undesirable people into the school grounds after school hours. These people will have no connection to the school and will not respect school facilities. The skateboard park will provide opportunities for rowdy behaviour, vandalism and graffiti—a den for criminal activities.

I request that the Council does not go ahead with plans for a skateboard park. It will make the school more inconvenient for staff, increase their workload and leave the school open to crime. The facility will only be used by a limited number of students. Why not spend the money on the library or gym? I cannot find any good reason for a skateboard park.

Yours sincerely
Jillian Cox (Year 7)

This text is beyond what would be expected of a typical Year 7 student. It is provided here as a model. The assessment comments are based on the marking criteria used to assess the NAPLAN Writing Test.

Structure

Audience
- The audience is readily identified (School Council members).
- Readers are quickly engaged in a relevant issue.
- A brief statement outlines the feelings of the writer.
- Background information is provided to give context to the writer's stance.

Character and setting
- Arguments for the writer's formal reaction are organised into separate paragraphs.
- Points raised are obviously important to the writer in a personal way.
- Evidence and examples are used to support the writer's stance.
- Objectivity is maintained throughout the writing.

Text structure
- The text contains a well-organised introduction, body and conclusion.
- The writer refers regularly to words used in the topic.

Paragraphing
- New paragraphs are used for new arguments and the summary.

Cohesion
- The final paragraph reiterates the writer's arguments and clearly shows where the writer stands on the issue.
- The concluding sentence is forceful and personal.

© Pascal Press ISBN 978 1 74125 209 5

WRITING
Persuasive text 1

The purpose of writing a persuasive text is to influence or change a reader's thoughts or opinions on a particular topic or subject. Your aim is to convince a reader that your opinion is sensible and logical. Successful persuasive writing is always well planned. Persuasive texts may include advertisements, letters to newspapers, speeches and newspaper editorials, as well as arguments in debates.

Before you start, read the General writing tips on pages 26–27 and the Tips for writing persuasive texts on page 28.

Today you are going to write a persuasive text, often called an exposition.

In public areas dog owners are required to keep their dogs on a leash. However, a group of dog owners want to let their dogs run free in national parks.

What do you think about this idea? Do you support or reject this proposal?

Write to convince a reader of your opinions.

Before you start writing, give some thought to:
- whether you strongly agree or strongly disagree with this opinion
- reasons or evidence for your arguments
- a brief but definite conclusion—list some of your main points and add a personal opinion
- the structure of a persuasive text, which begins with a well-organised introduction, followed by a body of arguments or points, and finally a conclusion that restates the writer's position.

Don't forget to:
- plan your writing before you start—make a list of important points you wish to make
- write in correctly formed sentences and take care with paragraphing
- choose your words carefully, and pay attention to your spelling and punctuation
- write neatly but don't waste time
- quickly check your persuasive text once you have finished—your position must be clear to the reader.

Remember: The stance taken in a persuasive text is not wrong, as long as the writer has evidence to support their opinion. How the opinion is supported is as important as the opinion itself.

Start writing here or type in your answer on a tablet or computer.

_____

_____

_____

_____

_____

_____

_____

_____

☞ **Marking guide on page 191**

The purpose of writing a persuasive text is to influence or change a reader's thoughts or opinions on a particular topic or subject. Your aim is to convince a reader that your opinion is sensible and logical. Successful persuasive writing is always well planned. Persuasive texts may include advertisements, letters to newspapers, speeches and newspaper editorials, as well as arguments in debates. Before you start, read the General writing tips on pages 26–27 and the Tips for writing persuasive texts on page 28.

Today you are going to write a persuasive text, often called an exposition.

Choose one of the following topics.

- **Banning contact team sports for children under nine years of age**
- **Litter along the roadside**
- **Shark nets for beaches**
- **Removal of peanut dishes from cafe menus**

What do you think about this idea? Do you support or reject this proposal?

Write to convince a reader of your opinions.

Before you start writing, give some thought to:
- whether you strongly agree or strongly disagree with this opinion
- reasons or evidence for your arguments
- a brief but definite conclusion—list some of your main points and add a personal opinion
- the structure of a persuasive text, which begins with a well-organised introduction, followed by a body of arguments or points, and finally a conclusion that restates the writer's position.

Don't forget to:
- plan your writing before you start—make a list of important points you wish to make
- write in correctly formed sentences and take care with paragraphing
- choose your words carefully, and pay attention to your spelling and punctuation
- write neatly but don't waste time
- quickly check your persuasive text once you have finished—your position must be clear to the reader.

Remember: The stance taken in a persuasive text is not wrong, as long as the writer has evidence to support their opinion. How the opinion is supported is as important as the opinion itself.

Start writing here or type in your answer on a tablet or computer.

_____

_____

_____

_____

_____

_____

_____

☞ **Marking guide on pages 191-192**

TIPS FOR WRITING RECOUNTS

A **recount** tells about events that have happened to you or other people. It is usually a record of events in the order they happened. If it is a personal recount you will use the personal pronoun *I*. You could also write a recount of an event in the third person. A recount can conclude with a personal opinion of the event. Recounts are always written in the past tense.

Before you start writing

- **Read the question and check the stimulus material carefully**. *Stimulus material* means the topic, title, picture, words, phrases or extract of writing you are given to base your writing on.
- Give some thought to:
  - ▶ where your recount takes place
  - ▶ the events that take place in your recount
  - ▶ the characters and what they do in your recount
  - ▶ the problems that have to be resolved
  - ▶ how you and others reacted to the event. You may make brief personal comments on events as you write about them.
- Remember that a recount is usually told **in the past tense** because the events have already happened.
- When you have chosen your topic it might be helpful to **jot a few ideas** quickly on paper so you don't forget them. Decide if you will write a first-person recount (using *I* as the main character) or a third-person recount.

Structure of informative texts (recounts)

The introduction
- The first paragraph of a recount is important as it must provide the reader with a **brief overview** of the event being recounted. It must inform the reader about who, what, when and where.
- The introduction may feature **proper nouns** such as the names of places and people—this helps orient the reader.

The body
- Recounts recall events **in the order in which they happened**. The body of a recount is a series of chronological paragraphs detailing important aspects of the event being recounted.
- **Conjunctions** and **connectives** must be used to indicate when events occur. These include *firstly, then, next, later* and *finally*.
- **Correctly paragraph your writing**. You need a new paragraph when there is a change in time or place or a new idea.
- **Include personal comments**, e.g. about your feelings, your opinions and your reactions, but only include comments that add to your recount.

The conclusion
- A conclusion is necessary as it **informs the reader of how the event ended**. It is also a good idea to include a final comment on the events or experiences. This may be as simple as reflecting on the impact that the event had on the individuals involved.

Language features of informative texts (recounts)

- **Engage the senses** of your reader through description of what can be seen, heard, felt, tasted or smelled. To do this you should include figures of speech such as similes, metaphors and personification.
- **Use strong action verbs** to capture mood and create tension. Instead of *The girl took the food* you could say *The girl lunged for the food.*
- **Use emotive words** to engage the emotions of your reader. It is important to consider what emotions you would like your reader to feel in a specific situation. Once you have decided, use emotive words and phrases to evoke these emotions, e.g. *Lee felt anxious having lost his wallet.*

Don't forget to:
- plan your recount before you start
- write in correctly formed sentences and take care with paragraphing
- choose your words carefully and pay attention to your spelling and punctuation
- write neatly but don't waste time
- quickly check your recount once you have finished.

Real Test and Tips

A recount is a retelling of an event. It usually retells an event in the order the incidents happened.

There is no way of knowing for certain what type of writing will be included in the NAPLAN Tests in years to come. This is an opportunity for you to practise different types of writing.

Before you start, read the General writing tips on pages 26–27 and the Tips for writing recounts on page 32.

Today you are going to write a personal recount.

Choose one of the following events and write several paragraphs, with a conclusion based on your opinion of the event.
- A wild bike or skateboard ride
- A theme park, show or fun park ride
- A ride on a lake in a kayak, canoe or jet ski

Before you start writing, give some thought to:
- where your personal recount takes place
- the events that take place in your personal recount and the problems that have to be resolved
- how you, and others, felt about the event—you may comment on events as you write about them.

Don't forget to:
- plan your personal recount before you start writing
- write in correctly formed sentences and take care with paragraphing
- choose your words carefully and pay attention to your spelling and punctuation
- write neatly but don't waste time
- quickly check your personal recount once you have finished.

Start writing here or type in your answer on a tablet or computer.

_____

_____

_____

_____

_____

_____

_____

_____

_____

_____

_____

_____

☞ **Marking guide on pages 192-193**

Real Test and Tips

WRITING
Recount 2

Recounts can also recall historical (real) events, the lives of interesting people and other events the writer may not be directly involved in. Such recounts are written from an impersonal point of view.

There is no way of knowing for certain what type of writing will be included in the NAPLAN Tests in years to come. This is an opportunity for you to practise different types of writing.

Before you start, read the General writing tips on pages 26–27 and the Tips for writing recounts on page 32.

Today you are going to write a recount.

Choose one of the following events and write several paragraphs, with a conclusion based on an opinion of or comment on the event.

- A school one-day excursion
- A short trip with the family to visit a place or person
- A visit to a particular place you found interesting

Before you start writing, give some thought to:
- where your recount takes place
- the characters and what they do in your recount
- the events that take place in your recount and the problems that have to be resolved
- how you, and others, felt about the event—you may comment on events as you write about them.

Don't forget to:
- plan your recount before you start writing
- write in correctly formed sentences and take care with paragraphing
- choose your words carefully and pay attention to your spelling and punctuation
- write neatly but don't waste time
- quickly check your recount once you have finished.

Start writing here or type in your answer on a tablet or computer.

_____

_____

_____

_____

_____

_____

_____

_____

_____

_____

_____

_____

_____

☞ **Marking guide on page 193**

Week

2

This is what we cover this week:

Day 1 **Number and Algebra/Statistics and Probability:**

◎ Fractions, decimals, percentages and probability

Measurement and Geometry: ◎ Length, time and mass

◎ Area, volume and capacity

Day 2 **Spelling:** ◎ Adding the suffixes 'ed', 'ing', 'er' and 'est'

◎ Common misspellings

Grammar and punctuation: ◎ Types of nouns, adjectives, adverbs and capitals

◎ Tenses, contractions and punctuation

Day 3 **Reading:** ◎ Understanding poetry

◎ Interpreting posters

◎ Understanding narratives

Day 4 **Writing:** ◎ Narrative texts

◎ Procedures

Test Your Skills

20 MIN

1 What is $\frac{17}{3}$ as a mixed numeral?

A $5\frac{2}{3}$ B $5\frac{2}{5}$ C $6\frac{1}{3}$ D $6\frac{1}{5}$

2 Which of these is not the same as $\frac{8}{12}$?

A $\frac{4}{6}$ B $\frac{2}{3}$ C $\frac{20}{30}$ D $\frac{1}{2}$

3 What fraction of the shape is shaded?

A $\frac{1}{5}$ B $\frac{5}{8}$ C $\frac{1}{10}$ D $\frac{1}{2}$

4 What is the sum of $\frac{1}{2}$ and $\frac{1}{4}$?

A $\frac{1}{6}$ B $\frac{1}{3}$ C $\frac{3}{4}$ D $\frac{1}{8}$

5 What is $2 - \frac{3}{4}$?

A $1\frac{1}{4}$ B $\frac{1}{4}$ C $1\frac{3}{4}$ D $2\frac{3}{4}$

6 What is $\frac{3}{4} + \frac{1}{2}$?

A $\frac{3}{8}$ B $\frac{4}{6}$ C $1\frac{3}{4}$ D $1\frac{1}{4}$

7 What is the product of $\frac{3}{4}$ and $\frac{2}{5}$?

A $\frac{3}{10}$ B $\frac{3}{20}$ C $\frac{4}{5}$ D $\frac{2}{3}$

8 What is $\frac{2}{5}$ of $20?

A $4   B $5   C $8   D $10

9 What is the value of the 8 in 21.978?

A 8 thousands   B 8 tenths
C 8 hundredths   D 8 thousandths

10 30.06 is the same as

A $3 \times 10 + 6 \times \frac{1}{10}$.   B $3 \times 10 + 6 \times \frac{1}{100}$.

C $3 \times 1 + 6 \times \frac{1}{10}$.   D $3 \times 1 + 6 \times \frac{1}{100}$.

11 What is 9.326 to the nearest hundredth?

A 933   B 9.32   C 9.33   D 9.40

12 How many hundredths are in 0.2?

A 2   B 12   C 16   D 20

13 Add 3.1, 0.42 and 6.

A 9.52   B 0.79   C 7.9   D 9.43

14 Find the difference between 1 and 0.72.

A 0.27   B 0.28   C 0.38   D 1.72

15 What is 1.5×0.3?

A 0.045   B 0.45   C 4.5   D 45

16 Find the answer to $5\overline{)3.15}$

A 0.61   B 0.63   C 0.65   D 6.3

17 What is 0.913×100?

A 0.00913   B 9.13
C 91.3   D 913

18 What is $3.6 \div 0.6$?

A 3   B 0.6   C 6   D 60

19 In a test, Jo scored 6 out of 10. What percentage did Jo score in the test?

A 6%   B 16%
C 60%   D 65%

20 A bag contains 15 balls of which 3 are red, 7 are blue and the remainder green. What is the probability of selecting a green ball?

A $\frac{2}{3}$ B $\frac{1}{5}$ C $\frac{1}{10}$ D $\frac{1}{3}$

☞ **Explanations on page 194**

Key Points

NUMBER AND ALGEBRA/ STATISTICS AND PROBABILITY
Fractions, decimals, percentages and probability

1 A fraction is written in the form $\dfrac{\text{numerator}}{\text{denominator}}$. An **improper fraction** can be rewritten as a **mixed numeral**.

Example: Convert $\dfrac{21}{4}$ to a mixed numeral.

4 into 21 is 5 and remainder 1,

it is written as $5\dfrac{1}{4}$.

2 Fractions can be **cancelled (or simplified)** by dividing the numerator and denominator by the same number.

Example: Simplify $\dfrac{6}{8}$

$$\frac{6}{8} = \frac{2 \times 3}{2 \times 4} = \frac{\cancel{2}^1 \times 3}{\cancel{2}^1 \times 4} = \frac{1 \times 3}{1 \times 4} = \frac{3}{4}$$

3 When we a**dd or subtract fractions** with **the same denominator**, we just add or subtract the numerator. *Examples:*

a $\dfrac{3}{8} + \dfrac{5}{8} = \dfrac{8}{8} = 1$ **b** $1 - \dfrac{3}{5} = \dfrac{5}{5} - \dfrac{3}{5} = \dfrac{2}{5}$

4 When we **add or subtract fractions** with **different denominators**, we first make the denominators the same.

Example: $\dfrac{4}{5} + \dfrac{3}{10} = \dfrac{8}{10} + \dfrac{3}{10} = \dfrac{11}{10} = 1\dfrac{1}{10}$

5 When we **multiply fractions** we **multiply the numerators together then the denominators together**. (We can cancel fractions if possible.)

Example: $\dfrac{3}{4} \times \dfrac{5}{6} = \dfrac{15}{24} = \dfrac{3 \times 5}{3 \times 8} = \dfrac{5}{8}$

6 The **place values of a digit in a decimal** are …
tenths   hundredths   thousandths
Example: What is the value of the 5 in 2.053?
The 5 is 5 hundredths.

7 When we round off to the nearest tenth (one decimal place) and hundredth (two decimal places) we use the rules identified earlier.

Example: Round off 4.761 to nearest tenth.
4.761 = 4.8 (to nearest tenth)

8 When **adding or subtracting decimals** take care with place value (add tenths to tenths, hundredths to hundredths, etc.).

Example: 3.1 + 0.023 + 0.802 + 0.07
= 3.995
(Place zeros on the ends to help.)

$$\begin{array}{r} 3.100 \\ 0.023 \\ 0.802 \\ + \ 0.070 \\ \hline 3.995 \end{array}$$

9 When **multiplying decimals** the number of decimal places in the question is the same as in the answer.
Example: What is 0.35 × 0.3?
As 35 × 3 = 105, and the question has 3 decimal places, the answer will be 0.105.

10 When **multiplying or dividing decimals by multiples of 10**, the decimal point moves to the right when multiplying, and to the left when dividing. The number of zeros in the multiple of ten is the same as the number of moves of the decimal point.
Examples:
a 7.6318 × 100 = 763.18 (right 2 places)
b 512.81 ÷ 10 = 51.281 (left 1 place)

11 When **dividing by a decimal**, multiply both numbers by the same multiple of ten to ensure we divide by a whole number.
Example: Divide 4.5 by 0.5.
4.5 ÷ 0.5 = 45 ÷ 5 = 9

12 A **percentage is a fraction** with a denominator of 100.
Example: What fraction is 47%?

$$47\% = 47 \text{ out of } 100 = \frac{47}{100}$$

13 Learn these **common conversions**:

$\dfrac{1}{2} = 0.5 = 50\%$ $\qquad$ $\dfrac{1}{4} = 0.25 = 25\%$

$\dfrac{1}{5} = 0.2 = 20\%$ $\qquad$ $\dfrac{1}{10} = 0.1 = 10\%$

Example: Mike scores 4 marks out of 5 in a quiz. What percentage is this?

Now $\dfrac{1}{5} = 20\%$, then $\dfrac{4}{5} = 4 \times 20\% = 80\%$

14 **Probability is the chance of something happening** and is expressed from 0 (impossible) to 1 (certain).
Example:
A dice is rolled. What is the probability of rolling a 5?

The probability is $\dfrac{1}{6}$.

Real Test

NUMBER AND ALGEBRA/ STATISTICS AND PROBABILITY
Fractions, decimals, percentages and probability

1 What number is the arrow pointing to?

1 ——————— 3 *Hint 1*

A $1\frac{1}{2}$ B $1\frac{3}{4}$ C $2\frac{1}{4}$ D $2\frac{1}{2}$

2 What percentage is 20c of $2? *Hint 2*
A 10% B 20% C 25% D 40%

3 Paperbacks were on sale for $9.97 each. What is the cost of 3 paperbacks?
A $29.81 B $29.87 C $29.91 D $29.97

4 During a cyclone, 75% of the houses in a town were damaged. If there were 120 houses in the town, how many were damaged? *Hint 3*
A 60 B 75 C 80 D 90

5 In one year the profit of a small business was $125 000. The owner of the business plans to increase his profit in the following year by 10%. What will be the new profit? *Hint 4*

A $12 000   B $12 500
C $137 000   D $137 500

6 What is 6.4 divided by 0.4?
A 0.16 B 0.4 C 1.6 D 16

7 The diagram shows some balls.

What fraction of the balls is purple? *Hint 5*

A $\frac{1}{16}$ B $\frac{3}{16}$ C $\frac{1}{6}$ D $\frac{3}{8}$

8 In the previous question, if the balls are placed in a bag and one is chosen at random, what is the probability that it is not black?

A $\frac{3}{16}$ B $\frac{1}{6}$ C $\frac{13}{16}$ D $\frac{5}{6}$

9 Two-thirds of the population watched the grand final on television. If the population was 21 million, how many people did not watch the grand final on television?
A 6 million   B 7 million
C 9 million   D 14 million

10 In five months, the price of a barrel of oil decreased from $160 to $40. What percentage decrease is this?
A 15% B 25% C 40% D 75%

11 Heather checks a carton of a dozen eggs at the supermarket. She finds that 25% of the eggs are cracked. How many eggs are cracked?
A 3 B 4 C 6 D 8

12 What number has the same value as $4\frac{1}{2}$?

A $2\frac{1}{4}$ B $4\frac{1}{4}$ C $4\frac{4}{6}$ D $4\frac{5}{10}$

13 What is 2.3 multiplied by 100?
A 23 B 230 C 2300 D 2.3

14 Marcos is building a pergola and needs 18.4 metres of timber. If the timber costs $16.30 per metre, what will be the total cost?
A $2.99   B $29.99
C $299.92   D $2999.90

15 Half the students in a class walked to school this morning, while a third caught the bus. If the remainder of the students travelled by car, what fraction of the class travelled in a car this morning?

A $\frac{1}{6}$ B $\frac{1}{5}$ C $\frac{1}{4}$ D $\frac{5}{6}$

16 The heights of four trees in the school playground were measured and the measurements recorded.

Tree	1	2	3	4
Height (m)	4.5	9.3	1.7	6.1

What was the average height of the trees? _____ m

Hint 1: Fill in the other values on the number line to help find the missing number.
Hint 2: Find the fraction and rewrite as a percentage.
Hint 3: Change the percentage to a fraction to find the number of houses.
Hint 4: Change the percentage to a fraction and then add the quantity on to the original amount.
Hint 5: Remember to cancel the fraction by dividing the numerator and denominator by the same number.

☞ **Answers and explanations on pages 194-195**

Test Your Skills

MEASUREMENT AND GEOMETRY
Length, time and mass

1 Change 7390 cm to metres.
A 0.739 m   B 7.39 m
C 73.9 m   D 739 m

2 In the long jump, Margot jumped 4.1 m while Caitlyn jumped 3.92 m. What is the difference in their jumps?
A 18 cm   B 22 cm   C 23 cm   D 180 cm

3 What is the perimeter of this shaded shape?

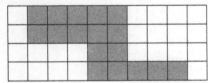

A 17 units   B 22 units
C 23 units   D 24 units

4 A square has a side length of 4.8 cm. What is the perimeter of the square?
A 1.2 cm   B 9.6 cm
C 14.2 cm   D 19.2 cm

5 An equilateral triangle has each side the same length. If the perimeter is 10.8 cm, what is the length of each side?
A 2.7 cm   B 3.6 cm
C 5.4 cm   D 32.4 cm

6 A map of the school has been drawn using a scale of 1 cm = 20 m. The flagpole and the canteen are 70 metres apart. How far apart are they on the map?
A 3 cm   B $3\frac{1}{2}$ cm   C 9 cm   D 11 cm

7 Abbotsfield to Buchanan is a distance of 120 km. A map is drawn and the distance between the towns is 5 cm. What scale has been used on the map?
A 1 cm = 4 km   B 1 cm = 20 km
C 1 cm = 24 km   D 1 cm = 25 km

8 Jack travels 450 km in 5 hours. What is his average speed?
A 85 km/h   B 90 km/h
C 110 km/h   D 120 km/h

9 How long will it take to travel 240 km at an average speed of 60 km/h?
A 180 min   B 4 hours
C 6 hours   D 6 h 25 min

10 Ronaldo travels at 70 km/h for 1 hour and 30 minutes. How far will he travel?
A 40 km   B 70 km   C 100 km   D 105 km

11 The time on a clock is showing 20 minutes to midnight. This time is the same as
A 11:20 am   B 11:40 am   C 23:20   D 23:40

12 Erica wants to see a movie. The screening times for the movie are 1420, 1750, 1905 and 2110. The clock on the wall shows the present time. How long is there before the next screening?
A 25 minutes   B 35 minutes
C 1 h 10 min   D 3 h 30 min

13 Mario is paid $2000 per week. How much is he paid per year?
A $24 000   B $52 000
C $100 000   D $104 000

14 Local time in Auckland is 2 hours ahead of local time in Hobart. When it is 11:30 am in Auckland, what will be the time in Hobart?
A 9:30 am   B 10 am   C 1 pm   D 1:30 pm

15 How many grams are there in 48.62 kg?
A 0.04862 g   B 4.862 g
C 4862 g   D 48 620 g

16 From a one kilogram bag of flour, 225 grams is poured out. What is the mass of the remaining flour?
A 675 g   B 685 g   C 775 g   D 785 g

17 If 1 litre of water has a mass of 1 kilogram, what is the mass of water in a 600-mL bottle?
A 6 grams   B 60 grams
C 600 grams   D 600 000 grams

☞ **Explanations on pages 195–196**

❶ Conversions involving length:

1000 mm = 1 m   1000 m = 1 km
10 mm = 1 cm   100 cm = 1 m

Example: How many m in 6.805 km?

6.805 × 1000 = 6805

❷ The **perimeter** is the distance around the outside of a shape.

Example: What is the perimeter of an equilateral triangle with side length 2.8 cm?
All 3 sides of triangle of equal length:
perimeter = 2.8 × 3 = 8.4 (8.4 cm)

❸ A **scale** is used on maps relating length on the map to length on the ground.

Examples:

a A map uses a scale of 1 cm = 10 km. If two towns are 5.4 cm apart on the map, find their actual distance apart.
As 5.4 × 10 = 54, the towns are 54 km apart.

b A road map uses a scale of 1 cm = 5 km. The distance from Duck's Crossing to Lake's Lagoon is 95 km. How far apart on the map are the two towns?
Map distance = 95 ÷ 5
= 19   (19 cm)

❹ Speed = $\dfrac{\text{Distance}}{\text{Time}}$ **Time** = $\dfrac{\text{Distance}}{\text{Speed}}$

Distance = Speed × Time

Examples:

a Find the speed if a car travels 400 km in 5 hours.

Speed = $\dfrac{400}{5}$ = 80   (80 km/h)

b How long does it take Jenn to travel 250 km at an average speed of 50 km/h?

Time = $\dfrac{250}{50}$ = 5   (5 hours)

c How far will a boy travel if he walks at 6 km/h for 30 minutes?

As 30 min = $\dfrac{1}{2}$ h, Distance = 6 × $\dfrac{1}{2}$ = 3

This means the boy travels 3 km.

❺ Morning time is am and afternoon/evening time is pm. **24-hour time** eliminates the need for **am or pm notation**.

Examples:

a Write 8:32 pm in 24-hour time.
8:32 pm = 2032

b What is the time 7 hours after 2130?

21:30 + 2$\dfrac{1}{2}$ h is midnight and then

another 4$\dfrac{1}{2}$ hours gives 0430.

❻ Conversions involving time:

60 s = 60 min   60 min = 1 h   24 h = 1 d
7 d = 1 week   52 weeks = 1 year
365 days = 1 year   366 days = 1 leap year
10 years = 1 decade   100 years = 1 century
1000 years = 1 millennium

❼ Time zones exist across the world. *Examples:*

a Local time in Adelaide is thirty minutes behind local time in Sydney. If it is 2:20 pm in Sydney, what is the local time in Adelaide?
2:20 minus 30 minutes
= 2:20 minus 20 min gives 2:00 then minus another 10 min is 1:50
The local time in Adelaide is 1:50 pm.

b The local time in Perth is 8 hours ahead of local time in London. If it is 10 pm Tuesday in London, what time is it in Perth?
10 pm plus 8 hours = 10 pm plus 2 is midnight plus 6 is 6 am
The local time in Perth is 6 am Wednesday.

❽ Conversions involving mass:

1000 mg = 1 g   1000 g = 1 kg   1000 kg = 1 t

Examples:

a How many kilograms in 321 grams?
321 ÷ 1000 = 0.321   (0.321 kg)
[as decimal point is after the 1 digit (hidden) and moves 3 places to the left]

b Write in words the number of milligrams in a tonne.
Number = 1000 × 1000 × 1000
= 1 000 000 000
There are one billion milligrams in a tonne.

❾ The mass of one litre of water is one kilogram.

Example: What is the mass of the 40 000 L of water in Tom's backyard swimming pool? Write your answer in tonnes.
40 000 L = 40 000 kg = 40 tonnes;
the water has a mass of 40 tonnes.

MEASUREMENT AND GEOMETRY
Length, time and mass

20 MIN

1 What time is the same time as the time shown on the digital clock? *Hint 1*

17:45

A 5:45 am   **B** 7:45 am
C 5:45 pm   **D** 7:45 pm

2 A paddock has dimensions 120 m by 80 m. A scale drawing is shown. What scale is used in the diagram?

A 1 cm = 10 m   **B** 1 cm = 40 m
C 10 cm = 1 m   **D** 20 cm = 1 m

3 Find the perimeter of the shape in question 2.

5 cm	6 cm	10 cm	12 cm	20 cm
A	**B**	**C**	**D**	**E**

4 Into his shopping bag Michael puts a 440 g tin of tomatoes and a 770 g box of muesli. What is the total mass in kg of the objects?

Write your answer in the box: ☐ kg

5 Trudi used her treadmill for fitness. She ran at a speed of 14 km/h for 30 minutes. What distance did she run? *Hint 2*

A 7 km   **B** 11 km   **C** 12 km   **D** 42 km

6 Prawns are $24 per kilogram. Alma bought $6 worth of the prawns. What mass of prawns did she buy?

A 25 grams   **B** 40 grams
C 200 grams   **D** 250 grams

7 Richie left home at 10:15 am and returned home at 10:00 pm on the same day? How long was he away from home?

A 11 h 15 min   **B** 11 h 45 min
C 12 h 15 min   **D** 12 h 45 min

8 1 kilogram and 80 grams is the same as
A 180 g.   **B** 1008 g.   **C** 1.08 kg.   **D** 1.8 kg.

9
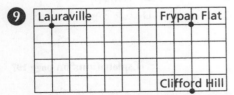

The map shows the location of three towns.

9 The distance from Lauraville to Frypan Flat is 160 km. How far is it from Frypan Flat to Clifford Hill? *Hint 3*

A 4 km   **B** 40 km   **C** 60 km   **D** 80 km

10 Ali walks at an average of 120 paces for every 100 metres. How many paces would he take for 75 metres?

A 60   **B** 70   **C** 80   **D** 90

11 The local time in Sydney is 2 hours ahead of Perth. Graeme leaves Perth at 10:40 am and his flight to Sydney takes 5 hours and 10 minutes. What time was it in Sydney when he arrived?

A 3:50 pm   **B** 5:50 pm
C 6:10 pm   **D** 6:50 pm

12 Isabella leaves home at 11 am and travels 240 km arriving at her destination at 3 pm. What was her average speed?

A 60 km/h   **B** 65 km/h
C 70 km/h   **D** 80 km/h

13 Bailey planned to exercise for three quarters of an hour. She jogged for 25 minutes 30 seconds, ran for 8 minutes 30 seconds and walked the remainder of the time. How long did Bailey walk for?

A 10 minutes   **B** 11 minutes
C 12 minutes   **D** 27 minutes

14 A train is travelling at an average speed of 150 km/h. How long would it take the train to travel 100 km?

A 30 min   **B** 40 min
C 45 min   **D** 1 h 30 min

15 How many decades are there in a millennium? ☐

16 6 millimetres is the same as ☐ metres. *Hint 4*

Hint 1: am is before midday, pm is after midday—in 24 hour time, 9:00 pm is 21:00.
Hint 2: Distance = Speed x Time
Hint 3: Determine the scale used on the map from known distances and then apply to new lengths.
Hint 4: Changing millimetres to metres we divide by 1000.

☞ **Answers and explanations on pages 196-197**

Test Your Skills

MEASUREMENT AND GEOMETRY
Area, volume and capacity

1 What is the area of a rectangle with dimensions 14 cm by 8 cm?
A 22 cm²   B 44 cm²
C 56 cm²   D 112 cm²

2 What is the area?
A 0.108 cm²
B 1.08 cm²
C 1.8 cm²   D 10.8 cm²

1.2 cm
0.9 cm

3 A rectangle has a length of 20 cm. If its area is 340 cm², what is its breadth?
A 17 cm   B 18 cm
C 34 cm   D 320 cm

4 A square has a side length of 4.8 cm. What is the best estimate of its area?
A 10 cm²   B 16 cm²
C 25 cm²   D 250 cm²

5 What is the area of the square?
A $\frac{1}{4}$ cm²   B $\frac{1}{2}$ cm²
C $\frac{3}{4}$ cm²   D 1 cm²

$\frac{1}{2}$ cm

6 What is the area of the triangle?
A 12 cm²   B 24 cm²
C 48 cm²   D 60 cm²

6 cm
8 cm

7 What is the area of the triangle?
A 27 cm²   B 80 cm²
C 85 cm²   D 170 cm²

10 cm
17 cm

8 What is the volume of a rectangular prism with length 7 cm, breadth 5 cm and height 6 cm?
A 18 cm³   B 105 cm³
C 210 cm³   D 420 cm³

9 How many kilograms are there in 39.05 tonnes?
A 390.5 kg   B 3905 kg
C 39 005 kg   D 39 050 kg

10 Find the volume:
A 27 cm³
B 60 cm³
C 600 cm³
D 1200 cm³

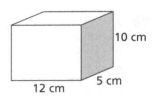
10 cm
12 cm
5 cm

11 A sporting complex is in the shape of a rectangle and measures 320 metres by 300 metres. What is the area?
A 9.6 hectares   B 96 hectares
C 960 hectares   D 9600 hectares

12 The diagram shows a cube with a grid placed over the front face. What is the total area of all the faces?
A 16 units²
B 32 units²
C 64 units²   D 96 units²

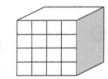

13 How many millilitres are there in 3.07 litres?
A 30.7   B 307   C 370   D 3070

14 An unopened jar of strawberry jam has a mass of 625 grams. When the jar is empty the mass is 175 grams. What is the mass of the strawberry jam?
A 450 grams   B 550 grams
C 575 grams   D 800 grams

15 How many litres are there in 5000 cm³?
A 5 L   B 50 L
C 500 L   D 5 000 000 L

16 The volume of a rectangular prism is 200 cm³. If the length is 10 cm and the breadth 5 cm, what is the height?
A 2 cm   B 4 cm   C 10 cm   D 40 cm

17 Which of these rectangular prisms has the greatest volume? (measurements in cm)
A 4 × 3 × 2   B 5 × 2 × 3
C 8 × 2 × 1   D 6 × 3 × 1

☞ **Explanations on page 197**

Key Points

MEASUREMENT AND GEOMETRY
Area, volume and capacity

1 The **area is a measure of space inside a shape**.

2 To find the **area of a rectangle** we multiply length by the breadth.

length
breadth

Examples:

a Find the area of a rectangle with sides 8 cm and 6 cm.

Area $= 8 \times 6$
$= 48$ The area is 48 cm²

b Find the area of a rectangle with sides 1.2 mm and 0.8 mm.

Area $= 1.2 \times 0.8$ $(12 \times 8 = 96)$
$= 0.96$ (2 digits after decimal point)
The area is 0.96 mm².

3 To find the **area of a square**, we can square the length of the side.

side
side

Example: Find the area of a square with side 7 cm.

Area $= 7^2$
$= 49$ The area is 49 cm².

4 To find the **area of a triangle**, we halve the base and multiply by the perpendicular height.

height
base

Examples:

a Find the area of a triangle with a base of 22 cm and a height of 9 cm.

Area $= \dfrac{1}{2} \times 22 \times 9$

$= 99$ The area is 99 cm².

b Find the area of a triangle with a base of 26 mm and a height of 2 cm.

First change 2 cm to 20 mm.

Now area $= \dfrac{1}{2} \times 26 \times 20$

$= 26 \times 10$
$= 260$ The area is 260 mm².

5 **Conversions involving area**:

10 000 m² = 1 ha (hectare)

Example: A rectangle measures 450 metres by 200 metres. Find the area in hectares.

Area $= 450 \times 200$
$= 90\,000$

No. of hectares $= 90\,000 \div 10\,000$
$= 9$
The area is 9 hectares.

6 **Large areas** are expressed in **square kilometres**.

Example:

A map has been drawn on the grid, where each square has an area of one square kilometre. Estimate the area of the island.

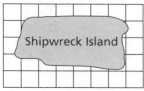

Shipwreck Island

The island is about 17 square kilometres.

7 The **volume is a measure of the space contained inside a solid or container**.

8 To find **volume of a rectangular prism**, multiply length by breadth by height.

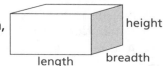

height
length   breadth

Example: Find the volume of a rectangular prism with dimensions 4 cm, 3 cm and 2 cm.

Volume $= 4 \times 3 \times 2$
$= 24$ Volume is 24 cm³.

9 The **capacity is a measure of the amount of liquid inside a container**.

10 **Conversions involving capacity**:

1000 mL = 1 L   1000 L = 1 kL
1000 kL = 1 ML (megalitre)

Example: How many litres in 7430 mL?
$7430 \div 1000 = 7.43$ (7.43 L)

11 **Conversions involving volume and capacity**:

1 cm³ = 1 mL (cubic centimetre = millilitre)
1000 cm³ = 1 L

Example: What is the capacity of a cube with side 10 cm?
Volume $= 10 \times 10 \times 10 = 1000$
As volume is 1000 cm³, then capacity is 1000 mL or 1 litre.

Real Test

MEASUREMENT AND GEOMETRY
Area, volume and capacity

1 The jug contains 750 mL of water. Leon pours out 300 mL. How many millilitres remain in the jug?

A 350 mL **B** 450 mL **C** 550 mL **D** 700 mL

2 A truck uses an average of 15 litres of fuel for every 100 kilometres. At that rate, how much fuel is used by the truck in a distance of 800 kilometres?

A 120 litres **B** 130 litres
C 150 litres **D** 160 litres

3 This is a scale drawing of a large floor.

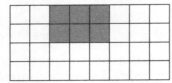

A rectangular rug with an area of 12 m² is placed on the floor. What is the area of the remainder of the floor?

A 6 m² **B** 12 m² **C** 52 m² **D** 64 m²

4 Every minute that Selena showers she uses 12 litres of water. How many millilitres does she use every second?

Write your answer in the box: ☐ mL/s

5 Jake draws a rectangle with an area of 24 cm². What could not be the dimensions of Jake's rectangle?

A 12 cm × 2 cm **B** 6 cm × 4 cm
C 8 cm × 3 cm **D** 20 cm × 4 cm

6 Find the volume of this rectangular prism.

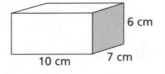

☐ cm³

7 What is the area of a square with side 0.1 cm? Write your answer in the box:

☐ cm²

8 A fish tank has dimensions 40 cm by 20 cm by 20 cm. How much water does the tank hold? *Hint 1*

☐ L

9 What is the area of the shaded section? Write your answer in the box:

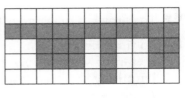

☐ units².

10 A rectangular prism has dimensions 3 cm × 2 cm × 4 cm. The solid prism is made of metal, which has a mass of 3 g for every 1 cm³. What is the mass of the prism?

A 24 g **B** 60 g **C** 72 g **D** 84 g

11 What is the area of a triangle with a base of 12 cm and a height of 10 cm?

A 30 cm² **B** 60 cm²
C 90 cm² **D** 120 cm²

12 Charlotte's rectangular garden measures 10 metres by 6 metres. If fertiliser is applied at the rate of 200 grams per square metre, what amount of fertiliser is needed?

A 1.2 kg **B** 2.4 kg **C** 12 kg **D** 24 kg

13 A 4-litre tin of paint costs $70 and 1 L costs $28. If Ben requires 10 litres of paint, what is the smallest amount he will pay? *Hint 2*

A $196 **B** $210 **C** $220 **D** $280

14 Eli filled a 10 L bucket with water in 12 seconds. At that rate, how long would it take to fill a 65 L container?

A 72 s **B** 73 s **C** 75 s **D** 78 s

15 A bag contains 1 kg of lawn seed. It is to be applied at the rate of 25 g for each square metre. What area can be covered?

A 4 m² **B** 40 m² **C** 16 m² **D** 25 m²

16 Harry poured the contents of a 2-litre bottle of soft drink into 7 glasses. What calculation finds the amount of millilitres in each glass if all glasses contain the same amount? *Hint 3*

A 2 × 100 ÷ 7 **B** 7 × 1000 ÷ 2
C 2 × 7 ÷ 1000 **D** 2 × 1000 ÷ 7

Hint 1: Estimate or use 1000 cm³ = 1 litre.
Hint 2: Try different combinations of cans to make at least 10 L.
Hint 3: Remember: 2 L = 2000 mL.

☞ **Answers and explanations on pages 197-198**

SPELLING
Adding the suffixes 'ed', 'ing', 'er' and 'est'

 With most spelling rules there are exceptions. English words have many different origins (e.g. 'bunyip' comes from Aboriginal Australian and 'sarong' comes from Malaysia).

Key Points

❶ To most 'short' words that end with two consonants or two vowels followed by a consonant you simply add the suffixes 'er', 'ing', 'ed' and 'est'.
Examples: camp → camping, camped, camper; load → loading, loaded, loader; fast → fasting, fasted (went without food), faster, fastest; light → lighter, lighting, lightest

❷ a For words that end with a consonant + 'y', simply add 'ing'.
Examples: try → trying, bury → burying, carry → carrying
 b When adding 'ed', 'er' and 'est' to words that end in a consonant + 'y', change the 'y' to 'i' before adding the suffix.
Examples: try → trier, tried; lazy → lazier, laziest; round → rounder, roundest

❸ For words ending with consonant + 'e', drop the 'e' and add the suffix.
Examples: hope → hoped, hoping; save → saver, saving, saved; safe → safer, safest

❹ For words ending in a single vowel + a consonant, simply double the last letter before adding the suffix.
Examples: shop → shopping, shopped, shopper; big → bigger, biggest
Main exceptions are words ending in 'w', 'x' and 'y'. (Note: 'w' and 'y' act as vowels in these words.)
Examples: row → rowed, rowing, rower; box → boxed, boxing, boxer; new → newer, newest; grey → greyer, greyest
Many common double syllable words do not double the last consonant.
Examples: ticketing, ticketed, entering, towered, widening, tutoring, balloting, sugared, budgeter, budgeting, budgeted

Test Your Skills

Learn the words below. A common method of learning and self-testing is the **LOOK, SAY, COVER, WRITE, CHECK** method. If you make any mistakes, you should rewrite the word three times correctly, immediately. In this way you will become familiar with the correct spelling. If the word is particularly troublesome, rewrite it several more times or keep a list of words that you can check regularly.

This week's theme word: ENTERTAINMENT

display	_____	displaying	_____
thrilled	_____	thrilling	_____
admitting	_____	admitted	_____
entertainer	_____	entertaining	_____
noisier	_____	noisiest	_____
rehearse	_____	rehearsing	_____
supporter	_____	supporting	_____
accompanied	_____	accompanying	_____

Write any troublesome word three times: _____ _____

_____ _____ _____

SPELLING
Common misspellings

Please ask your parent or teacher to read to you the spelling words on page 247.
Write the correct spelling of each word in the box.

1. The railways have hundreds of lost _____!

2. Morris _____ believes in the benefits of hypnosis.

3. Your _____ in the test will have to be readable.

4. Ask the attendant for a _____.

5. Any _____ team will have to play well!

6. My brother's _____ will be next weekend.

7. Aaron was _____ down a hill when he lost control.

8. Tina had a _____ smile and a soft voice.

9. We had a _____ experience in the caravan park.

10. The books had been _____ by a shady accountant!

11. The cruise ship _____ in the tranquil bay.

12. There was an _____ storm in the harbour.

13. What _____ does any official have ringing me this early?

14. _____ shirts were going at bargain prices at the sale.

15. The letter was a fake and the gentleman was not an _____.

Each sentence has one word that is incorrect.
Write the correct spelling of the underlined word in the box.

16. HG Wells has written a novel about an <u>invisable</u> person.

17. The salesman spent hours <u>persuadeing</u> us to sell our home.

18. Where is the cheapest <u>occommodation</u> in this village?

19. Tom's <u>admittence</u> is on the condition that he behaves.

20. Louise was <u>addresing</u> the envelope when her pen dried up!

☞ **Answers on pages 198–199**

Each sentence has one word that is incorrect.
Write the correct spelling of the word in the box.

21 You don't have your brooch? It can't have dissappeared!

22 We had our hotest day in the month of February.

23 Centuries ago shepheards were employed to care for sheep.

24 Just suppossing I give you a vehicle, what then?

25 You'll need a woolen jumper and a leather jacket.

☞ **Answers on pages 198-199**

Key Points
and
Test Your
Skills

GRAMMAR AND PUNCTUATION
Types of nouns, adjectives, adverbs and capitals

20 MIN

Key Points

1 There are four types of nouns.

a **Common nouns** are the names of everyday things around us.
Examples: coat, rat, clouds, toe, elephant, desert

b **Proper nouns** begin with a capital letter and are the names of particular persons, places or things. *Examples:* Napoleon, Melbourne, Ford, Opera House, Christmas Day, Russians
Titles only take capital letters when used for a specific person or thing.
Compare: 'We saw our *uncle*.' and 'Is *Uncle* Joe coming?'

c **Abstract nouns** are things that can be recognised by the five senses.
Examples: beauty, hate, amazement, sadness, peace, exhaustion, health

d **Collective nouns** are used to name groups of individuals, places or things.
Examples: crowd, batch, bunch, herd, flock, kit
Note: a collective noun is singular as it refers to just one group.

2 **a** **Adjectives** are words that tell us more about nouns or describe them.
Examples: <u>weak</u> cordial, <u>ugly</u> boxer, <u>ten</u> houses, <u>brown</u> paint, the sky is <u>blue</u>

b **Proper adjectives** are formed from proper nouns. *Examples:* Italy → Italian, France → French

c Adjectives have **three degrees of comparison**.
Example: Joan is tall. (One person is tall.)
Bill is taller than Joan. (Two people are compared.)
Helen is the tallest person in our class. (Three or more people are compared.)

d For longer words the convention is to add **more** or **most** to show degree.
Examples: dutiful, more dutiful, most dutiful; energetic, more energetic, most energetic

3 **Adverbs** are words that describe an adjective or another adverb. Adverbs can tell us the answer to the questions: How? To what extent? When? Where?
Most adverbs end in 'ly'.
Examples: softly, angrily, successfully, eerily, momentarily

Other adverbs do not have the 'ly' ending.
Examples: off, near, well, too, almost, quite, tomorrow, soon, outside, later

Test Your Skills

1 Name the types of nouns.
a thunder _____ , kindness _____ , bundle _____ , dogs _____
b Elvis _____ , length _____ , flame _____ , crew _____

2 Underline the adjectives in this sentence.
Torn raincoats were a useless item in the hopeless situation of cold, stinging rain.

3 What adjectives can be formed from these proper nouns?

Britain _____ , India _____ , Germany _____ , China _____

4 Underline the adverbs in this sentence.
Hawks often glide silently over the farm when searching desperately for food.

Answers: **1 a** common, abstract, collective, common **b** proper, abstract, common, collective **2** Torn, useless, hopeless, cold, stinging **3** British, Indian, German, Chinese **4** often, silently, desperately

Real Test

GRAMMAR AND PUNCTUATION
Tenses, contractions and punctuation

20 MIN

1 Which of the following correctly completes this sentence?

Dad says every worker should belong to _____ union wherever they work.

a	an	the	that
A	**B**	**C**	**D**

2 Which of the following correctly completes this sentence?

After completing the mowing I found the _____ chair on the deck to sit on.

comfortablest	more comfortable	most comfortable	comfortabler
A	**B**	**C**	**D**

3 Which of the following correctly completes this sentence?

We watched a _____ of naval ships leave the harbour.

bunch	fleet	mob	group
A	**B**	**C**	**D**

4 Which of the following correctly completes this sentence?

I was given _____ from everyone on how to do text messages!

advice	an advice	many advices	advices
A	**B**	**C**	**D**

5 Which of the following correctly completes this sentence?

Billiards _____ a game often played on a table in a hotel.

are	am	were	is
A	**B**	**C**	**D**

6 What part of speech is the underlined word?

The <u>Welsh</u> runner dashed over the line to win the marathon.

adverb	adjective	noun	preposition
A	**B**	**C**	**D**

7 Which sentence has the correct punctuation?

A The judge asked the foreman of the jury for, "Their verdict."
B The Judge asked the foreman of the jury for their verdict.
C The judge asked the foreman of the jury for their verdict.
D The judge asked, "The foreman of the jury for their verdict."

8 Which sentence has the correct punctuation?

A The British team out-played the fijians on their home ground in Suva.
B The British team out-played the Fijians on their Home Ground in Suva.
C The British Team out-played the Fijians on their home ground in Suva.
D The British team out-played the Fijians on their home ground in Suva.

9 Which of the following correctly completes the sentence?

The latest news was both incorrect _____ distressing.

and	yet	but	while
A	**B**	**C**	**D**

☞ **Answers and explanations on pages 199–201**

Real Test

10 Choose the words that complete this sentence.

The pony is fit and I know _____ age is important to you, but _____ not my rule.

its its	it's its	its it's	it's it's
A	**B**	**C**	**D**

11 Which sentence is correct?

A Yesterday, when the bell rang, the children was still working.

B Yesterday, when the bell rang, the children were still working.

C Yesterday, when the bell rang, the children are still working.

D Yesterday, when the bell ringed, the children were still working.

12 Which sentence has the correct punctuation?

A For lunch, Dana had an apple, banana and plum.

B For lunch, Dana had an apple, a banana and plum.

C For lunch, Dana had an apple, banana and a plum.

D For lunch, Dana had an apple, a banana and a plum.

13 Which sentence has the correct punctuation?

A We have an old newspaper, a magazine, a comic and a book to read.

B We have an old newspaper, a magazine, a comic, and a book to read.

C We have an old, newspaper, a magazine, a comic and a book to read.

D We have an old newspaper, a magazine, a comic, and a book, to read.

14 Which sentence has the correct punctuation?

A Im the groups leader and this dog is its mascot!

B I'm the groups' leader and this dog is its mascot!

C I'm the group's leader and this dog is its mascot!

D I'm the group's leader and this dog is it's mascot!

15 Which of the following correctly completes the sentence?

I _____ the teacher my homework before I left school.

give	had given	gives	had gave	began
A	**B**	**C**	**D**	**E**

16 Shade a bubble to show where the missing apostrophe (') should go.

Ⓐ   Ⓑ   Ⓒ   Ⓓ

Marilyn said it was her▾s but Mum▾s suspicion▾s were based on pas▾t experience.

17 Which sentence has the correct punctuation?

A Rusty, our friendly, red setter, barked, all through the night.

B Rusty our friendly, red setter barked all through the night.

C Rusty our friendly red setter barked, all through the night.

D Rusty, our friendly red setter, barked all through the night.

☞ **Answers and explanations on pages 199–201**

Real
Test

GRAMMAR AND PUNCTUATION
Tenses, contractions and punctuation

18 Which of the following correctly completes the sentence?

I saw that you _____ late but I was early!

were	was	is	are
A	**B**	**C**	**D**

19 Using as many boxes as you need list all the **adverbs** used in this sentence.

The moon always rises brilliantly over the bay, at this time of the year.

20 Where do the **two** missing speech marks (" and ") go?

Ⓐ   Ⓑ   Ⓒ   Ⓓ

"Sit on the seat, Judy directed, and I will read you a story. It will be my favourite."

21 Choose the subordinate clause in this sentence.

<u>I well remember</u>   <u>my little brother</u>   <u>winning a dress-up beauty contest</u>   <u>when he was in Year 1</u>!

     A   **B**   **C**   **D**

22 Which sentence has the correct punctuation?
  A We found the pepper, and salt, the bread, and butter and the honey but only one knife.
  B We found the pepper and salt, the bread and butter and the honey but only one knife.
  C We found, the pepper and salt, the bread and butter and the honey but only one knife.
  D We found the pepper and salt, the bread and butter and the honey, but only one knife.

23 Shade a bubble to show where the missing exclamation mark (!) should go.
I can't believe it ⟍ You have the $5 ⟍ that Dad gave you ⟍ I think you ⟍ should find that enough.
            Ⓐ   Ⓑ   Ⓒ   Ⓓ

24 Which sentence is correct?
  A The bands were so exciting I could of danced all night.
  B The bands were so exciting I could off danced all night.
  C The bands were so exciting I could've danced all night.
  D The bands were so exciting I could'er danced all night.

25 Write a word from this sentence in each empty box to match the given part of speech.

The sleek fox bounded effortlessly over logs and rocks.

verb		conjunction	

adverb		adjective	

☞ **Answers and explanations on pages 199–201**

Poetry can take many forms. It can tell a story (narrative verse), paint a word picture, or be the format for a play.

Poets create experiences that are shared with the reader. To do this the poet uses literary techniques such as figurative language (similes and metaphors), rhyme and rhythm. Poetry does not have to rhyme.

Poetry is often described as the most personal form of expression. Poets choose their words carefully and economically. They create images and feelings with words.

Read the extract from the poem *The Teams* by Henry Lawson (1867–1922) and answer the questions.

The Teams

A cloud of dust on the long white road,
And the teams go creeping on
Inch by inch with the weary load;
And by the power of the <u>green-hide</u>[1] <u>goad</u>[2]
The distant goal is won.
With eyes half-shut to the blinding dust,
And necks to the yoke bent low,
The beasts are pulling as bullocks must;
And the shining tires[3] <u>might almost rust</u>
While the spokes are turning slow.
With face half-hid 'neath a broad-brimmed hat
That shades from the heat's white waves,
And the shouldered whip with the green-hide plait,
The driver plods with a gait like that
Of his weary, patient slaves.
The rains are heavy on roads like these
And, fronting his lonely home,
For weeks together the settler sees
The teams bogged to their axletrees[4],
Or ploughing the sodden loam.

1 untanned leather cattle prod or whip
2 provoke or force something to do something
3 another spelling of *tyres*
4 the shaft or bar between the wheels

Test Your Skills

1 This poem
  A tells a story.
  B describes a landscape.
  C explains an incident along a bush road.
  D describes the life of a bullock team driver.

2 The life of the driver of the bullock team is
  A hard.
  B comfortable.
  C trouble-free.
  D dangerous.

3 How does the driver travel?
  A on horse
  B on foot
  C on a wagon
  D on a bullock

4 The 'green-hide goad' is
  A knowledge that the team will reach green pastures.
  B the need to find the shade of trees.
  C a whip used to make the bullocks pull.
  D dreams of better times ahead.

5 Why does the poet suggest the tyres 'might almost rust'?
  A The roads travelled have been flooded.
  B They are turning so slowly there will be time for them to rust.
  C The team has been travelling for a long time.
  D The road's surface is harsh on the wagon's steel tyres.

6 The poet compares the team under two different conditions. What are they?
  A dry and wet
  B summer and winter
  C night and day
  D town and country

7 The rhythm of the poem captures the
  A motion of horses.
  B rocking of the wagon load.
  C plodding, labouring effort of the team
  D beat of flooding rain.

Read the poem *Some Families of My Acquaintance* by Laura Elizabeth Richards (1850–1943) and answer the questions.

Some Families of My Acquaintance

The Rummy-jums, the Rummy-jums,
Are very funny people;
(Very, very, very, very,
Very funny people!)
They run as hard as they can go,
And clamber up the steeple;
(Clamber-climber, climber-clamber,
Clamber up the steeple!)
And when they get up to the top,
They say, "Good gracious, we must stop!"
    And turn about with grief and pain,
    And clamber-climber down again.
The Viddipocks, the Viddipocks,
Have very pretty bonnets*;
(Very, very, very, very,
Very pretty bonnets!)
And when they wear them upside down
They write most lovely sonnets;
(Lovely-dovely, dovely-lovely,
Lovely-dovely sonnets!)
And sitting on the new-mown hay,
They wirble-warble all the day;
    "For oh," they say, "at such a time,
    Our very ribbons flow in rhyme!"
The Wiggle-wags, the Wiggle-wags,
They never know their mind, sir;
(Never, never, never, never,
Never know their mind, sir!)
Sometimes they hook their frocks before,
(Hook them, crook them, crook them, hook them,
Hook them up behind, sir!)
And first they turn them inside out,
Then outside-inside with a shout;
    "For oh," they say, "there's no one knows
Which way the most our beauty shows!"

*a hat framing the face and tied under the chin with a ribbon

Real Test

1 The poet makes use of
A nonsense names.
B true-life events.
C tales of daring.
D mysterious happenings.

2 Look at the two poems: *The Teams* (page 52) and *Some Families of My Acquaintance* (page 54). For what purposes were these **two** poems written? Tick **two** boxes for each poem.

	The Teams	Some Families of My Acquaintance
to entertain	☐	☐
to portray an ordeal	☐	☐
to evoke respect	☐	☐
to indulge in nonsense	☐	☐

3 The Rummy-jums family
A wear pretty bonnets.
B have ribbons that rhyme.
C sit in newly mown hay.
D climb steeples.

4 People who '[n]ever know their mind' would be considered
A clever. B unsure. C argumentative. D trusting.

5 The Wiggle-wags family
A race about a lot.
B write poems about steeples.
C wear their bonnets upside down.
D fasten their frocks up at the back.

6 The Rummy-jum family discovered steeple climbing
A is difficult to do successfully.
B makes them laugh.
C meant finding a way back down.
D is all great fun.

7 Which family wears their frocks inside out? Write your answer on the line.

_____

8 The families mentioned in the poem are
A people the poet sees occasionally.
B neighbours of the poet.
C close friends of the poet.
D relatives the poet avoids.

☞ **Answers and explanations on page 201**

You may often see a poster like the one below. It is important that you can interpret graphics as well as read the text. A poster is often a form of persuasive text.

Study the poster on ladders and answer the questions.

WORK SAFE, STAY SAFE!
You don't have to fall far to be seriously injured!

Ladder sense
* Never lean out too far from the ladder—work well within arm's reach.
* <u>Don't use the ladder if you are alone</u>.
* Never use a ladder that is unstable.

Always check the ladder before use.
The ladder should be fitted with non-slip rungs.
Only climb to the second-top rung of a ladder.
Use ladders fitted with non-slip safety feet.
Make sure the ladder is sitting firmly on the ground.
Climb safely.

BUYING A LADDER FOR <u>DOMESTIC PURPOSES</u>?

Unpack and inspect the ladder in the shop before you buy.
It should:
- be the right **height** for your needs
- be a manageable **weight**
- be **rigid and secure** when set up
- have feet with a sure **grip**
- be labelled with clear **safety instructions**.

Check the ladder's **weight-bearing rating** (loads up to 100 kg).

A safe style of home ladder

Real Test

1 The main intent of the poster is to
 A increase awareness of ladder safety.
 B promote the sale of ladders.
 C advise on the types of ladders.
 D show how to use a ladder to change a light bulb.

2 A suitable place to display the poster would be
 A at a bus stop.
 B at a sports ground.
 C in a hardware store.
 D in a doctor's waiting room.

3 What reason could be offered for the advice: 'Don't use a ladder if you are alone'?
 A Ladders can be heavy items to lift.
 B A second person improves safety by supporting and stabilising the ladder.
 C Most people enjoy working with a friend.
 D A second person can pass tools to the ladder user.

4 The triangle with the exclamation mark is intended to
 A show that the information is a warning.
 B add a splash of colour to the poster.
 C add a similar shape to a stepladder.
 D encourage people to buy ladders.

5 Why are ladder users advised to climb only to the second-top rung?
 A It is difficult to stand unaided on a thin, round rung.
 B A person on the top rung is more likely to get a fear of heights.
 C The ladder can become difficult to steady for the person on the ground.
 D The top rung provides a firm rest and support for the legs when leaning forward.

6 What reason could there be for buying a ladder that can take a 100kg load?
 A Large people should not climb ladders.
 B A common use for using a ladder is to change light bulbs.
 C Most people weigh less than 100 kg.
 D Ladders that take a greater weight load cost a lot more.

7 When using a ladder the first requirement is to
 A make sure the feet have a non-slip grip.
 B check the ladder before you climb it.
 C tell a friend you are about to climb a ladder.
 D stop climbing near the top.

8 'Domestic purposes' refers to use
 A on a farm.
 B in a factory.
 C by professional builders.
 D around the home.
 E for tree lopping.
 F by electricians.

9 A special feature of the example of the safe ladder is the
 A safety rail around the top step.
 B colour of the steps.
 C number of steps.
 D width of the steps.

☞ **Answers and explanations on pages 201-202**

READING
Understanding narratives

In Week 1 you learned about understanding narratives. Here is another opportunity to practise your narrative comprehension skills.

Read this extract from *The Sylvia Mystery* by Penny Hall and answer the questions.

'I have been thinking about that shopping trolley you keep in your shed,' Sylvia said.

It was the next day, and Kat had just finished giving Sylvia another swimming lesson.

Kat immediately felt guilty, even though the shopping trolley had come with the house. 'It was there when we came here,' she said defensively.

'If the wheels will run straight,' Sylvia went on as if Kat had not spoken, 'we could use it to keep your boredom away.'

'What can you do with an old shopping trolley?' Kat asked lazily.

'Let us examine it and, if it still works, I will tell you of my idea.'

They trundled the wire basket, set low on its four wheels, out of the shed. The wheels did, indeed, still run true, if squeakily. Kat dribbled oil over the axles and the squeaks disappeared. It was covered in spider's webs so Kat turned the hose on it, while Sylvia scrubbed it with a laundry brush.

'Okay, Syl,' Kat said, 'the thing still functions. So tell me your latest bright idea.'

'If we were to put an old pillow in it we could take it in turns to sit in it and ride down your front driveway.'

'That's your worst idea yet!' Kat exclaimed. 'We'd go down that driveway at a rate of knots, over the road and <u>whammo</u>, into that brick wall round the place opposite.'

'We will tie this piece of rope onto your gatepost,' Sylvia said, in a voice like a teacher explaining an idea to a student who was refusing to think, 'and the one who is not in the trolley will hold it out. The one who is in the trolley will grab the rope and the trolley will swing around and go up the road. The slope on the road will make it slow down. The trolley will ...'

'Run back down the road towards the highway,' Kat cut in.

'In which case, the one who is not in the trolley will catch it. It will be fun, eh Kat?'

Kat took a deep breath. 'Now you listen to me, Sylvia. For starters, if you grab a rope at high speed, it'll burn the skin off your hands. And what if it doesn't slow down? What if it goes thundering into the gutter and throws its passenger out? What if a car comes by just at the moment the trolley hits the road? Goodbye trolley. Goodbye rider. Hello, big trouble.'

1 What was Sylvia's plan for the trolley?
  A Use it for rides down the driveway.
  B Put a pillow in it to make a seat.
  C Repair it and then put it back in the shed.
  D Clean it up and return it to the shop.

2 What problem most concerned Sylvia about the trolley in the shed?
  A It was covered in cobwebs.
  B It needed cleaning.
  C The wheels would squeak.
  D The wheels wouldn't run straight.

3 Sylvia was looking for something to do because
  A she was avoiding her swimming lesson.
  B she didn't want to clean the trolley.
  C Kat was bored.
  D Kat has just had an accident.

4 What was Sylvia's plan to stop the trolley from rolling away? Write your answer on the lines.

_____

_____

5 Why did Kat feel guilty about the trolley?
  A She hadn't cleaned it.
  B It hadn't been repaired.
  C It belonged to the previous owners of the house.
  D She feared Kat might think she had stolen it.

6 What does Kat mean when she says 'whammo'?
  A The trolley will smash the brick wall down.
  B Sylvia's idea would be a success.
  C There will be a loud forceful impact.
  D The ride will be exciting fun.

7 Circle **two** letters.

Kat's reaction to Sylvia's plan could best be described as
  A practical.   **B** timid.   **C** enthusiastic.
  D hasty.   **E** indifferent   **F** apprehensive

8 A suitable title for the extract would be
  A Cleaning a Trolley.   **B** A Crazy Idea.
  C Talking Sense.   **D** Goodbye Rider.

☞ **Answers and explanations on page 202**

TIPS FOR WRITING NARRATIVE TEXTS

A **narrative** is a fiction text and is also known as a **story**. The purpose of a narrative is to entertain, amuse or inform.

Before you start writing

- **Read the question and check the stimulus material carefully**. *Stimulus material* refers to the topic, title, picture, words, phrases or extract of writing you are given to base your writing on.
- **Decide if you are going to be writing in the first person** (you become a character in your story) or in **the third person** (you are writing about other characters). When writing in the first person be careful not to overuse the pronoun *I* (e.g. *I did this, I did that*).
- Take a few moments to **plan the structure of your story**. Remember: stories have a beginning, middle and end. It sounds simple but many stories fail because one of these three parts is not well written.

Structure of narrative texts

A narrative has a specific structure, containing:
- **Orientation**—the introduction of the setting and characters
- **Complication**—a problem faced by the character(s) that must be overcome
- **Climax**—a scene of increased tension where the character is faced with some kind of danger
- **Resolution**—the problem is overcome
- **Coda**—a lesson is learned and life returns to normal.

Language features of narrative texts

- **Engage the senses** of your reader through description of what can be seen, heard, felt, tasted or smelled. To do this you should include figures of speech such as similes, metaphors and personification.
- **Use strong action verbs** to capture mood and create tension. Instead of *The girl took the food* you could say *The girl lunged for the food*.
- **Use emotive words** to engage the emotions of your reader. It is important to consider what emotions you would like your reader to feel for a character in a specific situation. Once you have decided, use emotive words and phrases to evoke these emotions, e.g. *Lee sat alone feeling despair descend upon him* or *Rob's desire for the cookie caused his stomach to tangle*.
- **Use dialogue sparingly**. It should be used to develop a character or situation. Remember that dialogue tags should elaborate on the attitude of the speaker. Instead of writing *Jane said* you should be more specific, such as *Jane cried* or *Jane moaned, flicking her hair over her shoulder*.

Don't forget to:
- plan your narrative before you start
- write in correctly formed sentences and take care with paragraphing
- choose your words carefully and pay attention to your spelling and punctuation
- write neatly but don't waste time
- quickly check your narrative once you have finished.

Real Test and Tips

There is no way of knowing for certain what type of writing will be included in the NAPLAN Tests in years to come. This is an opportunity for you to practise different types of writing.

Before you start, read the General writing tips on pages 26–27 and the Tips for writing narrative texts on page 60.

Today you are going to write a narrative or story.
Look at the picture on the right.
The idea for your story is **the discovery of something unusual**. It could be a note hidden in a container, a wallet or small purse, a map, keys with a tag, a strange electronic device or some strange information.
Think about where your story takes place. It could be on a beach, or by a lake or river. It could be in a park or camping ground.
Think about when your story takes place—daytime or dusk, summer or winter, holidays or school days.
Your story might be amusing or it might be serious. Think about how the people in your story react.

Before you start writing, give some thought to:
- where your narrative takes place
- the characters and what they do in your narrative
- the events that take place in your narrative and the problems that have to be resolved
- how your narrative begins, what happens in your narrative, and how your narrative ends.

Don't forget to:
- plan your narrative before you start writing
- write in correctly formed sentences and take care with paragraphing
- choose your words carefully and pay attention to your spelling and punctuation
- write neatly but don't waste time
- quickly check your narrative once you have finished.

Start writing here or type in your answer on a tablet or computer.

_____

_____

_____

_____

_____

_____

_____

_____

_____

_____

☞ **Marking guide on page 203**

WRITING
Narrative text 2

There is no way of knowing for certain what type of writing will be included in the NAPLAN Tests in years to come. This is an opportunity for you to practise different types of writing.

Before you start, read the General writing tips on pages 26–27 and the Tips for writing narrative texts on page 60.

Today you are going to write a narrative or story.
Choose one of the following phrases and use it as a basis for your story.
- Shadows
- Shadow across the moon
- In the shade of a gum tree
- Valley of shadows

These phrases can relate to anything. Think of all the situations where shadows may play a part. Shadows across the moon could be birds, clouds or an aircraft. A valley of shadows might be the onset of night or something more sinister. Remember: if your writing is gross or weird and written just to shock, it may not be well received.

Before you start writing, give some thought to:
- where your narrative takes place
- the characters and what they do in your narrative
- the events that take place in your narrative and the problems that have to be resolved
- how your narrative begins, what happens in your narrative, and how your narrative ends.

Don't forget to:
- plan your narrative before you start writing
- write in correctly formed sentences and take care with paragraphing
- choose your words carefully and pay attention to your spelling and punctuation
- write neatly but don't waste time
- quickly check your narrative once you have finished.

Start writing here or type in your answer on a tablet or computer.

_____

_____

_____

_____

_____

_____

_____

_____

_____

_____

_____

_____

☞ **Marking guide on pages 203-204**

TIPS FOR WRITING PROCEDURES

Procedures tell us how to do something. This might include instructions on how to carry out a task or play a game. More complicated procedures involve several phases, directions for getting to a place or rules to be followed.

The purpose of a procedure is to provide instructions. Written procedures aim to tell the reader how to make or do something. Procedures usually have two main parts:

- the materials and tools needed (these are often called *requirements* or, in recipes, *ingredients*)
- the steps to be followed.

When writing procedures, it is best to keep the following points in mind. They will help you get the best possible mark.

Before you start writing

- **Read the question and check the stimulus material carefully**. *Stimulus material* means the topic, title, picture, words, phrases or extract of writing you are given to base your writing on.
- **Write about something you know**. Don't pick a complicated topic. Even the steps in a simple everyday procedure can be difficult to explain simply and precisely.

The introduction

- Start by **stating what will happen in the end**—the goal of the activity. This is often contained in the title.

The body

- **You may add personal opinions and comments** to brighten up the largely impersonal language used in procedures.
- **Follow the structure of procedures**. The materials and tools required are listed first, followed by short, concise sentences describing the steps in chronological order. The steps may be numbered.
- **Correctly paragraph your writing**. This is important: put each step in a separate paragraph.
- **Lay out your instructions clearly**. The reader must be able to follow the steps easily in order.
- **Add diagrams**. These can be very useful, as they can often clearly illustrate a step that would take many words to explain.
- **Include additional material** such as safety notes and explanations.
- **Use precise terms** such as *lukewarm, spread evenly, hold for two minutes* or *sharp turn right*.
- **Use command sentences**. These are sentences starting with infinitive verbs without *to*, such as *put, place* and *allow*. This is known as the imperative mood.
- **Use sequencing words**, such as *then, after* and *while*, that establish the sequence of steps clearly.
- **Include optional stages as necessary**, such as explaining reasons, providing alternative steps, giving warnings or mentioning possible consequences.

The conclusion

- The final paragraph may **include a comment** on what will have been achieved by following the steps.

When you have finished writing give yourself a few minutes to read through your procedure. Quickly check spelling and punctuation, and insert any words that have been accidentally left out.

There is no way of knowing for certain what type of writing will be included in the NAPLAN Tests in years to come. This is an opportunity for you to practise different types of writing.

In a procedure the aim is to describe to a reader exactly how to do or make something.

Before you start, read the General writing tips on pages 26–27 and the Tips for writing procedures on page 63.

Today you are going to write a procedure.

Choose one of the following topics and tell a reader exactly what to do.
- Preparing a slice of toast spread with your favourite topping
- Potting a small indoor plant
- Withdrawing cash from an ATM
- Writing and sending an email

Before you start writing, give some thought to:
- every step involved in carrying out the task
- any safety hints or precautions you can offer
- what you achieved by following the instructions.

Don't forget to:
- plan your procedure before you start writing
- make a list of materials needed and use command-type sentences in your instructions
- choose your words carefully and pay attention to your spelling and punctuation
- write neatly but don't waste time
- quickly check your procedure once you have finished.

Start writing here or type in your answer on a tablet or computer.

_____

_____

_____

_____

_____

_____

_____

_____

_____

_____

_____

_____

☞ **Marking guide on page 204**

Real
Test and
Tips

There is no way of knowing for certain what type of writing will be included in the NAPLAN Tests in years to come. This is an opportunity for you to practise different types of writing.

In a procedure the aim is to describe to a reader exactly how to do or make something.

Before you start, read the General writing tips on pages 26–27 and the Tips for writing procedures on page 63.

> Today you are going to write a procedure.
> Choose one of the following topics and tell a reader exactly what to do.
> - How to blow up and tie balloons for a party
> - How to make a cup of tea using a teabag
> - How to eat a hard-boiled egg
> - How to do a simple addition of three numbers (23 + 34 + 15)

Before you start writing, give some thought to:
- every step involved in carrying out the task
- any safety hints or precautions you can offer
- what you achieved by following the instructions.

Don't forget to:
- plan your procedure before you start writing
- make a list of materials needed and use command-type sentences in your instructions
- choose your words carefully and pay attention to your spelling and punctuation
- write neatly but don't waste time
- quickly check your procedure once you have finished.

Start writing here or type in your answer on a tablet or computer.

_____

_____

_____

_____

_____

_____

_____

_____

_____

_____

_____

_____

_____

_____

☞ **Marking guide on pages 204-205**

Week 3

This is what we cover this week:

Day 1 **Statistics and Probability:** ◎ Mean, graphs and tables
       Number and Algebra: ◎ Patterns and algebra
       Measurement and Geometry: ◎ 2D and 3D shapes and position

Day 2 **Spelling:** ◎ 'ie' and 'ei' words and the suffix 'ful'
       ◎ Common misspellings
       Grammar and punctuation: ◎ Verbs and commas

Day 3 **Reading:** ◎ Understanding recounts
       ◎ Following procedures

Day 4 **Writing:** ◎ Description of a scene
       ◎ Description of a person
       ◎ Book review
       ◎ Review of a production

Test Your Skills

STATISTICS AND PROBABILITY
Mean, graphs and tables

1 What is the mean of 11, 19, 33 and 17?
A 11   **B** 18   **C** 20   **D** 33

2 The heights of three students are 125 cm, 135 cm and 145 cm. What is the mean height?
A 125 cm **B** 135 cm **C** 145 cm **D** 305 cm

3 The total mass of 4 watermelons is 23.68 kg. What is the mean mass?
A 5.82 kg **B** 5.92 kg **C** 6.42 kg **D** 8.42 kg

4 What is the mean of $1\frac{1}{2}$ and $2\frac{1}{2}$?
A $\frac{1}{2}$ **B** 1   **C** 2   **D** 4

The column graph below shows the results of a quiz given to a class of 24 students.

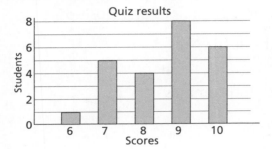

Quiz results

5 If a student was chosen at random, what is the chance that they scored 8?
A $\frac{1}{12}$ **B** $\frac{1}{8}$ **C** $\frac{1}{6}$ **D** $\frac{1}{4}$

6 What fraction of the class scored less than 8?
A one-fifth   **B** one-quarter
C one-half   **D** three-quarters

The divided bar graph shows the results of a survey of 100 people to find the most popular pets.

Popular pets

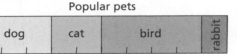

7 What is the most popular pet?
A bird   **B** cat   **C** dog   **D** rabbit

8 How many people preferred a cat?
A 2   **B** 10   **C** 20   **D** 25

9 What percentage of people preferred a dog?
A 10%   **B** 20%   **C** 30%   **D** 40%

The line graph shows the population of a town.

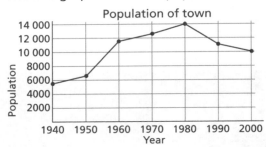

Population of town

10 Between what years was the population growing the fastest?
A 1940–1950   **B** 1950–1960
C 1960–1970   **D** 1970–1980

11 When did the population first reach 10 000?
A 1948   **B** 1951   **C** 1952   **D** 1957

The sector graph shows the distances from a school that 120 students live.

Distance between school and home

12 Estimate the number of students who live between 2 and 5 km from school?
A 20   **B** 30
C 45   **D** 60

13 What percentage of students live within 2 km of the school?
A 20%   **B** 25%   **C** 30%   **D** 40%

The graph shows the time taken for four cyclists to travel 48 kilometres.

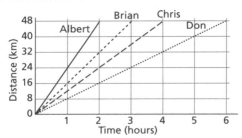

14 Which cyclist travelled the slowest?
A Albert   **B** Brian   **C** Chris   **D** Don

15 What was Chris's average speed?
A 12 km/h   **B** 16 km/h
C 24 km/h   **D** 32 km/h

☞**Explanations on pages 205–206**

Key Points

STATISTICS AND PROBABILITY
Mean, graphs and tables

1 The **mean is the average** and is found by adding quantities together and then dividing by the number of quantities.

Examples:

a Find the mean of 16, 12, 8 and 24.

$$\text{Mean} = \frac{16 + 12 + 8 + 24}{4} = \frac{60}{4} = 15$$

The mean is 15.

b If the mean of 6 scores is 5, what is the total of the 6 scores?

Mean = 5

Total = 6×5

= 30

The total of the scores is 30.

c The mean of 3 scores is 8. If another score is included, the mean increases to 10. What is the new number?

Total of the 3 scores = 8×3

= 24

Total of the 4 scores = 10×4

= 40

As 40 − 24 = 16, the new score was 16.

2 A **column graph** uses columns or bars to compare quantities.

Example: The graph shows the hair colour of students in a class.

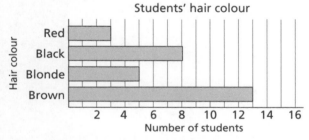

How many students were surveyed?

Students = 3 + 8 + 5 + 13

= 29

29 students

3 A **divided bar graph** is a bar divided into sections to show information.

Example: The graph shows how 80 students travelled to school.

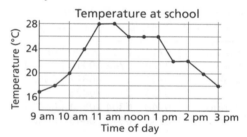

Student transport to school

Estimate the number who travelled by car.

Car travellers make up about one-quarter of the total length. As $\frac{1}{4}$ of 80 is 20, about 20 students travelled by car.

4 A **line graph** uses a line to join points which represent data.

Example: The temperature throughout the school day is recorded.

When was the temperature 20 degrees? From the graph, 10 am and 2:30 pm

5 A **sector (pie) graph** uses a circle and sections (sectors) to represent different categories.

Example: 600 people were surveyed to find their continent of birth. Estimate the number born in Asia.

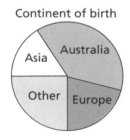

Continent of birth

The sector representing Asia measures about 60°, a sixth of 360°.

Number = $\frac{1}{6} \times 600 = 100$

About 100 people

6 A **conversion graph** converts currencies.

Example: Use the graph to convert 50 Australian dollars to US dollars.

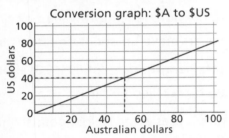

Conversion graph: $A to $US

The graph shows $50 Aus = $40 US

7 Use a **timetable** to make decisions.

Example: Harry uses the train timetable to plan a trip from Brakle to Yango.

Howarth	0714	0732	0800	0817
Portworth	0724	0742	0810	
Brakle	0731		0817	0832
Cooper	0739	0755	0825	
Yango	0748	0804	0834	0847
Warialta	0759	0815	0845	0856

What is the latest time Harry can catch the train if he wants to be in Yango by twenty to nine?

Harry catches the 8:17 at Brakle, to be in Yango at 8:34.

Real Test

STATISTICS AND PROBABILITY
Mean, graphs and tables

20 min

The table shows the number of vehicles in a parking area: *Hint 1*

Vehicle	Number
Car	40
Truck	2
Motorbike	3
Van	?
Total	50

1 What percentage of the vehicles were vans?

A 1%   **B** 5%   **C** 10%   **D** 20%

2 A vehicle is chosen at random. What is the probability that it is a motorbike?

A 0.03   **B** 0.06   **C** 0.3   **D** 0.6

This graph is used to convert Australian dollars to US dollars.

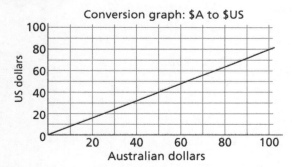

Conversion graph: $A to $US

3 How many Australian dollars are equal to 60 US dollars? *Hint 2*

A 10   **B** 20
C 50   **D** 75

4 How many US dollars are equal to 1000 Australian dollars?

A 80   **B** 600
C 800   **D** 1000

5 The table shows the number of push-ups Brad has completed each morning. *Hint 3*

Day	Mon.	Tue.	Wed.	Thu.	Fri.
Push-ups	12	15	15	10	8

What was the average (mean) number of push-ups?

Write your answer in the box:

Mitchell recorded his activities throughout a 24-hour period in a sector graph.

Mitchell's day

6 The 'Other' is represented by an angle of 60°. What fraction of the day was Mitchell involved in the other activities?

A $\frac{1}{6}$ **B** $\frac{1}{5}$ **C** $\frac{1}{4}$ **D** $\frac{1}{3}$

7 What percentage of the day was Mitchell at school?

A 6%   **B** 12%   **C** 25%   **D** 40%

8 Mitchell slept for 8 hours. What angle is used to represent sleeping? *Hint 4*

A 80°   **B** 100°
C 120°   **D** 180°

Kim's height is measured each year on her birthday and recorded in the chart.

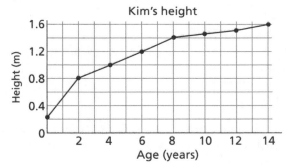

Kim's height

9 What is the difference in her height between 8 years and 14 years?

Write your answer in the box: _____ cm

10 How old was she when she reached 1.5 m?

A 11   **B** 12   **C** 13   **D** 14

☞ **Answers and explanations on page 206**

The graph shows the number of viewers of different channels at 7:15 pm.

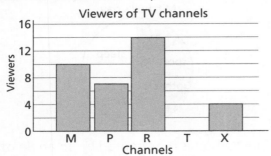

11 How many were watching channel P?

A 6   **B** 7   **C** 8   **D** 14

12 If there was a total of 40 viewers, how many were watching channel T?

A 5   **B** 6   **C** 7   **D** 8

The graph shows the way Sonia spends her $24 weekly allowance.

Allocation of allowance

food	savings	other

13 How much does she spend on food?

$ [   ]

14 What percentage of her allowance does she save?

[   ] %

15 If Sonia recorded the information on a sector graph, what angle would represent her savings?

[   ] degrees

16 Part of a train timetable is detailed.

Jeffersen	0802	0842	0859	0817
Ainsworth	0811	0851		0826
Phelan	0817		0912	
Bradley	0826	0903	0920	0836
Carment	0831		0925	0841

How long is the fastest trip from Jeffersen to Bradley?

Write your answer in the box: [   ] min

Hint 1: Find the missing value using subtraction.
Hint 2: Use horizontal and vertical lines on the conversion graph.
Hint 3: Monday to Friday is 5 days.
Hint 4: There are 360° in a circle.

☞ **Answers and explanations on page 206**

Test Your Skills

NUMBER AND ALGEBRA
Patterns and algebra

20 MIN

1 65, 78, 91, ____
What is the missing value?
A 13 **B** 103 **C** 104 **D** 106

2 $\frac{2}{5}$, $\frac{4}{5}$, ____, $1\frac{3}{5}$, 2
What is the missing value?
A $\frac{1}{5}$ **B** $\frac{2}{5}$ **C** 1 **D** $1\frac{1}{5}$

3 0.2, 0.9, 1.6, ____, ____, 3.7

What number goes here?
A 0.7 **B** 2.3 **C** 3 **D** 3.2

4 16, 12, 8, 4, …
What is the sixth number in the pattern?
A −12 **B** −8 **C** −4 **D** 0

5

Top	3	5	9
Bottom	X	17	25

The rule used to complete the table is 'bottom number is double the top number and then add 7'. What is the value of X?
A 11 **B** 12 **C** 13 **D** 14

Here is a pattern of triangles made from matches:

6 How many matches are needed to make 5 triangles?
A 10 **B** 11 **C** 12 **D** 15

7 The diagrams are used to complete a table.

Triangles	1	2	3	4	5	6	7	8	9
Matches	3	5	7	9				X	

What is the value of X?
A 13 **B** 16 **C** 17 **D** 24

8

Top	12	17	22	X	32
Bottom	48	43	38	Y	28

Which is correct?
A X = 27 and Y = 43 **B** X = 23 and Y = 35
C X = 27 and Y = 35 **D** X = 27 and Y = 33

1st 2nd 3rd 4th
The pattern of dots continues.

9 How many dots would be in the 5th figure?
A 11 **B** 12 **C** 13 **D** 15

10 A table summarises the figures and dots.

Figure	1	2	3	4	5	6
Dots	1	3	6	10		X

What is the value of X?
A 15 **B** 16 **C** 18 **D** 21

11 295 − ☐ = 86
What is the missing number?
A 209 **B** 211 **C** 219 **D** 229

12 4 × ☐ − 2 = 18
What is the missing number?
A 5 **B** 4 **C** 2 **D** 10

13 Jack is thinking of a number. He doubles it and adds six. His answer is twenty-four. What was Jack's original number?
A 6 **B** 9 **C** 12 **D** 16

14 A third of what number subtracted from ten is the same as six?
A 6 **B** 9 **C** 12 **D** 15

15 48 ÷ ☐ + 5 = 13
What is the missing number?
A 6 **B** 8 **C** 18 **D** 30

16 Lee started at 93 and counted forward by 5. His second number was 98. What is his fifth number?
A 5 **B** 103 **C** 108 **D** 113

Here is a pattern of dots:

Fig 1 Fig 2 Fig 3

17 How many dots will be in Fig 4?
A 13 **B** 14 **C** 15 **D** 16

18 Which figure will consist of 21 dots?
A Fig 5 **B** Fig 6 **C** Fig 7 **D** Fig 8

☞**Explanations on pages 206-207**

1 To complete a **pattern of numbers** we first determine the rule and then use it to find other numbers.

Examples:

a Complete the sequence 32, 51, 70, 89, ____.
The sequence is counting forward by 19.
Next number = 89 + 19
    = 89 + 20 − 1
    = 109 − 1
    = 108
The next number is 108.

b What is the missing number in this sequence? 256, 128, 64, ___, 16, 8
The pattern is dividing by 2.
Missing number = 64 ÷ 2
    = 32
The missing number is 32.

2 A **pattern of shapes** can be summarised in a table.

Example: Matches are used to form a pattern of squares.

a How many matches are needed to make 4 squares?
The matches used are 4, 7, 10, ?
The next number is 13.

b Complete the table:

Squares	1	2	3	4	5	6	7
Matches	4	7	10	13			

The three entries are 16, 19 and 22.

c Write in words the rule for the bottom row.
The bottom number is 3 times the top number plus 1.

d How many matches are needed for 20 squares?
Using the rule in **c**, 3 × 20 + 1 = 61.

3 A table can be completed by **determining the rule, or pattern**.

Example:

Top	1	2	3	4	5	6
Bottom	6	10	14	18	22	?

a What is the rule?
The bottom number is four times the top number plus 2.

b What is the missing number?
4 × 6 + 2 = 24 + 2 = 26

4 Number sentences can be completed by **finding the missing value**.

Examples: Find the missing value.

a 5 + ☐ = 3 × 4
As 3 × 4 = 12, then the missing number is 7 as 5 + 7 = 12.

b 6 × ☐ = 3
Replace the missing number with the phrase 'what number': 6 times 'what number' is 3.
This means the number is $\frac{1}{2}$.

5 An **unknown number** can be found.

Example: I am thinking of a number so that when I double it and add 5, I get 17. What is the number?
2 times 'what number' + 5 = 17
This means 2 times 'what number' = 12
The number is 6.

6 A solution can be checked by **substituting different numbers** in the original question.

Example: Half of a certain number plus six is equal to ten. Find the number.

A 2　　　　**B** 4　　　　**C** 6　　　　**D** 8

Check each of the choices:
2: Half of 2 + 6 = 1 + 6 ≠ 10
3: Half of 4 + 6 = 2 + 6 ≠ 10
6: Half of 6 + 6 = 3 + 6 ≠ 10
8: Half of 8 + 6 = 4 + 6 = 10
The number is 8.

7 **Inverse operations** are useful when solving number sentences. Inverse operations are addition and subtraction, multiplication and division.

Examples: Find the missing value in

a 95 + ☐ = 198
The inverse of addition is subtraction:

☐ = 198 − 95 = 103

b ☐ ÷ 0.4 = 0.6
The inverse of division is multiplication:

☐ = 0.6 × 0.4 = 0.24

Arjun is making this pattern of triangles using matches:

He summarised the information in the table:

Triangle	1	2	3	4	5	6
Matches	3	5	7			X

❶ What number replaces the X? *Hint 1*
  A 9   **B** 12   **C** 13   **D** 18

❷ How many matches are needed to make 10 triangles?
  A 20   **B** 21   **C** 26   **D** 30

❸ If Arjun continues the pattern, how many matches would he need for 50 triangles?
  A 51   **B** 81   **C** 86   **D** 101

❹ What is the missing number in this number sentence? $7 \times \Delta = 714$ *Hint 2*
  Write your answer in the box: ☐

❺ Suzie was thinking of a number. She said that if you multiplied the number by 4 and then added 8, the answer would be 32. What was Suzie's number? *Hint 3*
  A 6   **B** 8   **C** 12   **D** 28

❻ Kali wrote this number pattern.
  25, 33, 41, 49, ...
  If the rule remained the same, what was Kali's sixth number in the pattern?
  A 8   **B** 48   **C** 55   **D** 65

❼ Amaya thought of a number. When she doubled her number and subtracted 5, her answer was 17. Which of the following statements shows the correct way to work out Amaya's number?
  A Divide 17 by 2 and add 5.
  B Multiply 17 by 2 and add 5.
  C Add 5 to 17 and then multiply by 2.
  D Add 5 to 17 and then divide by 2.

❽ This pattern shows some missing numbers.
  21, 27, ____, 39, _____, 51. Which of these numbers are the missing numbers?
  Select **all** the correct answers.

32	33	44	45	46
A	B	C	D	E

❾ Sean used the same rule on each number in the top row to get the number below it in the bottom row. What rule did Sean use?

Top	6	11	16	21
Bottom	20	35	50	65

  A Add 14 to the top number.
  B Multiply top number by 3 and add 2.
  C Multiply top number by 4 and minus 4.
  D Multiply top number by 5 and minus 10.

❿ Look at this number sentence:
  $\triangle + \triangle + \bigcirc = 15$
  If $\triangle = 6$, what is the value of the $\bigcirc$?
  A 3   **B** 4   **C** 5   **D** 6

⓫ Gavin starts with a number. He multiplies it by 6 and then divides by 8. His answer is 3. What number did Gavin start with?
  A 2   **B** 3   **C** 4   **D** 6

⓬ 1, 4, ___, _____, 25, 36, 49
  What are the missing numbers?
  A 5 and 10   **B** 9 and 16
  C 10 and 15   **D** 7 and 10

⓭ If $45 = 2 \times$ ☐ $+ 5$, what is the missing value?
  Hint 4
  A 15   **B** 20   **C** 25   **D** 30

⓮ Shari thought of a number. She multiplied it by 8 and then added 8. Her answer was 64. What number did Shari start with?
  A 7   **B** 8   **C** 9   **D** 16

⓯ Start with 0.3 and count forward by 0.5. Which pattern shows this rule?
  A 0.3, 0.5, 0.7, 0.9, ...   **B** 0.3, 0.8, 1.3, 1.8, ...
  C 0.3, 0.8, 1.2, 1.6, ...   **D** 0.3, 0.8, 1.2, 1.7, ...

⓰ Teresa used the rule 'bottom number = 30 minus 2 times top number' to complete the table. Which of these are the missing numbers? Select **all** the correct answers.

Top	3	5	11	13
Bottom	24	?	?	4

7	8	10	12	20
A	B	C	D	E

Hint 1: *Use the first 3 numbers to develop a rule and then apply it.*
Hint 2: *The inverse operation of multiplication is division.*
Hint 3: *Sometimes it is easier to substitute the choices into the question to find the correct one.*
Hint 4: *The inverse operation of addition is subtraction.*

☞**Answers and explanations on pages 207-208**

MEASUREMENT AND GEOMETRY
2D and 3D shapes and position

20 min

1 Estimate the size of the angle.

A 30°   **B** 60°   **C** 120°   **D** 220°

2 What is the value of x?

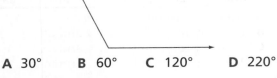

50° $x°$

A 20   **B** 50   **C** 110   **D** 130

3 What is the value of x?

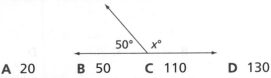

100°
30° $x°$

A 30   **B** 50   **C** 60   **D** 70

4 The triangle in question 3 is
A scalene.   **B** isosceles.
C right-angled.   **D** equilateral.

5 What is the size of each angle in an equilateral triangle?
A 30°   **B** 50°   **C** 60°   **D** 90°

6 Which four-sided shape has all sides equal and diagonals that are different lengths?
A square   **B** rhombus
C hexagon   **D** triangle

7 What is not shown on the diagram?
A segment   **B** sector
C quadrant   **D** arc

8 How many lines of symmetry has this shape?
A 1   **B** 2
C 3   **D** 4

9 What is the order of rotational symmetry of this shape?
A 1   **B** 2
C 3   **D** 4

10 A triangle has been enlarged. What is the value of x?

2   2.3
3

4   x
6

A 4   **B** 4.6   **C** 5   **D** 6.4

11 The ratio of lengths on a model car to the lengths on the actual car is 1:15. A tyre on the model car is 3 cm in diameter. What is the diameter of the actual tyre?
A 5 mm   **B** 5 cm   **C** 45 cm   **D** 50 cm

12 A 3D shape has 5 faces, 9 edges and 6 vertices. What could the shape be?
A triangular prism   **B** cube
C hexagonal prism   **D** square pyramid

13 A knife is used to cut a section of a cylinder. What shape is the cross-section?

A ☐   **B** ⬭   **C** ⬭   **D** ○

14 What is the top view of this shape?

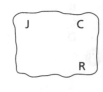

A   **B**

C   **D**

15 The net of a triangular prism consists of
A a triangle and 3 rectangles.
B 2 triangles and 3 rectangles.
C 2 triangles and 6 rectangles.
D 4 triangles.

16 On a map, Catherine is 10 metres east of Jackie and 10 metres north of Raynor. What direction is Raynor from Jackie?

J   C

R

A north-west   **B** north-east
C south-west   **D** south-east

☞ **Explanations on page 208**

MEASUREMENT AND GEOMETRY
2D and 3D shapes and position

1 A **protractor** measures angles.

The angle measures 60°.

2 **Angle types:** Acute: less than 90°; right: 90° obtuse: between 90° & 180°; straight: 180°; reflex: between 180° & 360°; revolution: 360°

3 The **angle in a straight line** is 180° and the **angles in a triangle** add to 180°.
Example: Find the values of x and y.

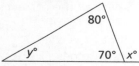

x = 110 as there is 180° in a straight line; y = 30 as there is 180° in a triangle.

4 Triangles can be classified:
Scalene: angles and sides of different sizes
Isosceles: 2 angles and 2 sides equal
Equilateral: 3 angles and 3 sides equal
Right-angled: 1 right angle
Obtuse-angled: 1 angle greater than 90°

5 Quadrilaterals can be classified:
Square: 4 equal sides, diagonals equal and a right angle
Rectangle: opposite sides equal and parallel, diagonals equal
Parallelogram: opposite sides equal and parallel
Rhombus: 4 equal sides, opposite sides parallel

6 **Parts of a circle:**

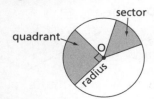
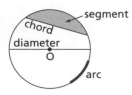

7 **Line symmetry** is where half an object is reflected on to the other half.

8 The **order of rotational symmetry** is the number of times an object matches its original position when it is being rotated through a revolution (360°).

Example: What is the order of rotational symmetry of a square?
Four (for every 90°, the square repeats)

9 An **enlargement** increases all dimensions of a shape by the same factor. Similarly, shapes can be reduced. A ratio can be used to express the enlargement factor (e.g. 1 : 3)
Example: A rectangle has dimensions of 4 cm by 3 cm. If it is enlarged by a factor of 2, what are the dimensions of the image? Image has dimensions 8 cm by 6 cm.

10 A **prism or pyramid** is named according to its base. This means a hexagonal prism has a hexagonal base.

11 A solid can be described in terms of the number of **faces**, **edges** and **vertices**:

Shape	Faces/ Surfaces	Vertices	Edges
Cube	6	8	12
Rectangular prism	6	8	12
Triangular prism	5	6	9
Square pyramid	5	5	8
Cylinder	3	0	2
Cone	2	1	1
Sphere	1	0	0

12 A **cross-section** is the face that is seen when a solid is cut through. If the solid is a prism, the cross-section parallel to the base is identical to the base.

13 A solid can be **viewed** from the top, front or side.
Example: Draw the top view of this solid:
Here is the top view:

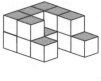

14 The **net of a solid** is a flat pattern that folds to form a 3D shape.
Example: What shape is formed using this net?
Octagonal pyramid

15 A **compass rose** shows directions north, south, east and west. In between there are directions north-east, south-east, south-west and north-west.

Real Test

MEASUREMENT AND GEOMETRY
2D and 3D shapes and position

1 Which dotted line is a line of symmetry? *Hint 1*

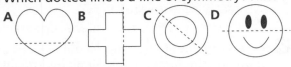

A   B   C   D

2 The net is used to make the cube. What number is missing from the top of the cube?

| 1 | 2 | 3 |
| 4 | 5 | 6 |

A 1   **B** 2   **C** 3   **D** 4

3 What is the size of the angle marked by the arrow?

A 40°
B 70°
C 110°
D 140°

4 The solid contains small cubes. What is the view from the right?

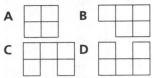

A   B
C   D

front

5 How many small cubes need to be added to the solid in question 4 to make a large cube?

| 1 | 4 | 15 | 17 | 19 |
| **A** | **B** | **C** | **D** | **E** |

6 Kurt rotates this shape 90° in a clockwise direction about the point. What is the new position?

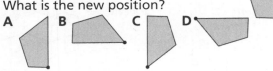

A   B   C   D

7 Which angle measures about 80°?

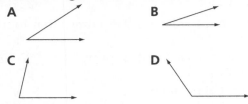

A   B   C   D

8 Alex measures two angles of a triangle as 40° and 70°. What is Alex's triangle? *Hint 2*

A isosceles   **B** equilateral
C right-angled   **D** obtuse-angled

9 The net of a pentagonal prism contains

A 1 pentagon and 5 rectangles.
B 2 pentagons and 5 rectangles.
C 1 pentagon and 5 triangles.
D 2 pentagons and 5 triangles.

10 The shape is rotated a quarter turn in an anticlockwise direction.

What is the new image?

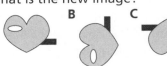

A   B   C   D

11 Ethan draws a hexagonal pyramid. Which of these statements is true? Select **all** the correct answers.

A It has 8 faces.   **B** It has 7 vertices.
C It has 12 edges.   **D** Its base has six sides.

12 Taylah is facing east. If she turns 135 degrees in a clockwise direction, which direction is she facing? *Hint 3*

A west   **B** south-west
C north-west   **D** south-east

13 What is the value of x in the diagram?

A 25   **B** 30
C 35   **D** 40

14 Part of the circumference of a circle is called

A an arc. **B** a radius. **C** a sector. **D** a quadrant.

15 Praena drew a triangle with rotational symmetry of order three. What type of triangle did she draw?

A scalene   **B** isosceles
C equilateral   **D** right-angled

16 What two types of angles are made by these intersecting lines?

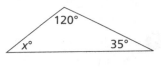

A right and obtuse   **B** reflex and obtuse
C reflex and acute   **D** acute and obtuse

Hint 1: *Line of symmetry cuts shape in half where one side reflects on to the other side.*
Hint 2: *In a triangle the angles add to 180 degrees.*
Hint 3: *Drawing a compass rose will help.*

☞**Answers and explanations on pages 208-209**

Key Points
and
Test Your
Skills

With most spelling rules there are exceptions. English words have many different origins (e.g. 'balaclava' comes from Central Europe and 'spaghetti' comes from Italy).

Key Points

1 a In **'ie'** and **'ei'** words, the 'i' usually comes before 'e' when the sound is 'ee'.
Examples: piece, niece, field, diesel *but* ceiling is an exception

b In words where the sound is not 'ee', the 'e' comes before 'i'.
Example: height

c In words where the sound is 'ay', the spelling is usually 'ei'.
Examples: neighbour, eight, eighty, feint

2 a The suffix **'ful'** means 'full' but is spelt with only one 'l'.
Examples: full of care → careful, full of use → useful, full of hate → hateful

b If the word ends with a consonant + 'y', then the 'y' is changed to 'i' before adding 'ful'.
Examples: beauty → beautiful, plenty → plentiful

3 Longer, common words ending in 'ice' and 'ise' can cause problems.
Many words ending in 'ice' are usually nouns.
Examples: practice, advice, device, office

Many words ending in 'ise' are usually verbs.
Examples: practise, advise, devise, utilise

In Australian English a number of verbs can take 'ise' or 'ize'. Some words must take the 'ise' spelling. When in doubt use the 'ise' spelling. However, a few words are always 'ize'.
Examples: capsize, prize, size.

Test Your Skills

Learn the words below. A common method of learning and self-testing is the **LOOK, SAY, COVER, WRITE, CHECK** method. If you make any mistakes, you should rewrite the word three times correctly, immediately. In this way you will become familiar with the correct spelling. If the word is particularly troublesome, rewrite it several more times or keep a list of words that you can check regularly.

This week's theme words: 'ie'/'ei' and 'ful' words

receipt	_____	eighth	_____
resourceful	_____	careful	_____
carefulness	_____	deceitful	_____
fieldsman	_____	siege	_____
seize	_____	ceiling	_____
reign	_____	weighty	_____
freighter	_____	sheik	_____
doubtful	_____	eventful	_____

Write any troublesome word three times: _____ _____ _____

_____ _____ _____

Real Test

20 MIN

Please ask your parent or teacher to read to you the spelling words on page 248.
Write the correct spelling of each word in the box.

1 Jude was as _____ as any person I know!

2 Luke was _____ in his decision to drop out of the team.

3 The _____ struck a tree near the shed.

4 For every _____ there is a logical explanation.

5 Any _____ would be appreciated.

6 This quick-setting _____ was designed for hobbyists.

7 Archie had an _____ reaction to the medicine.

8 Before use, twist the yellow _____ to OPEN.

9 The juice has a _____ taste. I just can't pick it.

10 After_____ the film, the critics made a quick decision.

11 It was _____ of Mr Amos to repair your picket fence.

12 I have _____ my obligations more than once!

13 Wayne was left friendless and _____ ruined after the sale.

14 Police warned the property owners about keeping _____ dogs.

15 The letter was forged and the agreement was _____.

Each sentence has one word that is incorrect.
Write the correct spelling of the underlined word in the box.

16 The <u>proffessor</u> showed university students how to do experiments.

17 The government had banned any <u>sceincetific</u> water quality tests.

18 There is no <u>gaurantee</u> that the watch is genuine.

19 The thief was caught with a steel bar in his <u>possesion</u>.

20 If you <u>realy</u> want a one-tonne utility you will have to earn it!

☞ **Answers on page 209**

Real Test

Each sentence has one word that is incorrect.
Write the correct spelling of the word in the box.

21 You have a broochure. Why don't you read it?

22 Uncle was hopping for fine weather for the celebration.

23 The junour team lost but the girls' team took out the trophy.

24 Now wait a minute! You have a neice and a nephew on the list!

25 If the craft capsises we will have to wade ashore.

☞ **Answers on page 209**

Key Points
and
Test Your
Skills

GRAMMAR AND PUNCTUATION
Verbs and commas

Key Points

① **a** **Verbs** are often called **doing** words or **action** words. Doing verbs include verbs for thinking and speaking. *Examples:* called, swam, collect, study, think, prepare, digest, compete

b There is a small group of verbs that are not doing or action verbs. These are often called **having** or **being** verbs. They do not involve actions or behaviour. *Examples:* is, are, am, was, were
Sometimes these verbs combine with other verbs to make a group of words.
Examples: was running, is eating, has been running

c Some verbs are used to express a thought or feeling.
Examples: dislike, enjoy, believe, understand, hope

② **a** Verbs can tell us when an action is, was or will be. This is called **tense**. Tense can be **past**, **present** or **future**. When an action happens can change the form of the verb.
Examples: Yesterday I <u>kicked</u> the ball. I <u>am kicking</u> the ball now. I <u>will kick</u> the ball soon.

b Some verbs change when the tense changes. *Example:* dig, dug, will dig

③ **Finite verbs** (or **complete verbs**) are verbs that can form a complete sentence when combined with a subject. (Jack swims.) The verb is *swims* and the subject is *Jack*.
Non-finite verbs are derived from other parts of speech. They cannot stand alone.
Examples: to see (It was the film *to see*.)

④ **Participles:** There are two types of participles: **present** participles and **past** participles. Participles are forms taken by verbs to indicate their tense. Participle verbs need **helper verbs** to form complete verbs. Helper verbs include am, are, is, was, were, has, have and had.
Examples: was hoping, had expected, is able, was lost, is running

⑤ **Commas** are used to:
a indicate where a reader should pause.
Example: You were told to wear shoes, and now you expect to be carried.

b separate a noun or phrase from the rest of the sentence.
Example: Trudy, my daughter, likes to paint.

c separate words or phrases in a list.
Example: We took pens, pencils, rulers, erasers and scrap paper.

d separate words that are spoken (quotations) from the rest of the sentence.
Example: The foreman yelled, 'Take care with that pipe!'

Test Your Skills

① Underline the six verbs in this passage.

The bell had rung and the children came out to watch the display. The teachers sat near the steps leading to the office. Everybody waited patiently.

② Write the tense for each of these sentences.
a Lucy caught the ball before it bounced into the pond. _____
b The club is going to see the match. _____
c Bruce is watching TV right now. _____

③ Choose *did*, *do*, *done*, *does* or *doing* to fill the space
All the students have _____ their homework.

④ How many commas should be used in this sentence?

Mandy said 'Did you bring the balloons streamers and flashing lights?' _____

Answers: **1** had rung, came, to watch, sat, leading, waited **2 a** past **b** future **c** present **3** (have) done **4** (two) Mandy said, 'Did you bring the balloons, streamers and flashing lights?'

Real Test

GRAMMAR AND PUNCTUATION
Verbs and commas

1 Choose the correct **articles** to complete this sentence. The spaces are numbered.

The farmer planted ☐1☐ elm, ☐2☐ eucalypt and ☐3☐ banksia by the creek.

Write your answer in the numbered boxes.

1	2	3

2 Which of the following correctly completes this sentence?

Carl gave a ░░░░░░ delivered address to the hushed school assembly.

attractively	stunningly	gorgeously	superbly
A	**B**	**C**	**D**

Read the text *New Students.* The text has some gaps.
Choose the correct word to fill each gap.

New Students

1 Two new boys enrolled at our school last week.
2 They want to be in our class. **3** They have ░░░░░░ the entrance test and are waiting for the results. **4** The boys were allowed to join the class for swimming training. **5** During summer we had ░░░░░░ twice during the week, then once on Saturday. **6** Now we only train on Friday. **7** Our coach told the boys not to leave their bags in the dressing room. **8** Jim Grey had his watch stolen.
9 When something is stolen, everybody ░░░░░░ a suspect until cleared by the police.

3
did	done	doing	does
A	**B**	**C**	**D**

4
practises	practise's	practice	practice's
A	**B**	**C**	**D**

5
are	am	were	is
A	**B**	**C**	**D**

6 Look at sentences 5 and 6 in *New Students* and answer the question.
Sentences 5 and 6 contain information about
A when something took place.
B why people behave as they do.
C how an event unfolded.
D where something took place.

7 Which sentence has the correct punctuation?
A Kelly the class captain asked for permission to speak to Inspector Sartor.
B Kelly, the class captain, asked for permission to speak to Inspector Sartor.
C Kelly the class captain, asked for permission to speak to inspector Sartor.
D Kelly, the class Captain, asked for permission to speak to Inspector Sartor.

8 Which sentence is correct?
A I have made the most perfect sauce for the meat.
B I have made a more perfect sauce for the meat.
C I have made the perfectest sauce for the meat.
D I have made the perfect sauce for the meat.

☞**Answers and explanations on pages 209–211**

Real Test

GRAMMAR AND PUNCTUATION
Verbs and commas

Read the text *Athletics Encounter*. The text has some gaps.
Chose the correct word to fill each gap.

Athletics Encounter

I'm Steele Avery, a sprinter. I was selected to represent our school at the yearly, interstate athletics carnival. I won my heat [____] my foot was badly blistered in an earlier race. There were competitors from every state. I meet a Tasmanian [____] name was also Steele!

9
	and	although	but	yet
	A	**B**	**C**	**D**

10
	who	who's	whose	which
	A	**B**	**C**	**D**

11 Which sentence is correct?
  A "I remember youse two used the sink after I had finished," protested Ryan.
  B "I remember you two used the sink after I have finished," protested Ryan.
  C "I remember you two used the sink after I has finished," protested Ryan.
  D "I remember you two used the sink after I had finished," protested Ryan.

12 Which sentence is correct?
  A On her long plane trip, Mum took a book, a crossword and an old diary.
  B On her long plane trip, Mum took a book, crossword and an old diary.
  C On her long plane trip, Mum took a book, a crossword and old diary.
  D On her long plane trip, Mum took a book, crossword and old diary.

13 Which sentence has the correct punctuation?
  A At the fete Jan, my sister played the violin, Kerry played the piano and I sang the songs.
  B At the fete Jan, my sister, played the violin, Kerry played the piano and I sang the songs.
  C At the fete Jan my sister, played the violin, Kerry played the piano and I sang the songs.
  D At the fete Jan, my sister, played the violin, Kerry played the piano, and I sang, the songs.

14 Which sentence has the correct punctuation?
  A He's the children's idol but Matts' songs are more memorable.
  B His the children's idol but Matt's songs are more memorable.
  C He's the children's idol but Matt's songs are more memorable.
  D He's the childrens' idol but Matt's song's are more memorable.

15 Which of the following correctly completes the sentence?

We watched as the model plane [____] out of control.

spun	span	spins	spinned	spend
A	**B**	**C**	**D**	**E**

16 Shade a bubble to show where the missing apostrophe (') should go.

Ⓐ Ⓑ   Ⓒ   Ⓓ

Both team▾s ▾mascot▾s were plastered on billboard ▾s down all major roads!

☞ **Answers and explanations on pages 209-211**

GRAMMAR AND PUNCTUATION
Verbs and commas

17 Which sentence has the correct punctuation?
  A The lonely old bent pensioner was given a handout of fruit, milk and tea.
  B The lonely, old, bent, pensioner was given a handout of fruit, milk and tea.
  C The lonely, old, bent pensioner was given a handout of fruit, milk, and tea.
  D The lonely, old, bent pensioner was given a handout of fruit, milk and tea.

18 Which of the following correctly completes the sentence?

The ten dollars on the table ▢ donated by a complete stranger.

were	is	was	are
A	**B**	**C**	**D**

19 Which sentence has the correct punctuation?
  A "That can't be right, can it?" Lindy asked.
  B "That can't be right? can it?" Lindy asked.
  C "That can't be right, can it? Lindy asked."
  D "That can't be right, can it," Lindy asked?

20 Shade **two** bubbles to show where the missing quotation marks (" and ") should go.

Ⓐ Ⓑ   Ⓒ   Ⓓ

"Take off your cap▼ ,▼ suggested the diver, "and bow to the guide.▼ It's good manners.▼

21 Which of the following correctly completes the sentence?

Looking through the telescope Mark could ▢ see the wreck.

easy	easily	easier	more easy
A	**B**	**C**	**D**

22 Which sentence has the correct punctuation?
  A "If two plus two is not four, then what is it?" questioned the examiner.
  B "If two plus two is not four? Then what is it?" questioned the examiner.
  C "If two plus two is not four, then what is it"? questioned the examiner.
  D "If two plus two is not four, then what is it? questioned the examiner."

23 Shade a bubble to show where the missing comma (,) should go.
"Stand by Hugh▲ "▲Father O'Brien said▲ to the new boy▲ in the choir.
  Ⓐ Ⓑ   Ⓒ   Ⓓ

24 Choose the word that is the verb.

through	verbose	recognise	crunchy
A	**B**	**C**	**D**

25 Which of the following correctly completes this sentence?

The weather was warm, but ▢ John nor Albert wanted to go swimming.

either	also	both	neither
A	**B**	**C**	**D**

☞**Answers and explanations on pages 209-211**

A recount is a record of events that happened in sequence. A recount has several forms. It can be personal or historical. It may also contain opinions or personal comments on the events. Many newspaper articles are recounts.

Read *China's Quake Lakes* and answer the questions.

China's Quake Lake

A quake lake is a natural lake formed by an earthquake which causes a mountainside to collapse and slide into a valley, blocking a river.

Rivers are recognised for carving valleys and canyons, not for their relationships with earthquakes. However, when the two natural forces (flowing water and movements in the earth's crust) blend, the result can be astounding and devastating.

In China, on Monday 12 May, 2008, an 8.0-magnitude earthquake and aftershocks triggered landslides that cut off rivers and streams, forming numerous 'quake lakes', with 34 in Sichuan, posing dangers to more than 700 000 of the people who survived the deadly quake.

Continuing landslides and heavy rains quickly increased the lake's water level. Authorities warned the banks could burst and flood nearby towns already devastated from the earthquake. People were evacuated.

The biggest concern was the Tangjiashan Lake, the largest of the quake lakes in Sichuan, whose water level rose rapidly by nearly two metres to 723 metres, only 29 metres below the lowest part of the barrier.

A problem arose because such lake walls are created by 'soft' landslide material—rubble, dirt and sand. When a lake fills and breaches the bank it then washes its bank away. Downstream floods can be sudden and dangerous. The problem was made worse by exceptionally heavy rains following the earthquakes, which rapidly filled the lakes.

Aftershocks caused access roads to be cut many times, hindering the arrival of relief teams.

All the barrier lakes (or quake lakes) formed after the massive May 12 earthquake in Sichuan Province are now 'under control', but the situation remained grim for some time.

More than 200 police officers worked round the clock for four days to drain the largest lake, which threatened one million residents living in the lower reaches of the river.

Their man-made spillway started draining the lake but it was not as effective as it should have been. The amount of water going into the lake was greater than the amount of water going out. Military engineers fired short-range missiles several times to blast boulders in the channel to speed up the outflow. Two massive blasts finally broke through a 'bottleneck' in the spillway.

Ironically, in July 2008 the Chinese Government made plans to turn the lake region into a tourist attraction and make it a feature of the distinctive local Qiang culture.

Sources:
http://www.channelnewsasia.com/stories/afp_asiapacific/view/352826/1/.html
http://www.thaindian.com/newsportal/world-news/china-to-turn-quake-created-
        lake-into-scenic-spot_10063755.html
Wikipedia: (http://en.wikipedia.org/wiki/Tangjiashan_Lake)
http://agonist.org/20080512/powerful_earthquake_hits_western_china

---

1 What is the initial cause of a quake lake?

A military explosions   **B** earthquakes

C flooding rains   **D** landslides

2 What **two** forces were involved in the creation of China's quake lake?
Write your answers on the lines.

1 _____

2 _____

3 Rescue attempts were made more difficult because

A police were employed to work on the spillway.

B the military had taken control.

C towns downstream were flooded.

D roads into the disaster area were cut.

4 What is meant by a 'bottleneck' in a river?

A an obstruction that causes one part of the river to flow at a slower rate

B any long, slow-flowing section of a river

C a deep and distinctive section of a riverbed

D a long lake that has become part of a river system

5 What fact did the writer find interesting about the largest quake lake?

A The police had to enlist military help to complete the spillway.

B Two different natural forces were required to create the lake.

C From being a disaster it may become a tourist attraction.

D It was just one of over thirty quake lakes.

6 The material in a quake lake barrier is described as 'soft' because it is

A the result of a natural disaster.

B saturated with floodwaters.

C created by natural forces.

D loose landslide material.

7 What was the threat to the people who survived the initial earthquakes?

A earth tremors

B flooding from burst lakes

C a military takeover

D movements in the earth's crust

8 The events in China could be best described as

A a human catastrophe.

B a planning shambles.

C an engineering failure.

D an environmental mistake.

Read this passage on the environmental disaster of a shipwreck in 1991 and answer the questions.

Wreck of the *Sanko Harvest*

Thursday 14 February, 1991

Just after 3 am the vessel, *Sanko Harvest*, hit a reef in the dangerous waters near Esperance, Western Australia. Cargo and fuel holds had been holed. The vessel was carrying 30 000 tonnes of fertilizer, 750 tonnes of fuel oil and 74 tonnes of engine diesel.

An urgent request for oil pollution equipment was issued because 'a small amount of oil was leaking'. The State Emergency Service (SES) responded quickly, as weather conditions were deteriorating. Winds pushed the vessel towards rocks.

At first, salvage operators thought the vessel could be towed to Esperance where its fuel oil and cargo could be unloaded. It may have been possible to 'refloat' the vessel if 2000 tonnes of cargo were dumped. Booms were rigged around the vessel to contain the fuel spill.

Friday 15 February, 1991

After 8 am, the situation deteriorated rapidly. The ship was resting on rocks and the movement on the rocks was causing increasing damage. Salvage operators recommended the unloading of the fuel oil. This was not attempted. Insurance companies would not permit another vessel to come in close in the dangerous conditions, as fuel oil is heavy and solidifies under cold conditions and would need heating before removal.

Rocks then pierced the fuel tanks and the hold itself. Fuel was lost. The closest available inflatable bags to contain the oil were in New Zealand.

The vessel listed as weather conditions deteriorated. The bow went under a metre of water. At 5 pm the ship was abandoned. Only the crew and documents were taken off.

Saturday 16 February, 1991

Aerial inspections of the vessel revealed that the ship was still firmly aground. Oil was leaking from the reef side. Dispersants were needed to break up the oil slick. Thirty-knot winds made the application of dispersants difficult. 18 000 tonnes of the cargo had been lost. By mid-afternoon some liquid dispersant was pumped into the damaged fuel hold.

Sunday 17 February, 1991

The vessel settled further onto the rocks. Oil reached a nearby island wildlife sanctuary and seal pups were covered in oil. An exclusion order was put around the wreck to prevent well-intentioned locals from boarding the vessel to remove oil.

At 3:30 pm the vessel slipped off the rocks. Within hours the ship's bow was on the bottom of the sea. The sea was too rough for a tug. A lone helicopter sprayed dispersant on the spill.

Monday 18 February, 1991

Overnight the ship split into two. A hatch lifted off and the remaining cargo and oil was lost, except for 100 tonnes of oil sealed in the engine room.

Follow-up

A massive clean-up followed involving hundreds of volunteers. Twenty-five kilometres of pure white beach had turned black. Gulls and other birds struggling in the water were rescued and cleaned. Seals responded to treatment. Even kangaroos on coastal beaches suffered.

Some good came of the disaster, however. The wreck site was declared a marine sanctuary and wildlife within 500 m of the wreck was protected from spear fishing. The Sanko Harvest is now the largest wreck within 'diveable' depth off the Australia coast. Rarely is a marine sanctuary the result of an environmental accident, but the Sanko Harvest story is one.

Source: Mackenzie's Island Cruises, January 2003

Real Test

1 Which group was informed first of problems aboard the *Sanko Harvest*?

A the State Emergency Service **B** the insurance company

C environmental volunteers **D** the New Zealand inflatable bag supplier

2 The reason the *Sanko Harvest* got into difficulties was because it

A was passing through a marine park. **B** was carrying too much cargo.

C sailed into dangerous waters. **D** encountered extreme weather conditions.

3 On what day and date did the crew of *Sanko Harvest* abandon ship? Write your answer on the line.

_____

4 Dispersants were intended to

A keep the ship afloat. **B** stop the ship from drifting.

C prevent the oil from solidifying. **D** break up the oil slick.

5 Why did the writer mention kangaroos?

A Kangaroos are not marine animals.

B Kangaroos usually avoid oil spills.

C Kangaroos keep themselves clean.

D Kangaroos are not affected by pollution.

6 The SES abandoned salvage attempts because

A more oil had spilled than was first advised.

B the weather conditions worsened.

C the insurance company would not permit the operation.

D the disaster happened over a weekend.

7 What was the final condition of the *Sanko Harvest*?

A It lost a hatch letting cargo escape into the ocean.

B The bow ended up a metre under water.

C A tug towed it to deeper water.

D It split into two on the rocks.

8 The passage could be best described as a

A police report. **B** factual recount. **C** newspaper report.

D warning to coastal shipping. **E** personal diary. **F** manual article.

9 The writer found that it was interesting that the *Sanko Harvest*

A sank so quickly.

B carried fuel oil through a marine park.

C had a larger cargo of fertilizer than fuel oil.

D was a disaster that produced a beneficial outcome.

10 Why did locals board the *Sanko Harvest*?

A to rescue injured marine life

B to see what damage had been done to the ship

C to take off as much oil as possible to prevent pollution

D to illegally remove oil that was going to be wasted

☞ **Answers and explanations on pages 211-212**

READING
Understanding recounts

Read *Ben Hall* and answer the questions.

Ben Hall

Ben Hall was a bushranger who led a notorious gang in the 1860s in NSW.

Born near Tamworth in 1837 to convict parents, he became a stockman, running a lease near the village of Wheogo. He and his partner, John McGuire, sold cattle to the miners on the gold diggings.

In 1862, Hall was falsely arrested for being an accomplice in a hold-up near Forbes and languished in jail for a month before the charges were dropped. While in detention, his wife ran off with a former policeman, his home was vandalised and his cattle either strayed or were stolen. Hall's life had been turned upside down and he wanted revenge.

Devastated by circumstances, Hall <u>took up the gun</u> and joined Frank Gardiner's bushranger gang, taking part in the infamous Eugowra Rocks robbery (1862), stealing gold and cash. When the gang separated, Hall took over leadership of the remaining bushrangers.

For three years the Hall gang audaciously plundered a large area around Forbes, Canowindra, Bathurst, Goulburn, Yass and Carcoar. 'Stand and Deliver' was often heard on the goldfields highways.

Besides the stealing, Hall wanted to embarrass police as much as possible for the wrongs he felt had been committed against him. He often humiliated local police by stealing their uniforms. When Police Inspector Sir Frederick Pottinger gave chase, the gang stole his horse.

The authorities called on Hall to surrender or be branded an outlaw. Hall's reply was "They'll never hang Ben Hall". He became the first bushranger to be outlawed.

A week later he was dead, aged all of 27 years. Hall was shot by the police on 6 May 1865, after former friend Mick Connolly informed police of his whereabouts at Billabong Creek. Mick had been tempted by the thousand-pound reward.

When shot, Ben appealed to tracker Billy Dargin to finish him off but a hail of bullets fired by the police did the job. Later, 36 bullet wounds were found in his body.

Ben Hall was buried at Forbes cemetery, two days before his 28th birthday. Nearly two hundred people attended his funeral. A neat picket fence appeared around the grave and in the 1920s a headstone was erected.

In recent times a small National Park in the Upper Hunter Valley (NSW) was named The Ben Hall Gap National Park.

Source: http://www.cultureandrecreation.gov.au/articles/benhall/

Real Test

1 Ben Hall became a bushranger because
  A his parents were convicts.
  B his friends were in a bushranger gang.
  C some bushrangers needed a new leader.
  D he felt he had been badly treated by the law.

2 The writer says Ben Hall 'took up the gun'. This means he
  A commenced a life of crime.
  B learned to use a gun.
  C needed to protect himself.
  D stole a gun.

3 How did Ben Hall's gang embarrass Sir Frederick Pottinger?
  A They took his guns.
  B They stole his horse.
  C They chased him away.
  D They told him to stand and deliver.

4 What fact indicates that Ben Hall was well regarded by the people of Forbes?
Write your answer on the line.

_____

5 When injured in a gunfight, who did Ben Hall turn to?
Write your answer on the line.

_____

6 Circle **two** letters. Ben Hall could best be described as
  A careful.   B brash.   C foolish.
  D cruel.   E assertive.   F merciful.

7 This writing could be best defined as
  A a personal explanation.
  B an official record.
  C a newspaper report.
  D a historical recount.

8 Ben Hall's exploits are regarded as
  A understandable.
  B merciless.
  C foolish.
  D irrational.

☞ **Answers and explanations on pages 212-213**

Real Test

A procedure is a set of instructions on how to do something. These are often called steps. Read the passage and answer the questions. It begins as a report and ends with general instructions on egg decorating.

Egg Decorating

Egg decorating is the art or craft of decorating eggs. It is quite a popular art/craft form because of the attractive, smooth, oval shape of the egg. Any bird egg can be used but most often the larger and stronger the eggshell, the more it is favoured by decorators. Egg carving is a delicate art not for the faint-hearted. Egg carvers create designs on eggs that range from the size of tiny quail eggs, to emu and ostrich eggs, about the size of a grapefruit. Designs might include a ribbon design or stencilled hearts, while elaborate designs might include nature scenes or lacy patterns.

Are eggs too fragile for carving? Some eggs are very sturdy. Ostrich eggs are so sturdy that chicks cannot hatch from them without their mother's help. Smaller eggs require careful handling. Carvers can break 10% of the eggs they attempt to carve. Most eggs used for carving come from hatcheries that sell infertile eggs for this purpose. Eggs from hatcheries are already cleaned and disinfected. Decorators using fresh eggs must clean them.

In Australia, in the 19th century, emu egg carving was widely practised by both Indigenous and European artists. A few Aboriginal artists from Western Australia maintained the tradition in the last century. Though no longer a popular activity, Peter Harris, a NSW artist, learned emu egg carving from an Aboriginal practitioner, Sam Kirby. One of Harris's best-known eggshell carvings illustrates the explorers, Burke and Wills.

There are two forms of egg carving. In one form, 'lacing', designs are cut out of the eggshell. In the other form of carving, the egg is 'sculpted'. Sculpting removes layers of the shell, often revealing different colours as the artist cuts deeper into the egg. Thicker shells provide more options for creating designs. However, both forms of carving can produce designs of outstanding detail.

If you don't want to be a carver you can simply decorate hard-boiled eggs or emptied eggshells. Hard-boiled eggs are sturdier than empty shells and easier to work with. If your hard-cooked egg does crack or the design isn't good enough to keep, you can eat the egg!

Emptied eggshells are lightweight. You can hang them on a mobile, an Easter egg tree or a Christmas tree. Emptied eggshells have nothing inside to spoil, so you can keep them on display for years. The white and yoke can be used in cooking.

If your finished dyed or decorated egg is a masterpiece, you can protect the design with an outer coating. Evenly coat the egg with thinned white glue, clear nail polish or craft finish.

Food safety tips:

■ Wash your hands in warm, soapy water before handling eggs at all four main steps: cooking, cooling, dyeing and decorating. This rule, of course, applies to all food-handling operations.

■ If the decorated hard-cooked eggs are to be eaten then:
  ● keep decorated, hard-boiled eggs refrigerated
  ● for health and safety reasons only use food colouring or food-grade egg dyes
  ● ensure the eggs aren't cracked. Cracked eggs should be disposed of properly. Eggs that crack during dyeing or decorating are liable to 'go off'.

Sources: http://www.aeb.org/kidsandfamily/eastereggs/decoratingtips.asp
http://www.smh.com.au/articles/2004/02/27/1077676969735.html?from=storyrhs
http://nga.gov.au/Exhibition/Tactility/Default.cfm?MnuID=6&Essay=5

1 Choose **two** options. Egg decorating could be described as
  A an ancient art.
  B a traditional craft.
  C a common pastime.
  D a guarded secret.
  E a multinational pursuit.
  F a passing fad.

2 If you intend to eat a decorated hard-boiled egg, you should
  A remove the design.
  B be careful of cracked shells.
  C make sure the dye is dry.
  D keep the egg in a fridge when not in use.

3 What is the main difference between laced eggs and sculpted designs?
  A Sculpted designs take off layers of eggshell.
  B Sculpted designs are mainly on hard-boiled eggs.
  C Sculpted designs are more delicate than laced designs.
  D Sculpted designs are for large eggs.

4 If you intend to keep your decorated egg, you should
  A hang it from a tree.
  B use it as an Easter egg.
  C coat the shell with protective coating.
  D save it as a hard-boiled egg.

5 What is the effect of using *you* in paragraph 5?
  A to assure the reader that the writer is well informed
  B to make the information pertinent to the reader
  C to persuade the reader to take up egg carving
  D to inform the reader of other people's experiences

6 The advantage of using emptied eggs is that
  A it doesn't matter if they get broken.
  B the eggs come from hatcheries.
  C they can be kept for years.
  D the insides can be used for cooking.

7 In the first paragraph you read 'Egg carving is a delicate art not for the faint-hearted'.

  What does the adjective 'faint-hearted' imply? Write your answer on the lines.

  _____

  _____

☞ **Answers and explanations on page 213**

TIPS FOR WRITING DESCRIPTIONS

Descriptions function as pictures in words of people, places or things. In a description you aim to give the reader a clear and vivid picture of what you are describing. After reading your description the reader should be able to close his or her eyes and picture the subject.

Descriptions are seldom written to stand alone in the same way as, say, narratives or recounts. Descriptions are often part of another kind of writing; they help to make other text types interesting.

When writing descriptions, it is best to keep the following points in mind. They will help you get the best possible mark.

Before you start writing

- **Read the question and check the stimulus material carefully**. *Stimulus material* means the topic, title, picture, words, phrases or extract of writing you are given to base your writing on.
- **Decide how you are going to present your description**. It could be in the first person or third person. Take care when using the first person not to overuse the pronoun *I*.
- **Decide on the tense you are going to use**. Descriptions are usually written in the present tense but feel free to use past or future tenses if this suits your purpose.

The introduction

- **Introduce the subject early** in your writing. The title should put the subject in focus.

The body

- **Always include some facts**. Descriptions in an information report may consist entirely of facts.
- **Don't just focus on what can be seen**. Enhance your writing by adding 'imagined' sounds and smells—you can even describe how something feels.
- **Make full use of adjectives and adverbs**. Use a short series of adjectives to paint a vivid picture.
- **Use action verbs to describe behaviour**. This adds interest to your description.
- **Use figurative language such as similes and metaphors** to make your description clear and interesting. Avoid clichés.

The conclusion

- The final paragraph may **include some brief personal opinions** in your description—the best place for this is often in the form of a concluding comment.

When you have finished writing give yourself a few minutes to read through your description. Quickly check spelling and punctuation, and insert any words that have been accidentally left out.

Real Test

There is no way of knowing for certain what type of writing will be included in the NAPLAN Tests in years to come. This is an opportunity for you to practise different types of writing.

The aim of a description is to give the reader a clear and vivid word picture of a person, thing, place or scene. Descriptions of scenes are often important in narratives. They can help create different moods and atmosphere.

Before you start, read the General writing tips on pages 26–27 and the Tips for writing descriptions on page 94.

Today you are going to write a description of a **garden**. Think of a garden you know well. Is it a private garden or a public garden? Is it a big or little garden? Is it well maintained? Is it a flower garden, a vegetable garden or a native garden? Start your description with a sentence naming what you are about to describe. Then think about colours, sounds and smells. Think about how the garden is used and the effort required to care for it. What birds and other animals enjoy the garden? Is the weather important?

Before you start writing, give some thought to:
- the setting—what you are describing
- the special features of the garden
- what value the garden has to the owners and the community.

Don't forget to:
- plan your description before you start writing.
- write in correctly formed sentences and take care with paragraphing
- choose your words carefully and pay attention to your spelling and punctuation
- write neatly but don't waste time
- quickly check your description once you have finished.

Start writing here or type in your answer on a tablet or computer.

_____

_____

_____

_____

_____

_____

_____

_____

_____

_____

_____

☞ **Marking guide on pages 213-214**

There is no way of knowing for certain what type of writing will be included in the NAPLAN Tests in years to come. This is an opportunity for you to practise different types of writing.

The aim of a description is to give the reader a clear and vivid word picture of a person, thing, place or scene. Descriptions of scenes are often important in narratives. They can help create different moods and atmosphere.

Before you start, read the General writing tips on pages 26–27 and the Tips for writing descriptions on page 94.

Today you are going to describe **a person**. Choose one of these options.
- An admired community worker
- A person you see often (e.g. bus driver, shop assistant, lady walking a dog)
- A brother or sister (or neighbourhood friend)
- A fictional superhero

Think about what makes the person interesting or different. You can write about the person's appearance. Think about their hair, eyes, their stature (height and size) and anything you notice or remember about them. Then think about their mannerisms (the way they do things), habits and their behaviour. Think about what they like doing and what seems to upset them. What do they do for relaxation? How do they speak? Are they noisy and outgoing, or quiet? Do they have other interests?

Before you start writing, give some thought to:
- where the person spends some or a lot of their time
- the character of the person
- how you or other people relate to the person.

Don't forget to:
- plan your description before you start writing.
- write in correctly formed sentences and take care with paragraphing
- choose your words carefully and pay attention to your spelling and punctuation
- write neatly but don't waste time
- quickly check your description once you have finished.

Start writing here or type in your answer on a tablet or computer.

_____

_____

_____

_____

_____

_____

_____

_____

_____

_____

_____

☞ **Marking guide on page 214**

There is no way of knowing for certain what type of writing will be included in the NAPLAN Tests in years to come. This is an opportunity for you to practise different types of writing.

The aim of a review is to give readers information about a book, play, film, electronic game or concert. Reviews are often found in newspapers.

Before you start, read the General writing tips on pages 26–27.

> Today you are going to write a review of a novel or children's story you have read recently.

Before you start writing, give some thought to:
- the material you are reviewing: the strengths and weaknesses of the subject matter
- the style, setting, characters, illustrations and main events of the book
- a concluding personal judgement and recommendation.

Don't forget to:
- plan your book review before you start writing
- identify the book and author, and the type of book
- write in correctly formed sentences and take care with paragraphing
- choose your words carefully and pay attention to your spelling and punctuation
- write neatly but don't waste time
- quickly check your book review once you have finished.

Start writing here or type in your answer on a tablet or computer.

Book/Story: _____ Author: _____

_____

_____

_____

_____

_____

_____

_____

_____

_____

_____

_____

_____

_____

_____

_____

_____

_____

_____

☞ **Marking guide on pages 214-215**

42 MIN

There is no way of knowing for certain what type of writing will be included in the NAPLAN Tests in years to come. This is an opportunity for you to practise different types of writing.

The aim of a review is to give readers information about a book, play, film, electronic game or concert. Reviews are often found in newspapers.

Before you start, read the General writing tips on pages 26–27.

> Today you are going to write a review of a television show, film or play you have recently seen.

Before you start writing, give some thought to:
- the name of the production, its location and who was in it
- your reaction to the staging, cost and enjoyment of the show, and the ability of the participants (actors).

Don't forget to:
- plan your review before you start writing
- write in correctly formed sentences and take care with paragraphing
- choose your words carefully and pay attention to your spelling and punctuation
- write neatly but don't waste time
- quickly check your review once you have finished.

Start writing here or type in your answer on a tablet or computer.

Name of film/show: _____

_____

_____

_____

_____

_____

_____

_____

_____

_____

_____

_____

_____

_____

_____

_____

_____

_____

☞ **Marking guide on pages 215-216**

Week 4

This is what we cover this week:

Day 1   **Number and Algebra:** ◎ Calculator allowed test

          Measurement and Geometry: ◎ Calculator allowed test

          Number and Algebra/Measurement and Geometry/

          Statistics and Probability: ◎ Calculator allowed test

Day 2   **Spelling:** ◎ Words ending in 'y', 'ible'/'able' words and homophones

                 ◎ Common misspellings

          Grammar and punctuation: ◎ Pronouns, prepositions, subject/verb

                                   agreement and apostrophes

                             ◎ Pronouns, prepositions and punctuation

Day 3   **Reading:** ◎ Understanding explanations

Day 4   **Writing:** ◎ Explanations

                ◎ Report from an outline

                ◎ Response to a picture

Test Your Skills

NUMBER AND ALGEBRA
Calculator allowed test

20 min

1 What is the sum of 153, 786, 987 and 11?
A 1926 **B** 1937 **C** 2031 **D** 2032

2 What is the difference between 8007 and 2398?
A 5609 **B** 5069 **C** 5672 **D** 5618

3 235 + ☐ = 986
What is the missing number?
A 749 **B** 751 **C** 1221 **D** 1222

4 896 ÷ ☐ = 7
What is the missing number?
A 128 **B** 129 **C** 6272 **D** 6273

5 Margaret thinks of a number. She divides the number by 5 and her answer is 42. What was Margaret's original number?
A 8 **B** 201 **C** 210 **D** 2100

6 What is the remainder when 1000 is divided by 7?
A 2 **B** 3 **C** 5 **D** 6

7 A number divided by 4 gives a remainder of 3. Which of the following might the number be?
A 51 **B** 62 **C** 76 **D** 85

8 What is three-quarters of 600?
A 150 **B** 200 **C** 400 **D** 450

9 Grant rewrote the mixed number as an improper fraction: $9\frac{1}{6} = \frac{x}{6}$. What is the value of x?
A 55 **B** 56 **C** 57 **D** 58

10 What is the middle (or average) of $2\frac{1}{5}$ and $3\frac{4}{5}$?
A $2\frac{4}{5}$ **B** 3 **C** $3\frac{2}{5}$ **D** $3\frac{3}{5}$

11 What is the product of $\frac{3}{4}$ and $\frac{1}{2}$?
A $\frac{3}{8}$ **B** 1 **C** $\frac{2}{3}$ **D** $\frac{5}{8}$

12 $1\frac{1}{4} -$ ☐ $= \frac{3}{4}$
What fraction should be placed in the box to make the number sentence true?
A $\frac{1}{4}$ **B** $\frac{1}{2}$ **C** $\frac{2}{3}$ **D** $\frac{3}{4}$

13 $\frac{15}{35}$ is the same as
A $\frac{1}{3}$ **B** $\frac{2}{7}$ **C** $\frac{5}{6}$ **D** $\frac{3}{7}$

14 What percentage is $12 of $48?
A 20% **B** 24% **C** 25% **D** 40%

15 What is $\frac{3}{4}$ of $60?
A $34 **B** $40 **C** $42 **D** $45

16 A book has 100 pages and each page is numbered commencing at page 1. How many 2s will be used?
A 10 **B** 19 **C** 20 **D** 21

17 20% of the students at a school purchase lunch each day from the canteen. If there are 740 students at the school, how many buy lunch every day?
A 74 **B** 94 **C** 148 **D** 158

18 The price of a computer game is $79. If the price is discounted by 10%, what is the new price?
A $71.10 **B** $72.10 **C** $73.10 **D** $73.90

19 What is 3.75 × 1.07 rounded to the nearest hundredth?
A 4.01 **B** 4.02 **C** 40.1 **D** 40.2

20 What is 37^2 to the nearest hundred?
A 1300 **B** 1370 **C** 1400 **D** 1500

21 25% of spectators at a netball game were males. If there were 60 males, how many spectators were at the game?
A 15 **B** 120 **C** 180 **D** 240

☞**Explanations on pages 216-217**

NUMBER AND ALGEBRA
Calculator allowed test

1 Certain words and symbols are used to represent mathematical operations.
Examples:

a Find the **sum** of 3.25 and 1.058.
    3.25 + 1.058 = 4.308

b Find the **total** of 30.1, 1.09 and 9.89.
    30.1 + 1.09 + 9.89 = 41.08

c What is the **difference** between 9.81 and 0.981?
    9.81 − 0.981 = 8.829

d By how much does 98.1 **exceed** 81.3?
    98.1 − 81.3 = 16.8

e Find the **product** of 19.672 and 0.065.
    19.672 × 0.065 = 1.27868

f What is 97 **times** 2.05?
    97 × 2.05 = 198.85

g Find the **quotient** of 60 and 0.005.
    60 ÷ 0.005 = 12 000

h What is 16 **divided** by 0.02?
    16 ÷ 0.02 = 800

2 The **remainder** is the amount left over when one number divides into another.
Examples: Find the remainder if:

a 158 is divided by 5.
    Now 158 ÷ 5 = 31.6.
    As 31 × 5 = 155, and 158 − 155 = 3, we can say 158 ÷ 5 = 31 and remainder 3

b 2010 is divided by 32.
    Now 2010 ÷ 32 = 62.8125.
    As 62 × 32 = 1984, and
    2010 − 1984 = 26, we can say
    2010 ÷ 32 = 62 and remainder 26

3 The calculator can be used when **simplifying fractions**. On many calculators the fraction key is shown as this. $\boxed{a^b/_c}$
Examples:

a Rewrite $\frac{21}{4}$ as a mixed numeral.

    Enter 21 $\boxed{a^b/_c}$ 4 =   The answer is $5\frac{1}{4}$.

b Simplify, or cancel, $\frac{76}{100}$.

    Enter 76 $\boxed{a^b/_c}$ 100 =   The answer is $\frac{19}{25}$.

c Simplify $\frac{3}{4} + \frac{1}{2} - \frac{4}{5}$.

    Enter 3 $\boxed{a^b/_c}$ 4 + 1 $\boxed{a^b/_c}$ 2 − 4 $\boxed{a^b/_c}$ 5 =

    The answer is $\frac{9}{20}$.

d Find the product of $4\frac{1}{2}$ and $5\frac{2}{3}$.

    Enter 4 $\boxed{a^b/_c}$ 1 $\boxed{a^b/_c}$ 2 × 5 $\boxed{a^b/_c}$ 2 $\boxed{a^b/_c}$ =

    The answer is $25\frac{1}{2}$.

e Find $\frac{3}{4}$ of $300.
    As 'of' means times, enter 3 $\boxed{a^b/_c}$ 4 × 300 =

    The answer is 225, or $225.

f What is the average of $2\frac{3}{4}$ and $5\frac{1}{2}$?

    Enter 2 $\boxed{a^b/_c}$ 3 $\boxed{a^b/_c}$ 4 + 5 $\boxed{a^b/_c}$ 1 $\boxed{a^b/_c}$ 2 =

    This is the total of $8\frac{1}{4}$.

    Now divide by 2: the average is $4\frac{1}{8}$.

4 When using a calculator, a **percentage** can be changed to a decimal.
Examples: Express as decimals:

a 75% = 0.75   **b** 5% = 0.05

5 When a **fraction or decimal** are to be **written as percentages**, we **multiply by 100**. (It is actually multiplying by 100% = 1.)
Examples:

a What percentage is 0.73?
    0.73 × 100 = 73%

b What percentage is 35 out of 50?

    $\frac{35}{50}$ × 100 = 35 $\boxed{a^b/_c}$ 50 × 100
            = 70, or 70%

c What percentage is 20c of $2?
    Change $2 to 200c,

    $\frac{20}{200}$ × 100 = 20 $\boxed{a^b/_c}$ 200 × 100
            = 10, or 10%

6 We can find **percentages of quantities**:
Example: Find 15% of $400
    Amount = 0.15 × 400
           = 60   ($60)

Real Test

NUMBER AND ALGEBRA
Calculator allowed test

20 MIN

1 What is the sum of 2.304 and 23.04?
A 25.344 B 25.404
C 26.308 D 26.404

2 What is added to 18.76 to make 51.27?
A 32.51 B 33.51 C 33.59 D 70.03

3 26.513 × ☐ = 26 513.
What is the missing number?
A 10 B 100 C 1000 D 10 000

4 Jason shared his 100 soccer cards equally among his 6 friends. How many did he have left over? *Hint 1*

A 2 B 3
C 4 D 5

5 12 × ☐ = 96 × 2
What is the missing number?
A 8 B 14 C 16 D 24

6 What fraction has the same value as $7\frac{5}{9}$?
A $\frac{64}{9}$ B $\frac{68}{9}$ C $\frac{68}{7}$ D $\frac{68}{5}$

7 What is the answer to 9.009 ÷ 0.03?
A 3.003 B 30.03 C 300.3 D 30 003

8

A farmer wanted to put 16 cows in each of 5 pens. He has 7 cows left over. How many cows did he have altogether?
A 73 B 87 C 88 D 97

9 What mixed numeral is $\frac{100}{3}$?
A 33 B $33\frac{1}{100}$ C $33\frac{1}{3}$ D $33\frac{2}{3}$

10 Esau wrote these equivalent fractions:
$\frac{2}{3} = \frac{12}{18} = \frac{48}{X}$. What is the value of X? *Hint 2*
A 72 B 84 C 96 D 108

11 Ruby was thinking of a number. When she divided the number by 8 her answer was 5 with a remainder of 6. What was the number Ruby was thinking of?

19	34	43	46	53
A	B	C	D	E

12 Sarah's school tank was empty. After a thunderstorm the tank was 20% full of water and contained 800 litres. How much water will the tank hold when it is full? *Hint 3*
A 160 litres B 1600 litres
C 3200 litres D 4000 litres

13 Brianna has a younger brother named Jacob. At present, Jacob is half Brianna's age and the total of their ages is 24. How old will Jacob be when Brianna is 21?
A 13 B 14 C 29 D 42

14 Avery recorded the amount of savings in the first four months of the year:
Jan: $9; Feb: $17; Mar: $21; Apr: $4.
How much more money did she save in the first 2 months than the final 2 months?
A $1 B $2 C $9 D $26

15 In a triathlon, Jocelyn swam a quarter of the distance and then cycled two thirds of the remainder of the race. The distance that remains is the run section. What fraction of the overall distance will she run? *Hint 4*
A $\frac{1}{4}$ B $\frac{1}{3}$ C $\frac{1}{2}$ D $\frac{2}{3}$

16 The smaller of two numbers is 298 and their difference is 211. What is the other number?
☐

Hint 1: The number left over is the remainder.
Hint 2: Check the rule that is being used for the numerators, and then use the rule for the denominators.
Hint 3: As 20% is one-fifth, the answer is found by multiplying by 5.
Hint 4: Draw a diagram—swim one-quarter, she still has three-quarters of the race to go. Find two-thirds of this distance first.

☞ **Answers and explanations on page 217**

Test Your Skills

MEASUREMENT AND GEOMETRY
Calculator allowed test

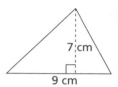

1 Change 2 metres 5 centimetres to metres.
A 2.005 m **B** 2.05 m **C** 2.5 m **D** 250 m

2 How many millimetres are there in 0.04 cm?
A 0.004 mm **B** 0.4 mm
C 4 mm **D** 40 mm

3 How many minutes are there in 6 hours 27 minutes?
A 327 minutes **B** 367 minutes
C 387 minutes **D** 627 minutes

4 Maria's heart beats at the rate of 72 per minute. At this rate, how many times would her heart beat in an hour?
A 132 **B** 1728 **C** 3600 **D** 4320

5 Add 56 minutes and 52 minutes. What is the answer?
A 1 hour 8 minutes **B** 1 hour 18 minutes
C 1 hour 38 minutes **D** 1 hour 48 minutes

6 The table shows the number of hours Gordon worked.

Day	Mon.	Tues.	Wed.	Thu.	Fri.
Hours	8	8.5	7.5	4	10.5

How many hours did he work?
A 38.5 **B** 39 **C** 39.5 **D** 40

7 The mass of two objects is 871 grams and 739 grams. What is the total mass of the objects?
A 1540 grams **B** 1600 grams
C 1610 grams **D** 1620 grams

8 A 10-litre bucket is filled with water. If 7 L 200 mL is poured out, how much water remains in the bucket?
A 800 mL **B** 2 L 800 mL
C 3 L 200 mL **D** 3 L 800 mL

9 What is the area of the rectangle?
A 0.02 hectares
B 0.2 hectares
C 2 hectares
D 20 hectares

100 m
200 m

10 Find the area of the triangle.
A 16 cm² **B** 31.2 cm²
C 31.5 cm² **D** 63 cm²

7 cm
9 cm

11 Find the volume of a rectangular prism with dimensions 12 cm, 10 cm and 9 cm.
A 31 cm³ **B** 108 cm³
C 120 cm³ **D** 1080 cm³

12 The area of a rectangle is 360 cm². If the breadth is 18 cm, what is the length of the rectangle?
A 18 cm **B** 20 cm **C** 40 cm **D** 60 cm

13 A car uses petrol at the rate of 9 litres for every 100 km travelled. How much petrol is used to travel 450 kilometres?
A 40.5 litres **B** 45 litres
C 55 litres **D** 60 litres

14 Jo is paid $14 per 100 pamphlets she delivers. What will she be paid if she delivers 150 pamphlets?
A $17 **B** $20 **C** $21 **D** $29

15 Goran cycled at a constant speed of 12 m/s. How far will he travel in one minute?
A 72 m **B** 500 m **C** 600 m **D** 720 m

16 The ratio of bus travellers to car travellers was 3 to 2. If there were 60 car travellers, how many bus travellers were there?
A 20 **B** 40 **C** 90 **D** 180

17 A cricket team needed 6.8 runs per over for their 20 overs. How many runs were required?
A 136 **B** 140 **C** 146 **D** 148

18 How far will Gerard travel at a speed of 66 km/h for 3 hours?
A 22 km **B** 69 km
C 188 km **D** 198 km

19 What is the area of a square with each side 100 cm?
A 1 m² **B** 10 m²
C 100 m² **D** 1000 m²

☞ **Explanations on page 218**

Answers: 1B **2**B **3**C **4**D **5**D **6**A **7**C **8**B **9**C **10**C **11**D **12**B **13**A **14**C **15**D **16**C **17**A **18**D **19**A

Excel Revise in a Month Year 7 NAPLAN*-style Tests

103

1 For **conversions between units of length** use:
1000 mm = 100 cm = 1 m
1000 m = 1 km.
Examples:
a Change 12 m 2 cm to metres.
As 2 cm = 0.02 m, 12 m 2 cm = 12.02 m
b Change 69 metres to kilometres.
To change m to km we divide by 1000:
As 69 ÷ 1000 = 0.069, so 0.069 km

2 We need to add and subtract times or time taken using different units
Example: The table shows the time taken by Aiden walking each morning:

Day of week	Distance
Monday	46 minutes
Tuesday	1 hour 11 minutes
Wednesday	38 minutes
Thursday	59 minutes
Friday	1 hour 2 minutes
Saturday	44 minutes
Sunday	17 minutes

a What was the total time Aiden walked during the week?
First change each time to minutes.
Sum = 46 + 71 + 38 + 59 + 62 + 44 + 17
= 337

Now $\frac{337}{60} = 5\frac{37}{60}$, or 5 hours 37 minutes

b What was the difference between the longest time he walked and the shortest?
Difference = 71 − 17
= 54, or 54 minutes

3 For **conversions between units of mass** use
1000 mg = 1 g
1000 g = 1 kg
1000 kg = 1 t
Example: Change 12 kg 21 g to kilograms.
For 21 g, 21 ÷ 1000 = 0.021,
so 12.021 kg

4 Learn the **area formulae**:
area of rectangle = length × breadth
area of square = side × side
area of triangle = $\frac{1}{2}$ × base × height

Example: Find the area of a triangle with a base of 17 cm and a height of 9 cm.
Area = 0.5 × 17 × 9
= 76.5   Area is 76.5 cm²

5 The **volume** of a rectangular prism is found by multiplying length by breadth by height.
Example: Find the volume of a rectangular prism with length $1\frac{1}{2}$ cm by $\frac{3}{4}$ cm by $\frac{1}{2}$ cm.

Volume = $1\frac{1}{2} \times \frac{3}{4} \times \frac{1}{2}$

= 1 $\boxed{a^{b/}c}$ 1 $\boxed{a^{b/}c}$ 2 × 3 $\boxed{a^{b/}c}$ 4 × 1 $\boxed{a^{b/}c}$ 2

= $\frac{9}{16}$ Volume is $\frac{9}{16}$ cm³.

6 For **conversions between units of capacity** use:
1000 mL = 1 L
1000 L = 1 kL
1000 kL = 1 ML.
Example: Change 6 litres 15 millilitres to litres.
For 15 mL, 15 ÷ 1000 = 0.015,
so 6.015 L

7 A **rate is the comparison of two measurements**.
Example: A bricklayer is paid $900 for every thousand bricks he lays. How much is he paid when he lays 2500 bricks?
His pay rate is $900/1000 bricks.

As there are $2\frac{1}{2}$ thousands in 2500,
Pay = $2\frac{1}{2}$ × 900
= 2250
His pay is $2250.

8 A ratio is the comparison of two numbers.
Example: In a class, the ratio of males to females is 5 to 3. If there are 15 females, how many males are there?
The ratio is 5 parts to 3 parts.
This means 3 parts represents 15 females.
This means 1 part represents 5 females.
Finally, 5 parts represent 25 males.
There are 25 males in the class.

Real Test

MEASUREMENT AND GEOMETRY
Calculator allowed test

20 MIN

1 Jack cycled for 2 hours at a speed of 18 km/h. How far did he travel? *Hint 1*

A 9 km **B** 20 km **C** 34 km **D** 36 km

2 A car uses 9 litres of petrol per 100 km. If the petrol tank has a capacity of 54 litres, how far will the car travel on a full tank of petrol?

A 500 km **B** 540 km
C 600 km **D** 630 km

3 The grid contains the net of a rectangular prism. Each square of the grid has an area of 4 cm².

What is the sum of the areas of each face on the prism?

Write your answer in the box: ☐ cm²

4 A ream of paper contains 500 sheets. If the mass of each sheet is about 4.5 grams, what is the best estimate of the mass of the ream?

A 0.225 g **B** 2.25 g
C 0.225 kg **D** 2.25 kg

5 A water tap fills an 8-litre bucket in 12 seconds. At this rate, how long would it take to fill a 40-litre container? *Hint 2*

A 1 min **B** 1 min 12 seconds
C 1 min 46 seconds **D** 1 min 56 seconds

6 A cube has a side of 5 cm. Each face of the cube is to be painted. What is the total area to be painted?

A 150 cm² **B** 180 cm²
C 250 cm² **D** 600 cm²

7 What is the sum of 1 hour 21 minutes and 49 minutes? *Hint 3*

A 2 hours **B** 2 hours 10 minutes
C 2 hours 20 minutes **D** 3 hours

8 What is the length of each side of a square if its area is 64 cm²?

A 4 cm **B** 8 cm **C** 16 cm **D** 32 cm

9 There are 21 balls in a bag. Some of the balls are red and the remainder are blue.

If the ratio of red balls to blue balls is 4 to 3, how many red balls are in the bag?

A 3 **B** 4 **C** 9 **D** 12

10 Jan babysits from 6:30 pm to 10:00 pm and is paid at the rate of $6 per hour. How much will she be paid?

Write your answer in the box: $ ☐

11

Whitebridge

Glendale

Hamilton

The distance from Hamilton to Whitebridge is 6 kilometres. What is the shortest distance from Whitebridge to Glendale? *Hint 4*

A 8.5 km **B** 17 km **C** 21 km **D** 23 km

12 On a house plan, the scale used is 1 cm = 2 m. What is the actual length of a wall that measures 15 mm on the plan?

A 2 m **B** 3 m **C** 4 m **D** 7 m

13 A recipe requires 250 grams of sugar. Kahlia uses a set of scales and pours 415 grams into a container. How many grams will she need to remove?

☐ grams

14 The price of sausages is $6.99/kg. What is the best estimate for the price Glenn will pay for 600 grams of the sausages?

A $4.05 **B** $4.10 **C** $4.20 **D** $4.55

15 The exchange rate is $1 Australian equals 70 c US. How many US dollars will Mitchell receive for $150 Australian?

☐

16 How many hectares in 62 000 m²?

☐ hectares

Hint 1: *Distance = Speed x Time*
Hint 2: *First determine the number of 8s in 40.*
Hint 3: *Change to minutes before adding.*
Hint 4: *Determine the scale used on the map by using known information.*

☞ **Answers and explanations on pages 218-219**

Test Your Skills

NUMBER AND ALGEBRA/
MEASUREMENT AND GEOMETRY/
STATISTICS AND PROBABILITY
Calculator allowed test

20 MIN

1 What is the mean (average) of 14, 17, 45 and 16?

A 14   B 23   C 43   D 78

2 What is the mean (average) of 2.5, 4.5, 5.5, 6.5 and 8.5?

A 5   B 5.5   C 6   D 20.7

3 What is the mean (average) of

$1\frac{1}{2}$, 3, $2\frac{1}{4}$, $1\frac{1}{4}$?

A $\frac{1}{4}$ B 2   C $2\frac{1}{4}$ D $2\frac{3}{4}$

4 The table shows the masses of vegetables:

Vegetable	Mass
Pumpkin	2 kg 40 g
Sweet Potato	810 g
Cucumber	245 g
Carrot	110 g
Eggplant	270 g

What is the mean (average) mass of the vegetables?

A 695 g   B 745 g   C 767 g   D 3259 g

5 The table shows the capacity of containers in a garden shed:

Container	Mass
Engine oil	5 litres
Brake fluid	450 mL
Lawnmower fuel	4 litres
Kerosene	750 mL
Methylated spirits	800 mL

What is the mean (average) capacity of the containers?

A 401.8 mL   B 580 mL
C 2.2 L   D 10.36 L

6 The table shows the heights of the children in Lin's family. What is the mean (average) height of the children?

Child	Height
Lin	1.41 m
Jianguo	1.16 m
Huidai	1.07 m
Quon	96 cm

A 1.15 m   B 1.2 m   C 1.21 m   D 1.24 m

7 What is the missing number?
31, 85, 139, ___, 247

A 193   B 196   C 197   D 199

8

Top	4	5	6	7	8
Bottom	17	26	37	50	

What is the missing number?

A 62   B 63   C 64   D 65

9

Top	2	4	6	8	10
Bottom	12	22	32	42	

What is the missing number?

A 44   B 48   C 52   D 54

10

Top	1	2	3	4	5
Bottom	7	13	19	25	31

If the top number was 8, what would the bottom number be?

A 48   B 49   C 50   D 51

11 When two numbers are multiplied, the answer is 12. When the same numbers are added, the answer is 7. What are the two numbers?

A 2 and 6   B 6 and 6
C 1 and 12   D 3 and 4

12 Penelope thinks of a number. She doubles it and adds 5. Her answer is 23. What was her original number?

A 7   B 8   C 9   D 10

13 A triangle is drawn and two of its angles are 70° and 30°. What is the other angle?

A 20°   B 60°   C 80°   D 100°

14 Renai drew a triangle and one angle measured 70°. The triangle cannot be

A isosceles.   B scalene.
C right-angled.   D equilateral.

15 A right-angled triangle has one angle measuring 40°. What is the size of the other angle?

A 20°   B 40°   C 140°   D 50°

☞**Explanations on pages 219-220**

Answers: 1 B **2** B **3** B **4** A **5** C **6** A **7** A **8** D **9** C **10** B **11** D **12** C **13** C **14** D **15** D

106   *Excel* Revise in a Month Year 7 NAPLAN*-style Tests

Key Points

NUMBER AND ALGEBRA/ MEASUREMENT AND GEOMETRY/ STATISTICS AND PROBABILITY
Calculator allowed test

❶ The **mean is the average** and is found by adding quantities together and then dividing by the number of quantities.
Example: Jessica recorded the number of points her basketball team scored.

Game	1	2	3	4	5
Points	63	45	51	43	38

What is the average number of points per game?

Average $= \dfrac{63 + 45 + 51 + 43 + 38}{5}$

$= 48$

❷ The data in a **column graph** can be interpreted.
Example: The column graph shows the number of people who live in each apartment in a building.

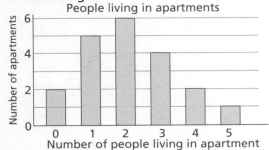

How many people live in the building?
People $= 0 + 5 + 12 + 12 + 8 + 5$
$= 42$ 42 live in the building.

❸ When finding **missing numbers in a number sentence**, use these techniques.
Examples: Find the missing value:

a 9.4 + ☐ = 12.2
As 12.2 − 9.4 = 2.8, then 9.4 + 2.8 = 12.2
The missing value is 2.8.

b $2\dfrac{1}{2} -$ ☐ $= 1\dfrac{3}{4}$

As $2\dfrac{1}{2} - 1\dfrac{3}{4} = \dfrac{3}{4}$, then $2\dfrac{1}{2} - \dfrac{3}{4} = 1\dfrac{3}{4}$,

The missing value is $\dfrac{3}{4}$.

c 5.1 × ☐ = 45.9
As 45.9 ÷ 5.1 = 9, then 5.1 × 9 = 45.9
The missing value is 9.

d 85 ÷ ☐ = 17
As 85 ÷ 17 = 5, then 85 ÷ 5 = 17.
The missing value is 5.

❹ When a **pattern exists in a series of diagrams we can summarise the information in a table**. The table can be used to make predictions.

Example: A series of shapes is formed using matchsticks.

a Complete the table:

Squares	1	2	3	4
Matches	4	7	10	

The 4th diagram has 13 matches.
The missing number is 13.

b Complete the rule linking the number of matches with the number of squares:
Matches = ____ × no. of squares + ____
By considering the table,
Matches = 3 × no. of squares + 1

c Use the rule in **b** to find the number of matches needed for 10 squares.
Matches = 3 × no. of squares + 1
$= 3 × 10 + 1$
$= 31$
31 matches are needed for the 10 squares.

d Use the rule in **b** to find the number of squares that can be made from 301 matches using the pattern in the question.
Matches = 3 × no. of squares + 1
301 = 3 × no. of squares + 1
This means the no. of squares is 100.

❺ The angle in a straight line is 180° and the angles in a triangle add to 180°.
Examples: Find the values of x and y:

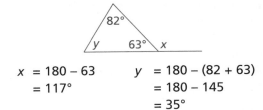

$x = 180 − 63$ $y = 180 − (82 + 63)$
$= 117°$ $= 180 − 145$
$= 35°$

1 What is the average (mean) of the following masses? 2.3 kg, 1.6 kg, 200 g, 750 g, 1.09 kg
A 1.188 kg B 1.91 kg
C 2.3 kg D 5.068 kg

2 The table shows the length of four ribbons in Mercia's sewing kit. What is the mean (average) length?

Ribbon colour	Length
Pink	2.6 m
White	98 cm
Yellow	3.3 m
Green	72 cm

A 180 cm B 185 cm C 190 cm D 7.06 m

3 A survey of 80 students was held to find the number of books read during a recent vacation.

	None	One	Two	More than 2
Male	11	16	8	2
Female	8	?	13	3

How many females read one book? *Hint 1*
A 19 B 20 C 21 D 22

4 From the survey in question 3, a student is chosen at random. What is the probability that the student was a male who read more than 2 books?

A $\frac{1}{40}$ B $\frac{3}{80}$ C $\frac{2}{35}$ D $\frac{3}{5}$

5 What is the value of x?
Hint 2
A 53 B 63
C 133 D 143

6 What is the value of y?
Hint 3
A 25 B 35
C 45 D 55

7 In a triangle, one angle is twice the size of another. If one angle is 20°, what could be the size of another angle? Select **all** the correct answers.
A 120° B 130° C 140° D 150°

8 11, 24, 37, 50, 63, ___
What is the missing number?
A 13 B 66 C 76 D 79

9 113, 109, 105, 101, …
What is the sixth number in the pattern?
A 98 B 97 C 93 D 92

10

Top	3	6	9	12	15
Bottom	12	24	36		60

What is the missing number? *Hint 4*
A 44 B 48 C 52 D 54

11 Using the table in question 10, if the top number was 20, what would be the bottom number?
A 72 B 80 C 84 D 88

12 The diagrams contain squares.

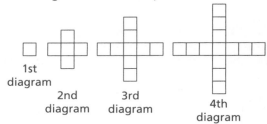

1st diagram
2nd diagram
3rd diagram
4th diagram

The information is summarised in the table.

Diagram	1	2	3	4	5
Square	1	5	9	13	

What is the missing value?

Write your answer in the box: ☐

13 From question 12, if the pattern continued, how many squares would be in the 6th diagram?
A 20 B 21 C 22 D 23

14 The scale on a map is 1 cm to 10 km. If the length of a road is 30 cm, how long is the actual road?

☐ km

15 Sigrid starts at 100 and counts backwards by 5. If the first number she calls out is 100, what is the sixth number?

16 1640 ÷ ☐ = 205
What is the missing number?
Write your answer in the box: ☐

Hint 1: All numbers in the table add to 80.
Hint 2: 180 degrees in a straight angle
Hint 3: 180 degrees in a triangle
Hint 4: Find the pattern linking the top and bottom numbers and apply the pattern to find the missing number.

☞ **Answers and explanations on pages 220-221**

Key Points
and
Test Your
Skills

SPELLING
*Words ending in 'y',
'ible'/'able' words and homophones*

20 MIN

With most spelling rules there are exceptions. English words have many different origins
(e.g. 'siesta' comes from Spain and 'kayak' is an Inuit word from North America).

Key Points

❶ To add a suffix to a word ending with a 'y', change the 'y' to an 'i' before adding the suffix.
Some common suffixes are 'ly', 'less', 'ness', 'est', 'ful' (See page 79 for 'ful'.)
Examples: happiness, happily, tidily, penniless, dizziness, laziest, angrily
An exception to this rule is adding 'ing' (keep the 'y').
Examples: bullying, partying, annoying, carrying, curtsying
Words to watch: ageing, taxiing, skiing

❷ Homophones are words that sound the same but have different spelling. You need to be able to
use them correctly in context.
Examples: forth, fourth; stationary, stationery; current, currant; morning, mourning; bight, bite, byte

❸ Words with 'ible' or 'able' endings can cause confusion. There is no clear rule but 'able' is a more
common ending than 'ible'. When 'able' is added to a word ending with an 'e' the 'e' is often
dropped unless the word ends with 'ge' or 'ce'.
Examples: noticeable, knowledgeable, manageable, changeable, embraceable
Examples of common 'ible' words: eligible, feasible, responsible, compatible
Many dictionaries give alternative spelling for some 'able' words: loveable, lovable; moveable,
movable; sizeable, sizable

Test Your Skills

Learn the words below. A common method of learning and self-testing is the **LOOK, SAY, COVER,
WRITE, CHECK** method. If you make any mistakes, you should rewrite the word three times correctly,
immediately. In this way you will become familiar with the correct spelling. If the word is particularly
troublesome, rewrite it several more times or keep a list of words that you can check regularly.

This week's list: Troublesome words

parallelogram	_____	kindergarten	_____
handkerchief	_____	accommodation	_____
government	_____	environment	_____
committee	_____	quarrelsome	_____
independent	_____	thoroughly	_____
technique	_____	physician	_____
flammable	_____	burglary	_____
guerrilla	_____	confidential	_____
behaviour	_____	intrigue	_____
professional	_____	parliament	_____
technological	_____	yachting	_____

Write any troublesome word three times: _____ _____ _____

_____ _____ _____

Real Test

SPELLING
Common misspellings

20 MIN

Please ask your parent or teacher to read to you the spelling words on page 248.
Write the correct spelling of each word in the box.

1 Jane was as fast a _____ as any person in the office!

2 The circus _____ was applauded at the end of the show.

3 Try this _____ for making a knot.

4 For every _____ there is a pile of forms to complete.

5 The blacksmith was _____ horses for the rodeo.

6 Put the _____ next to the sword.

7 This film is no longer _____! It is too silly for words!

8 They play with _____ at my brother's preschool.

9 If you must _____ at the tourists, try to be less obvious.

10 After _____ out, the plane turned towards Darwin.

11 The financial institution is _____ credit.

12 The _____ beating of rival tom-toms was a distraction.

13 History is nothing more than a list of _____ facts!

14 From a distance we could hear the _____ of the creek.

15 The gearbox was _____ as we struggled up the steep hill.

Each sentence has one word that is incorrect.
Write the correct spelling of the underlined word in the box.

16 The eleventh and <u>twelvefth</u> person did not participate.

17 I said, 'Where<u>ever</u> you go your obedient pup will follow.'

18 If you are <u>responsable</u> then you should pay the account.

19 The <u>thiefs</u> were discovered huddled under a blanket!

20 The short <u>rein</u> of the monarch lasted a few meagre years.

☞ **Answers on page 221**

Each sentence has one word that is incorrect.
Write the correct spelling of the word in the box.

21 Put the athletics equiptment in the cupboard.

22 The visitors demanded we turn the volumn down.

23 The principal was strick when it came to fair play.

24 They are issueing a stamp for the Olympic Games in 2012.

25 It is fashionible to wear board shorts to the disco.

☞ Answers on page 221

**Key Points
and
Test Your
Skills**

GRAMMAR AND PUNCTUATION
Pronouns, prepositions, subject/verb agreement and apostrophes

Key Points

① **Pronouns** are words that take the place of nouns.
Example: John gave the ball to Jill. He gave it to her. ('He' and 'her' are pronouns.)
Here are some common pronouns: I, we, me, us, you, they, them, he, she, him, her, it.

② **Prepositions** show the relationship between a noun or pronoun and another word. They show the position (preposition).
Examples: at, above, among, under, off, until, into, up, beside, between

③ **Apostrophes** have two uses.
  a **To show ownership**: when something belongs to an individual (or thing), ownership is shown with **'s**. *Examples:* dog's collar, Holden's tyre, doctor's fee, table's leg, team's mascot
  When ownership belongs to more than one individual (or thing), ownership is shown by **s'**.
  Examples: boys' noses, dogs' tails, teachers' staffroom, babies' playroom
  Care must be taken with plurals that do not have an **s** ending. For these add **'s**.
  Examples: children's toys, men's room, mice's holes

  b To indicate **contractions** (shortened words): when letters are left out of a word, an apostrophe is put in its place.
  Examples: was not → wasn't, he will → he'll, they are → they're, I am → I'm, it is → it's
  Note: the word **it's** stands for 'it is'. (It's a fine day.) **Its**, without an apostrophe, is a pronoun like 'hers', 'his' and 'their'. (The cat licked its fur.)

④ **Colons** introduce a quotation or a list.
Example: Your diet should include the following: grains, fruit and greens.
Semicolons let the reader know when to pause, often before an added clause.
Example: Jim was late home from school; therefore he was forbidden to watch TV.

⑤ **Subject/verb agreement:** it is essential to ensure that the subject and the verb agree, that is, they are both plural or both singular. *Examples:* the girls go/the girl goes; the bomb explodes/the bombs explode; Jack walks/Jack and Jill walk; the price is/the prices are
Note: many mistakes occur when the subject is a pronoun. *Examples:* you was late (wrong)/you were late (correct); she don't agree (wrong)/she doesn't agree (correct)
Note: some pronouns always take a singular verb. *Examples:* each, every, everyone, someone, nobody, no-one, everybody, anybody, anyone, somebody
Subjects that name quantities take a singular verb. *Example:* Two metres of string is enough.

Test Your Skills

① Underline the **pronouns** in this passage.
Tony and Anna were lost. They could not see the house. It was hidden in the valley. Tony tried to climb a tree but he was too small. Anna sat on a log. Her head ached.

② Underline the **prepositions** in this passage.
Rover hid behind the kennel when he saw the family cat coming round the corner. The cat stopped by the door, looked at the kennel and then went into the house. Her tail was in the air.

③ Choose the correct **preposition** to fill the spaces.
  a I picked the apple _____ the tree. (at, from, by)
  b The kangaroo jumped _____ the fallen log. (over, below, in)

④ Write these words in **shortened** form.
  we are _____   where is _____   I will _____   you have _____

⑤ Underline the correct **verb**.
  a The trees (was, were) swaying in the breeze.
  b A flock of sheep (is, are) on the road.

Excel Revise in a Month Year 7 NAPLAN*-style Tests

GRAMMAR AND PUNCTUATION
Pronouns, prepositions and punctuation

1 Which of the following correctly completes this sentence?

A fleet of ships _____ the harbour as we watch.

enters	enter	entered	entering
A	**B**	**C**	**D**

2 Write a word from this sentence in each empty box to match the given part of speech.

Quickly the snake coiled itself around the surprised deer.

verb			adverb	
preposition			adjective	

3 Which of the following correctly completes this sentence?

The extra paint _____ a splendid job covering the scratches.

do	done	has done	have done	has did
A	**B**	**C**	**D**	**E**

Read the text *Carnival*. The text has some gaps.
Chose the correct word or words to fill each gap.

Carnival

We were on the beach by eight o'clock. The flags were out. Huge waves were breaking right on the beach. The captain of the life-savers had more than enough _____ for the team, even before the carnival started.

It was wasted. Nobody _____ prepared to go into the surf until they had to.

Wesley Jones, an amateur photographer, was determined to get some action shots during the day.

He not only takes photos _____ prints them.

He sells prints to competing surf clubs.

4
advice	advise	advises	advise's
A	**B**	**C**	**D**

5
are	is	were	was
A	**B**	**C**	**D**

6
but	and	but also	however
A	**B**	**C**	**D**

7 Which sentence has the correct punctuation?
  A Jason's team's two wins' were a shock to the supporters.
  B Jason's team's two wins were a shock to the supporters.
  C Jason's team's two wins were a shock to the supporters'.
  D Jason's teams' two wins were a shock to the supporters.

8 Which sentence is correct?
  A His intentions are good, but his rough manner tends to intimidate.
  B His intentions is good, but his rough manner tends to intimidate.
  C His intentions are good, but his rough manner tend to intimidate.
  D His intentions is good, but his rough manner tend to intimidate.

☞ **Answers and explanations on pages 221-223**

Real Test

GRAMMAR AND PUNCTUATION
Pronouns, prepositions and punctuation

9 Which of the following correctly completes the sentence?

The shed was ▓▓▓▓▓ with a whole range of power tools.

equiping	equipt	equipted	equipped
A	**B**	**C**	**D**

10 Write an appropriate pronoun in the box to complete the sentence.

We saw many frogs but we also saw a frog ☐ is on the endangered list.

11 Which sentence is correct?

A 'I know youse two used the computer after I left!' accused Georgia.
B 'I know you two ust the computer after I had left!' accused Georgia.
C 'I know you two used the computer after I had left!' accused Georgia.
D 'I know you two useded the computer after I had left!' accused Georgia.

12 Which sentence is correct?

A Peter said to 'stop work,' so we put our pens down.
B Peter said to stop work so we put our pens down.
C Peter said to 'Stop work.' so we put our pens down.
D Peter said, 'to stop work so we put our pens down.'

13 Which sentence has the correct punctuation?

A If anybody thinks dogs are worser than cats then they are right!
B If anybody thinks dogs are more worse than cats then they are right!
C If anybody thinks dogs are worse than cats then they are right!
D If anybody thinks dogs are worst than cats then they are right!

14 Which sentence has the correct punctuation?

A They departed on Thursday 22 January.
B They departed on Thursday the 22 January.
C They departed on Thursday 22 of January.
D They departed on Thursday the 22 of January.

15 Which of the following correctly completes the sentence?

As the teenagers ▓▓▓▓▓ on the beach, the sun went behind clouds.

laid	lay	lied	layed
A	**B**	**C**	**D**

16 Shade a bubble to show where the missing apostrophe (') should go.

Ⓐ   Ⓑ   Ⓒ   Ⓓ

The rein▾s are not your▾s, they belong to the stable and it▾s owner▾s family.

17 Which sentence has the correct punctuation?

A Joseph asked, 'which position do you play?'
B Joseph asked, 'Which position do you play'?
C Joseph asked, 'Which position do you play?'
D Joseph asked? 'which position do you play.'

☞ **Answers and explanations on pages 221-223**

Real Test

GRAMMAR AND PUNCTUATION
Pronouns, prepositions and punctuation

18 Which of the following correctly completes the sentence?

Toby leant the shovel ▨▨▨ the wall.

against	up	to	onto	by
A	**B**	**C**	**D**	**E**

19 Which sentence has the correct punctuation?
A John has requested a full report? hasn't he.
B John has requested a full report? hasn't he?
C John has requested a full report, hasn't he.
D John has requested a full report, hasn't he?

20 Shade two bubbles to show where the missing commas (,) should go.

The chair ⌃ made of wood ⌃ belongs to my aunt ⌃ who is living ⌃ in Adelaide.
ⓐ   ⓑ   ⓒ   ⓓ

21 Which of the following correctly completes the sentence?

Lyn wrote ▨▨▨ inside the card.

careful	most careful	carefully	carefuller
A	**B**	**C**	**D**

22 Write any of the **correctly** used contractions from these sentences in the boxes.
You may choose more than one box.
The boy <u>who's</u> name is missing has had <u>he's</u> money refunded.
The officials have stated that <u>they've</u> sorry and <u>won't</u> penalise the boy.

23 Which of the following correctly completes the sentence?

All the stationery ▨▨▨ now stacked on the office shelves.

are	is	were	has
A	**B**	**C**	**D**

24 Which word or words should have capital letters in this sentence?
You may choose more than one box.

if you go to wattle grove you must visit my uncle on his dairy farm.

25 Which of the following correctly completes this sentence?

On the table you will see a pen, ▨▨▨ but no writing paper.

a envelope	the envelope	an envelope	envelope
A	**B**	**C**	**D**

☞ **Answers and explanations on pages 221-223**

READING
Understanding explanations

The purpose of an explanation is to tell how and why something happens or came about. Explanations can be about natural, scientific and social phenomena, how things work or events. Read *The Parson's Cat* and answer the questions.

The Parson's Cat

In the Victorian period, a period during which Queen Victoria of Great Britain reigned (1840–1900), word games were popular. In the late 1800s, well before radio and television, people had to find ways of amusing themselves. Singing around the piano was a family or party activity. Games (non-electronic!) were popular—from board games such as chess or jigsaws, to word games that required a little more imagination and skill.

Lewis Carroll (1832–1898) was alive during this period. Although famous for *Alice in Wonderland*, he also invented a number of word games, some of which are still popular today. He appears to have invented, or at least made popular, the Word Ladder—a game of changing one word into another by altering one letter at a time, each successive change always resulting in a genuine word. For instance, CAT is transformed into DOG by the following steps: CAT, COT, DOT, DOG.

There were many word games and most had simple rules. One such game was The Parson's Cat. It is described in the 1898 book *Games for Parlours and Playground*:

The first player begins by saying, 'The parson has an ambitious cat', the next player, 'an affable cat', the next player 'an amiable cat', and so on until all players have named an adjective beginning with A. The next time of going round the adjective must begin with the letter B, the next time C, and so on until the whole alphabet, or as much as possible, has been gone through. The game is made more difficult and more interesting by each player having to repeat what the previous players have said, then adding his or her own contribution.

Sometimes the players have to name the cat as well as describe it, so the first player might say, 'The parson has an agile cat and its name is Archibald'. The next time round the player could say, 'The parson had a black cat and his name was Baubles'. The letter *X* was usually omitted in most games. However, a smart person might say, 'The parson had a xenophobic (fear of foreigners) cat and his name was Xavier'. Options for *X* would run out very quickly!

Of course, people still play board games, more often than not on a computer screen with an opponent that is a computer program. At least today's players can pick the level they compete at!

1 Why was the game 'The Parson's Cat' popular?
  A It was a board game.
  B It was a simple word game.
  C It was readily converted to a computer game.
  D It only required a knowledge of everyday words.

2 The Word Ladder game involves
  A making words of increasing numbers of letters.
  B a knowledge of animal names.
  C a skill in remembering what competitors have done.
  D modifying words one letter at a time.

3 Which statement is true?
  A Lewis Carroll was alive during the reign of Queen Victoria.
  B Lewis Carroll played Word Ladders with Queen Victoria.
  C Lewis Carroll was the first to convert board games to screen games.
  D Lewis Carroll's word games are no longer played.

4 Which could be a correct response for a competitor in The Parson's Cat game?
  A The parson had a black cat and his name was Puss.
  B The parson had a lazy cat and his name was lost.
  C The parson had a small cat and his name was Kitty.
  D The parson had a cruel cat and his name was Claws.

5 The game is made more interesting when
  A the players get close to the end of the alphabet.
  B the players have to repeat all the answers of previous players.
  C it is played on a computer screen.
  D no player knows how to start the game.

6 For what reason could the letter *X* pose problems?
  A It is almost at the end of the alphabet.
  B Most young players don't know the complete alphabet.
  C Not many common words start with *X*.
  D Most people haven't heard of the name Xavier.

7 Which word could come next in a Word Ladder after HOP?
You may choose more than one option.
  A HOPE
  B SHOP
  C HEN
  D HOG
  E HAG
  F TOP

Read *What is a phobia?* and answer the questions.

What is a phobia?

Are you really scared of something that can in no way harm you? Entering a small space? Standing on a lookout? Small spiders? Snakes? You might just have a phobia.

A phobia is an abnormal and absurd, even morbid, fear of a situation, living thing or even an object. That is a very 'composed' explanation of a phobia, but a person coping with a phobia attack may be close to uncontrolled panic with a pounding, racing heart, legs like jelly and gasping for air. The person may break out in a cold sweat. They can fear for their life. The word *phobia* comes from the Greek word for *fear*.

Phobias most likely affect about ten per cent of the population and are usually a little more common in females than in males. They can develop any time, anywhere and can happen to almost anyone.

Some phobias may develop from an unpleasant experience. A person involved in a car accident may develop a fear of car travel.

Some phobias are particularly related to childhood and simply pass away as the child gets older. Nyctophobia is a fear of darkness. Most adults don't need a light on to go to sleep! Other people might have photophobia: fear of light!

Some things most people take for granted or are able to do easily, other people find almost impossible. There are drivers who won't drive through a tunnel even though the tunnel is used by thousands of other drivers each day. They will find an alternate route to their destination.

Here are some common phobias.

heights—acrophobia

small or confined spaces—claustrophobia

crowded places (like markets)—agoraphobia

blood—haemophobia

water—hydrophobia

spiders—arachnophobia

strangers and foreigners—xenophobia

dogs—cynophobia

snakes—ophidiophobia

There are hundreds of phobias. Many older adults may have technophobia—an extreme dislike of new technology.

There is even a phobia for the fear of work—ergophobia. Tell your teacher you suffer badly from it and can't do any homework!

Real Test

READING
Understanding explanations

1 A phobia is a
  A distressing anxiety.
  B loathing of someone or something.
  C lack of understanding.
  D feeling of concern.

2 The writer describes most phobias as being absurd. This is because
  A people can avoid those things that cause the fear.
  B most phobias are not based on reason or sense.
  C only ten per cent of people have a phobia.
  D a person with a phobia requires specialist treatment.

3 The fear of the dark
  A is often accompanied by a fear of lights.
  B causes nightmares.
  C makes people afraid to open their eyes.
  D passes as a person gets older.

4 Draw a line to match the phobia with the fear it refers to.

| 1 arachnophobia | 2 agoraphobia | 3 hydrophobia | 4 haemophobia |

| A water | B blood | C spiders | D crowded spaces |

5 Where might a person experience claustrophobia?
  A on a hike   B at the beach   C in a football stadium   D in a car

6 People with a particular phobia often
  A go to extreme measures to avoid the feeling.
  B pass it on to other people.
  C overcome their phobia when they see it does not affect others.
  D accept their phobia as an amusing inconvenience.

7 Which person may be in a difficult situation if they had haemophobia? Choose **two** options.
  A a construction worker
  B an ambulance driver
  C an orchardist
  D a nightwatchman
  E a hairdresser
  F a veterinarian

8 According to the passage, which symptom can a phobic person experience?
  A sleepiness   B thirstiness   C cold sweat   D aching joints

☞ **Answers and explanations on pages 223-224**

Real Test

Read *Lava Tubes* and answer the questions.

Lava Tubes

Lava tubes are natural conduits (tunnels) through which lava travels beneath the surface of a covering lava flow from a volcano during an eruption. They can be actively draining lava from the volcano, or can be extinct, meaning the lava flow has ceased and the rock has cooled, leaving a long, cave-like channel.

Lava tubes are formed under a lava flow, which has developed a continuous, thick and hard crust, forming a roof above a lava 'stream'.

The Undara Lava Tubes, 275 km south-west of Cairns, are one of Australia's great geological wonders. They are the largest, longest and most accessible lava tubes on earth.

The Undara Volcano erupted 190 000 years ago and spewed 23 cubic kilometres of molten lava onto the surrounding country. Streams of lava flowed over the land, spilling out like boiling golden syrup into depressions and creek beds.

When the lava ceased flowing at the end of an eruption, lava in the tube system drained away, leaving empty underground tunnels. The drained tubes often have 'high-lava' marks on their walls and flat floors. Many of the tubes have stalactites ('lavacicles') formed from lava dripping from the ceiling.

By the time the volcano subsided, over 160 km of lava flow streaked the countryside and the 20 m diameter tubes had been formed.

Over centuries the roofs of the tubes, in places, collapsed, leaving fertile soakages that protected ancient rainforest from the ravages of bushfires. In these fertile pockets, rainforest plants and animal species now thrive. From the air, the pockets of dark green rainforest make the tube line stand out in stark contrast to the vast golden plains that stretch away to the horizon on all sides.

Eighteen metres below ground level at the tube's entrance, the temperature is cooler. There is the pungent smell of underground life. Bat droppings have accumulated with silt and leaf litter to form a false floor, which in places is six metres thick.

The tubes are homes to creatures previously unknown to science, including two species of insect-eating bats. Unique blind insects and colourless shrimps and beetles have evolved without need for sight or for colour camouflage in the black basalt tubes. Among the twenty-four cave-adapted species discovered are two new snail varieties.

Sources: Undara Expereience; Geoscience: the Earth; The State of Queensland (Environmental Protection Agency)

1 The Undara Lava Tubes are significant because
  A they were created by a volcano.
  B they are a few hundred kilometres south of Cairns.
  C they are the world's longest lava tubes.
  D the volcano ceased erupting 190 000 years ago.

2 A lava tube tunnel forms
  A from water erosion in creek beds.   B when surface lava cools to form a crust.
  C while the surface lava is flowing.   D after a volcanic eruption.

3 Which statement is true about the Undara site?
  A Sections of the Undara Tubes have collapsed.
  B The original Undara lava flow was 23 kilometres wide.
  C The Undara Tubes are difficult to access.
  D Birds have adapted to the Undara Tube environment.

4 The rainforest at Undara
  A has been destroyed by bushfires.   B is now part of a national park.
  C has become part of the 'golden plains'.   D follows the line of the lava tube.

5 The smell in the Undara tubes comes from
  A the breakdown of volcanic rock.
  B decomposing animal and vegetable matter.
  C the trapped smell of solidified lava.
  D overuse by visitors to the tubes.

6 What is unusual about many of the animals living in the tubes? Write your answer on the line.

_____

7 What colour is the basalt tunnel?
  A black   B red   C orange   D white

8 The floor of the lava tube tunnel
  A is a deep, rounded depression.
  B is hot to walk along.
  C is covered in ancient stalactites.
  D in places, has a flat 6-m thickness of non-volcanic matter.

9 How wide are the Undara tubes?

Write your answer in the box. ☐ metres

☞ **Answers and explanations on page 224**

READING
Understanding explanations

Read *Jigsaws* and answer the questions.

Jigsaws

A jigsaw is a power-driven saw with a narrow vertical blade, used to cut sharp curves in pieces of wood.

A jigsaw is also a puzzle. As a puzzle it is a tiling challenge that involves the assembly of numerous small, oddly shaped, interlocking pieces. Each piece has a small part of a picture on it. A completed puzzle produces a picture or design.

Jigsaw puzzles were originally created by producing a picture on a flat, rectangular piece of wood, then cutting that picture into small pieces with a jigsaw—that's where the name comes from!

Typical images found on jigsaw puzzles include scenes from nature, rural and city life and repetitive designs. Castles, mountains and water scenes with reflections are also traditional subjects. However, any kind of picture can be used to make a jigsaw puzzle. Cartoon-style pictures are popular. There are companies that create puzzles from personal photographs. Completed puzzles can also be pasted onto plywood or cardboard to make a wall hanging.

How did the power-driven saw and the puzzle get the same name? We must look to the history of the jigsaw puzzle to answer this question.

The first jigsaw puzzles were designed as geography teaching devices, by John Spilsbury, in 1767. His 'jigsaw' was a map puzzle. It was a hand-painted map of England on a piece of wood. It was a successful teaching method. He went on to make over thirty other map puzzles. The pieces were not interlocking.

Before the end of the 1700s pictorial 'jigsaws' began to appear. Instead of maps, the puzzles had pictures on them. The first of these had a picture of a dairymaid offering a young man some fresh milk. The pieces were not interlocking.

With the invention of power tools more than a century later, jigsaw puzzles with fully interlocking pieces come into being. The jigsaw machine could cut neat, sharp curves. Hence the name jigsaw puzzles.

Today there are jigsaws of all sizes. Jigsaw puzzles typically come in 300-piece, 500-piece, 750-piece and 1000-piece sizes. However, the largest commercial puzzle has 24 000 pieces and spans an area 428 cm by 157 cm. The most common layout for a 1000-piece puzzle is 38 pieces by 27 pieces, for a total of 1026 pieces. The majority of 500-piece puzzles are 27 pieces by 19 pieces. The largest jigsaw is said to have 40 000 pieces! Jigsaws for children come in a variety of sizes, rated by the number of pieces to suit various age groups.

Some jigsaws are quite tricky. Try doing one with all blank pieces. A few puzzles are made double-sided, so that they can be solved from either side. This increases the difficulty, because the puzzle solver cannot be certain which way up each particular piece goes. Some jigsaws do not have straight edges. The edge pieces could be any interlocking piece. Others deliberately have a piece or two missing or a few pieces too many. Jigsaws are no longer educational toys but entertainment and a hobby.

Sources:
http://en.wikipedia.org/wiki/Jigsaw_puzzlehttp://inventors.about.com/gi/dynamic/offsite
htm?site=http://www.jigsaw%2Dpuzzle.org/jigsaw%2Dpuzzle%2Dhistory.html

Real Test

1 How many meanings does the word 'jigsaw' have?

Write your answer in the box. ☐

2 The special feature of a jigsaw for cutting is
 A the speed at which it operates.
 B the type of timber it cuts.
 C the width of the blade.
 D its size.

3 What was the purpose of the first jigsaw puzzles? Write your answer on the lines.

_____

_____

4 A significant advance in jigsaw puzzles was the
 A use of cardboard instead of wood.
 B size increase to 1000 pieces.
 C use of pictures instead of maps.
 D introduction of interlocking pieces.

5 The first jigsaw picture was supposedly a picture of a
 A milkmaid and a young man.
 B water scene with a reflection.
 C castle in the mountains.
 D farming scene.

6 The size of a child's jigsaw puzzle depends a lot on the
 A subject matter of the picture.
 B age of the child.
 C quality of the cardboard.
 D size of the interlocking pieces.
 E educational value of the subject.

7 Which of these puzzles would most likely be the most difficult?
 A a puzzle made from a photograph
 B a 1000-piece puzzle
 C a puzzle with a reflection in water
 D a puzzle without a picture or design

8 The largest commercial jigsaw has
 A 1000 pieces.   B 1026 pieces.   C 24000 pieces.   D 40000 pieces

☞ **Answers and explanations on pages 224-225**

TIPS FOR WRITING EXPLANATIONS

Explanations tell us why things occur in scientific and technical fields. They are used in all the arts and sciences. Explanations are designed to help readers understand a topic but are not necessarily serious.

When writing explanations, it is best to keep the following points in mind. They will help you get the best possible mark.

Before you start writing

■ **Read the question and check the stimulus material carefully.** *Stimulus material* means the topic, title, picture, words, phrases or extract of writing you are given to base your writing on.

■ **Write about something you know.** Don't try to write about something outside your experience.

The introduction

■ **Inform your reader early of the topic of your explanation.** The title can be in the form of a question. The first few sentences or first paragraph may expand this idea—a statement about what is to be explained.

The body

■ Once you have introduced your topic, **use a sequence of paragraphs** to explain how your subject works, operates, grows or performs—the how and why part.

■ If possible, **include simple definitions of any scientific or technical words** you use. Definitions include the meaning of the word, a description of selected features and an example. Avoid common words that carry little or no meaning, such as *good*.

■ **Only add information that helps the reader better understand the subject** of the explanation. 'Waffle' and unnecessary detail don't improve an explanation. Detail must be selected carefully.

■ Many explanations are written in the **simple present tense** and **passive voice**, e.g. *The camera is designed to be lightweight …*

■ **Paragraphing is important**. Take care not to include too much information in each paragraph. Separate paragraphs work well even for small points. Paragraphing may explain where, when and how. Cause and effect can be part of an explanation.

■ Explanations may include **diagrams and pictures**.

The conclusion

■ Many explanations **end with a short comment**. This is a way to round off your writing.

■ **Make your writing interesting and informative** by using words and phrases precisely.

When you have finished writing give yourself a few minutes to read through your explanation. Quickly check spelling and punctuation, and insert any words that have been accidentally left out.

Real Test and Tips

42 min

There is no way of knowing for certain what type of writing will be included in the NAPLAN Tests in years to come. This is an opportunity for you to practise different types of writing.

An explanation tells **how** or **why** something happens or works. Explanations are often about scientific, technical or natural phenomena. The importance of the subject matter is stated.

Before you start, read the General writing tips on pages 26–27 and the Tips for writing explanations on page 124.

Today you are going to write an explanation of one of these objects.
- A school ruler
- A home letterbox
- A crash helmet

Before you start writing, give some thought to:
- what you are describing
- the special features of the object and how it operates
- the value or importance of the object.

Don't forget to:
- plan your explanation before you start writing
- write in correctly formed sentences and take care with paragraphing
- choose your words carefully and pay attention to your spelling and punctuation
- write neatly but don't waste time
- quickly check your explanation once you have finished.

Start writing here or type in your answer on a tablet or computer.

_____

_____

_____

_____

_____

_____

_____

_____

_____

_____

_____

_____

_____

_____

☞ **Marking guide on page 225**

There is no way of knowing for certain what type of writing will be included in the NAPLAN Tests in years to come. This is an opportunity for you to practise different types of writing.

An explanation tells **how** or **why** something happens or works. Explanations are often about scientific, technical or natural phenomena. The importance of the subject matter is stated.
Before you start, read the General writing tips on pages 26–27 and the Tips for writing explanations on page 124.

Today you are going to write an explanation of one of these objects.
- A bike bell or doorbell
- A bike tyre pump
- A pressurised insect spray

Before you start writing, give some thought to:
- what you are describing
- the special features of the object and how it operates
- the value or importance of the object.

Don't forget to:
- plan your explanation before you start writing
- write in correctly formed sentences and take care with paragraphing
- choose your words carefully and pay attention to your spelling and punctuation
- write neatly but don't waste time
- quickly check your explanation once you have finished.

Start writing here or type in your answer on a tablet or computer.

_____

_____

_____

_____

_____

_____

_____

_____

_____

_____

_____

_____

_____

_____

_____

☞ **Marking guide on pages 225-226**

Real Test and Tips

WRITING
Report from an outline

42 min

There is no way of knowing for certain what type of writing will be included in the NAPLAN Tests in years to come. This is an opportunity for you to practise different types of writing.

A report is an account based on research or investigation of a particular topic or incident. In some reports, information is collected from a number of sources. Before you start, read the General writing tips on pages 26–27.

Read the notes of the following incident and then write a report of what happened.

Date: 26 January (Australia Day)

Time: mid-afternoon

Location: Smiths Lake

Persons involved: young boys—Jim and Mark Eggins, Frank Paccini (tourist)

Incident: Two boys wearing life jackets, kayaking on calm waters of the lake. Jet ski rider creates waves, capsizes kayak. Boys in water. Manage to hang onto upturned kayak. Rescued by tourist fishing from boat nearby. Tourist rights the kayak and follows boys back to shore.

Outcome: Incident report to marine authorities. On arrival the jet skier is identified.

Before you start writing, give some thought to:
- the details of the report: what, where, when, why and who
- which aspects of the scene are relevant to the incident (these are what you should write about).

Don't forget to:
- plan your report before you start writing
- use mostly short sentences that contain one fact each
- choose your words carefully and pay attention to your spelling and punctuation
- write neatly but don't waste time
- quickly check your report once you have finished.

Start writing here or type in your answer on a tablet or computer.

Title: _____

_____

_____

_____

_____

_____

_____

_____

_____

_____

_____

_____

☞ **Marking guide on pages 226-227**

There is no way of knowing for certain what type of writing will be included in the NAPLAN Tests in years to come. This is an opportunity for you to practise different types of writing.

You may be asked to write a response to a picture or some other stimulus, such as lines of poetry or the beginning of a story.

Before you start, read the General writing tips on pages 26–27.

> Today you are going to write a response to a picture.
> Look at the picture on the right and write your response to it.

Before you start writing, give some thought to:
- what you see in the picture and what you think about this
- what you feel about the picture: your impressions when you look at it
- what will happen next.

Don't forget to:
- plan your response before you start writing
- write in correctly formed sentences and take care with paragraphing
- choose your words carefully and pay attention to your spelling and punctuation
- write neatly but don't waste time
- quickly check your response once you have finished.

Start writing here or type in your answer on a tablet or computer.

_____

_____

_____

_____

_____

_____

_____

_____

_____

_____

_____

_____

_____

_____

_____

_____

☞ **Marking guide on page 227**

Sample NAPLAN Online-style tests

DIFFERENT TEST LEVELS

- There are eight tests for students to complete in this section. These sample tests have been classified as either Intermediate or Advanced according to the level of the majority of questions. This will broadly reflect the NAPLAN Online tailored testing experience where students are guided into answering questions that match their ability.
- The following tests are included in this section:
  - one Intermediate-level Test for each of Reading, Conventions of Language and Numeracy
  - one Advanced-level Test for each of Reading, Conventions of Language and Numeracy
  - two Writing Tests.

CHECKS

- The NAPLAN Online Reading, Conventions of Language and Numeracy tests will be divided into different sections.
- Students will have one last opportunity to check their answers in each section when they have reached the end of that section.
- Once they have moved onto a new section, they will not be able to go back and check their work again.
- We have included reminders for students to check their work at specific points in the Sample Tests so they become familiar with this process before they take the NAPLAN Online tests.

EXCEL TEST ZONE

- After students have consolidated their topic knowledge by completing this book, we recommend they practise NAPLAN Online–style questions on our website at www.exceltestzone.com.au.
- Students will be able to gain valuable practice in digital skills such as dragging text across a screen, using an onscreen ruler, protractor and calculator to answer questions, or listening to audio recording of a spelling word which they then type into a box.
- Students will also become confident in using a computer or tablet to complete NAPLAN Online–style tests so they will be fully prepared for the actual NAPLAN Online tests.

The School Council is considering converting the staff car park into a skateboard park.

Write to the School Council supporting or rejecting this proposal.

Address: President
Palmdale School Council
Palmdale High School

Before you start writing, give some thought to:
- the students (including you) that this decision could affect
- the effect the decision may have on the school's reputation
- how you or other people, including parents, relate to the decision.

Don't forget to:
- plan your arguments before you start—make a list of important points you wish to make
- write in correctly formed sentences and take care with paragraphing
- choose your words carefully, and pay attention to your spelling and punctuation
- write neatly but don't waste time
- quickly check your writing once you have finished—your position must be clear to the reader.

Start writing here or type in your answer on a tablet or computer.

☞ **Marking guide on pages 227-228**

Read *How to Make Finger Puppets* and answer questions 1 to 7.

How to Make Finger Puppets

Make these for your younger brother or sister. They are easy to make and provide hours of fun for bored youngsters—and they make use of those single, lonely gloves or holey gloves.

Things You'll Need
- An old glove
- Fabric glue
- Glitter and glitter glue
- Felt
- Yarn/wool/string, cotton wool balls, steel wool, etc., for hair
- Fabric off-cuts
- Sequins, tiny buttons, unwanted jewellery
- Marking pens

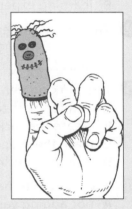

Steps

1   Cut the fingers off the old gloves. Discard fingers that have a hole in the top unless you are creating a 'bald' puppet (your fingertip will be the bald patch).

2   Edge the base of the fingers to prevent unravelling with a simple hand-sewn stitch. Quick drying glue works just as well if you cannot sew. Turn up the base a couple of millimetres and glue it. Small paper slides will hold it in place until it dries.

3   Decorate the puppets:

   Hair: glue on hair and beard. Use yarn, wool or string for hair. It can be loose, tied into ponytails, braided, left long or cut short. Add a beard to one or two with small pieces of cotton wool.

   Eyes: cut small eye shapes, or circles, from felt or buy stick-on eyes from a craft shop.

   Nose: glue on a nose made from felt, sequins or tiny buttons.

   Mouth: a glitter strip is great for this, or cut a felt smile and glue it on.

4   Dress the puppets. Use fabric, glue or stitching and your imagination. Add bow ties, scarves, caps and buttons. Draw on features with fine-line marking pens.

Helpful Tips

A finger puppet theatre can be made from a shoebox or a cereal box. Up-end the box and cut out a small window at the top of the box, this will become the puppets' stage. Make sure your arm can fit up into the box.
Decorate the box with curtains and pretend 'lights'. Screwed-up bits of coloured foil work well.

Warnings

- Don't cut up someone's new gloves. They won't be impressed!
- Take care with the scissors.

Sources:
http://www.internationalfolkart.org/eventsedu/education/muertos/skeletonpuppets.html
http://familyfun.go.com/arts-and-crafts/sew/feature/famf19puppet/famf19puppet3.html

1 Finger puppets, as described, are intended as a
   A way to earn pocket money.
   B means of recycling old clothes
   C playthings for young children.
   D family activity.
   E learning experience.

2 What is suggested as a beard for a finger puppet? Write your answer in the box.

3 The marking pen is used to
   A add features to the puppets' attire.
   B create the facial features.
   C mark the shape of the puppet theatre.
   D draw the outline of the finger puppet.

4 It is possible to have a puppet that has a bald head by
   A not adding yarn to the tip of the glove finger.
   B using a finger from the glove that has a hole in the end.
   C gluing a small piece of felt on the tip of the glove finger.
   D painting the tip of the glove finger in a pale colour.

5 It can be concluded that younger children would not make finger puppets because it is
   A boring.
   B extremely complicated.
   C fiddly.
   D time consuming.

6 This information would most likely be found in a
   A craft book.
   B recycling guide.
   C book of children' games.
   D holiday activities book.

7 It is suggested that a cereal box may be useful for playing with finger puppets.
   What is suggested that the cereal box be used for?
   Write your answer on the line.

_____

☞ **Answers and explanations on page 228**

Read *Rough Riding* and answer questions 8 to 14.

Rough Riding

The three standard events in rodeo are classified as 'rough riding' events. They are saddle bronc riding, bareback bronc riding and bull riding.

Bull riding involves a rider getting onto a large bull and attempting to stay mounted for eight seconds while the animal attempts to buck the rider off. It is a high-risk contest and has been called 'the most dangerous eight seconds in sports'. It has been around longer than most modern extreme sports.

A rider mounts a bull and grips a flat braided rope. After he secures a good grip on the rope, the rider nods to signal he is ready. The bucking chute (a small enclosure which opens from the side) is opened and the bull storms into the arena. The rider attempts to stay on the bull for the eight seconds, while only touching the bull with his riding hand. His other hand must remain free for the duration of the ride.

The bull bucks, rears, kicks, spins and twists in an effort to throw the rider. A loud buzzer announces the completion of the ride.

Throughout the ride, 'bull fighters' move about the bull in an effort to influence its movements and enhance the ride. When the ride ends, intentionally or not, the bull fighters move in to protect the rider from harm.

Bull riding is the ultimate test of courage and strength. It is the most dangerous event in rodeo—not only because of danger during the ride, but also danger from the bull after the eight-second ride. Danger increases if the bull rider has been bucked off, and lies injured and defenceless on the ground. Bull riding has the highest rate of injury of any rodeo sport and bull fighters have the highest injury rate of any non-contestant group.

Debate rages between animal rights organisations and bull riding enthusiasts. Critics claim that electric cattle prods harm the bull, while supporters claim that a brief shot simply gets the bull out of the chute quickly and is only a small irritation. The animal has a thick hide. Cattle prods are losing favour at large competitions. At smaller locations, prods are sometimes used to ensure the bull leaves the chute when the rider nods.

Spurs also cause controversy. Modern rodeo rules have strict regulations on the type and use of spurs. Participants point out that spurs are commonly used in equestrian events other than rodeos.

Sources:
http://en.wikipedia.org/wiki/Bronc_riding, http://en.wikipedia.org/wiki/Bull_riding,
http://www.prorodeo.asn.au/Events.htm

8 To be considered successful, a bull rider must remain mounted

A for eight seconds.

B for eight minutes.

C until he is bucked off.

D until rescued by the bull fighters.

9 According to the text, which **two** of these events are considered a part of rough riding?

A steer wrestling events

B saddle bronc riding events

C rope and tying events

D team roping events

E bullock racing events

F bareback bronc riding events

10 What is the basic responsibility of the bull fighters? Write your answer on the lines.

_____

_____

11 Bull riders feel they are justified in using spurs because

A they are just a brief irritation.

B less dangerous horse events use spurs.

C they make the bull react violently.

D bulls have extremely thick hides.

12 The most dangerous time for a rider is when

A the bull feels the spurs.

B he leaves the chute.

C the bull fighters torment the bull.

D he lies hurt upon the ground.

13 The main purpose of the electric prod is to

A encourage the bull to quickly leave the chute.

B force the bull to react to pain

C get the bull mad and bucking wildly.

D make the ride thrilling for spectators.

14 Write the numbers 1, 2, 3 and 4 in the boxes to show the order of the action when a bull rider's turn to compete comes.

☐ The bull breaks clear of the chute.

☐ The competitor nods his head.

☐ A buzzer announces the completion of a successful ride.

☐ The enclosed bull is mounted by the rider.

**It would be a good idea to check your answers to questions
1 to 14 before moving on to the other questions.**

☞ **Answers and explanations on page 229**

Read the poster about a car boot sale and answer questions 15 to 22.

Get along to

**Cambulla Public School's
next Biannual
Giant Car Boot Sale for 2020**

and support our school library.

WHEN: Sunday 10 September, 9 am–1 pm

WHERE: Cambulla Community Hall (next to the Post Office)

WHAT'S THERE:

- Over 20 mini garage sales
- Junior School Art Festival
- Inaugural pet show
- Native plant stalls
- Kids' Toy stalls
- Pony rides
- Lucky dips
- Food for every taste
- Jumping castle
- Face painting
- Cake stalls

Drawing of monster raffle (12 noon)   Live Music!
Rural Bushfire Truck on display

**Here's a chance to clean out the cupboards and
have your own garage sale in a friendly place.**

Return the slip below along with money to Cambulla School office by noon, Friday.

Car Space: (including Insurance) and a free coffee $12
Mini stalls: (blanket size and toys only) $5
Total $_____
Name: .... Contact address: ....

Credit card payments to Cambulla School Library Fund. Thank you.

Further details: Murray Jones, Cambulla Beach Newsagency

15 How often is the Cambulla School Car Boot Sale held? Write your answer on the line.

_____

16 The Cambulla Car Boot Sale is being held
   A in front of the Post Office.
   B in Cambulla School library.
   C at Cambulla Community Hall.
   D in Cambulla School grounds.

17 According to the text, a mini stall is
   A for small cars only.   B a stall run by kids.
   C a stall selling small items.   D blanket-sized.

18 The Cambulla School Car Boot Sale includes many activities.
   Which activity or activities were new for this 2020 sale? Circle as many options as you need.
   A a pet show   B live music   C a jumping castle
   D kids' toy stalls   E face painting   F monster raffle

19 The organisers are promoting the sale as a
   A sporting event.   B safe driving event.
   C social event.   D gourmet food event.

20 To take part in the Car Boot Sale participants must
   A pay before the day of the car boot sale.
   B take out insurance.
   C hand the slip in at the Newsagency.
   D have toys to sell.

21 The Junior School Art Festival most likely refers to artwork by
   A Cambulla School's best artists.
   B students in the lower grades.
   C young, aspiring artists from Cambulla.
   D a professional children's art teacher

22 You are going to compare the texts *Rough Riding* (page 133) and *Car boot sale* (page 135).
   For what purposes were these texts written? Tick **two** options for each text.

	Rough Riding	*Car boot sale*
to persuade	☐	☐
to explain	☐	☐
to describe	☐	☐
to advise	☐	☐

☞ **Answers and explanations on page 229**

For some reason many Australians have a soft spot for bushrangers and lawbreakers and in many cases they have become folk heroes. 'The Wild Colonial Boy' is a popular bush ballad, a story in verse or song that appeals to an Irish streak in many Australians.

Read the poem and answer questions 23 to 29.

The Wild Colonial Boy

There was a wild Colonial Boy,
Jack Doolan was his name,
Of poor but honest parents,
He was born in Castlemaine.
He was his father's only hope
His mother's pride and joy,
And dearly did his parents love
The Wild Colonial Boy.

At the age of sixteen years
He left his native home,
And to Australia's sunny shores
A bushranger did roam.
They put him in the iron gang
In the government employ,
But never an iron on earth could hold
The Wild Colonial Boy.

In sixty-one this daring youth
Commenced his wild career,
With a heart that knew no danger
And no foreman did he fear.
He stuck up the Beechworth mail coach
And robbed Judge MacEvoy
Who, trembling cold, gave up his gold
To the Wild Colonial Boy.

He bade the Judge good morning
And he told him to beware,
That he'd never rob a needy man
Or one who <u>acted square</u>,
But a Judge who'd robbed a mother
Of her one and only joy
Sure, he must be a worse outlaw than
The Wild Colonial Boy.

One day as Jack was riding
The mountainside along,
A-listening to the little birds
Their happy laughing song.
Three mounted troopers came along,
Kelly, Davis and Fitzroy
With a warrant for the capture of
The Wild Colonial Boy.

'Surrender now! Jack Doolan,
For you see it's three to one;
Surrender in the Queen's own name,
You are a highwayman.'
Jack drew his pistol from his belt
And waved it like a toy,
'I'll fight, but not surrender,' cried
The Wild Colonial Boy.

He fired at trooper Kelly
And brought him to the ground,
And in return from Davis,
Received a mortal wound,
All shattered through the jaws he lay
Still firing at Fitzroy,
And that's the way they captured him,
The Wild Colonial Boy.

Chorus
So come away me hearties
We'll roam the mountains high,
Together we will plunder
And together we will die.
We'll scour along the valleys
And we'll gallop o'er the plains,
And scorn to live in slavery,
Bound down by iron chains.

23 The verse is described as a ballad. A ballad is
   A the life story of an important, respected hero.
   B any song that has survived since colonial times.
   C the traditional telling of a story in poetry or song.
   D the tale of the exploits of a villain.

24 The verse treats Jack Doolan as
   A fearless and foolhardy.
   B lawless and flamboyant.
   C dashing and careless.
   D cruel and ruthless.

25 Write the numbers 1, 2, 3 and 4 in the boxes to show the order of events in which Jack Doolan lived his life.

☐ Doolan robbed Judge MacEvoy of his gold.

☐ Doolan left Castlemaine for Australia.

☐ Doolan engaged in a gunfight with three troopers.

☐ Doolan was faced with a warrant for his arrest.

26 Jack Doolan considered the law to be

heartless.	incompetent.	sensitive.	reputable.	superfluous.
A	B	C	D	E

27 Draw a line to match the person with the fact from the lyrics of the song.

1 Judge MacEvoy	2 Trooper Davis	3 Jack Doolan	4 Trooper Kelly

A held up a coach.	B was robbed of gold.	C brought down Doolan.	D was shot by Doolan.

28 The writer portrays Jack Doolan as a
   A hopeless drifter.   B callous murderer.
   C loveable rogue.   D evil schemer.

29 Doolan states he'd never rob a man who 'acted square'. By this he means anyone who
   A was a judge.   B lived a fair and honest life.
   C had spent time harassed by the law.   D didn't have much money.

It would be a good idea to check your answers to questions
15 to 29 before moving on to the other questions.

☞ **Answers and explanations on pages 229-230**

Read *What is wildlife rehabilitation?* and answer questions 30 to 36.

What is wildlife rehabilitation?

Helping wild creatures to recover from injury, or raising orphans to be released back into their natural environment, requires more than kindness. Practical caring for wildlife is very different from caring for domesticated animals. It requires specialised knowledge and expertise to house, feed and rehabilitate them.

Wildlife rehabilitation is physically, emotionally and financially demanding and it requires considerable time. An animal may require anywhere from one hour's attention to weeks of round-the-clock care. Access to veterinary care and medicines is often needed, as are both indoor and outdoor housing facilities.

A variety of specialised equipment is necessary and there are a myriad of tasks to undertake, from cleaning cages to administering medical treatments.

In Victoria, wildlife rehabilitators require a permit to care for native wildlife. Wildlife rehabilitators spend considerable time, energy and resources of their own, often operating from their own homes, to provide the necessary care for needy wildlife. They are trained and skilled to firstly assess the rescue needs of an animal and then to safely capture, handle and transport it. Further expertise and knowledge is required to provide a high quality of care for the injured, distressed and/or orphaned animal.

Although wildlife rehabilitation is a rewarding and valuable thing to do, it must be stressed that it is also difficult and requires commitment, patience and emotional stamina.

Rehabilitation is not about 'cuddling wildlife' or keeping wildlife as pets. It is about allowing native animals to remain wild and to live freely according to their own will and in their own environment.

Wildlife carers often need people willing to use their properties as release sites. This might mean anything from simply opening a cage and releasing animals to being involved in monitoring and supporting a newly released animal and reporting back to the wildlife carer. Wildlife carers inspect properties, as very specific requirements are needed. A property may be unsuitable for some types of animals and so inspection is necessary.

Thanks to Wildlife Victoria for permission to use this information.

30 What special attribute does a successful wildlife carer require?
A kindness
B a large property
C patience and emotional stamina
D knowledge of caring for domestic animals

31 Wildlife rehabilitation is mostly about
A cuddling animals.
B keeping native animals as pets.
C inspecting properties.
D returning native animals to their environment

32 The passage is mainly concerned with
A explaining the complexities of wildlife rehabilitation.
B encouraging people to become wildlife carers.
C finding properties for the release of wildlife.
D warning people not to keep native animals as pets.

33 According to the text which statement is true?
A All animal care is conducted in special veterinary clinics.
B Wildlife carers often put animals in cages.
C Most animals require the same level of care.
D Animals released into the bush no longer require a carer's attention.

34 You are going to compare the texts *The Wild Colonial Boy* (page 137) and *What is wildlife rehabilitation?* (page 139). For what purposes were these texts written? Tick **two** options for each text.

	Colonial Boy	*Wildlife rehabilitation*
to entertain	☐	☐
to explain	☐	☐
to inform	☐	☐
to retell an event	☐	☐

35 Under what conditions might a wildlife carer use his own home?
A when the carer has the medical supplies
B when the animal is too stressed to return to the bush
C when caring for a young orphaned animal
D when there are insufficient cages at the workplace

36 Select **all** correct answers. In Victoria, to become a wildlife carer a person needs
A a permit.
B a supply of veterinary medicines.
C a permanent home.
D a place for injured animals.
E a uniform.
F training.

☞ **Answers and explanations on page 230**

Read *Going Down Canal Locks* and answer questions 37 to 43.

Going Down Canal Locks

Locks are a part of canals in the United Kingdom. A lock is a section of canal closed off by gates to control the water level and enable the raising and lowering of boats that pass through it. Canals, once used for commercial transportation, are now used for enjoyment—travelling with family or friends on a canal system. People using canals must know how the locks operate.

How to descend through a lock

If the lock is empty, first shut the bottom gates and fill the lock by opening the top paddles (and closing the bottom ones). Paddles are common on locks. They provide a means to control the water flow in and out of the lock.

When the lock is full, open the top gates and the boat can sail into the lock.

With the top paddles down and the top gates closed, open the bottom paddles and the water level inside the lock equalises with that of the lower level in the canal below the lock. There is often a sill underneath the top gates, which extends out into the lock about a metre. Care must be taken to avoid getting caught up on the sill.

Once the water inside the lock is the same level as the water below the lock, open the bottom gates and the boat sails off.

Word of warning: it is bad, if not dangerous practice, to moor when in a lock.

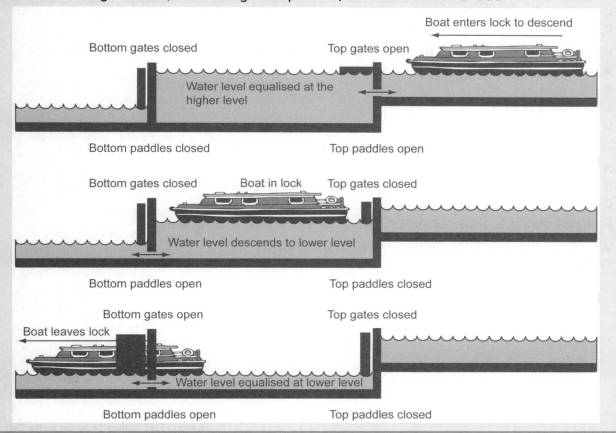

37 Choose **two** options. The information would be relevant to a person on a voyage
  A over a lake.
  B along a canal.
  C across an ocean.
  D into a harbour.
  E along a river.
  F over flooded land.

38 The best description of the style of writing in this passage would be
  A casual.
  B emotive.
  C dramatic.
  D informative.
  E simplistic.
  F verbose.

39 When going downstream and approaching an empty lock, what is the order of procedures?
Write the numbers 1 to 4 in the boxes to show the order of operations required.

☐	open the top gates
☐	open the top paddles and close the bottom paddles
☐	shut the bottom gates
☐	allow the water to fill the lock

40 The paddles are used to
  A control water flow in and out of the lock.
  B manipulate the boat through the lock.
  C prevent the lock gates bursting open.
  D allow the boat to pass into the lock.

41 Boat operators descending through a lock must take care
  A of passing boats coming up.
  B to avoid the paddles.
  C leaving the lock.
  D crossing the sill.

42 A descending boat can leave the lock when the
  A lock is full of water.
  B water level in the lock is the same as the water level below the lock.
  C mooring rope has been released.
  D water begins to flow out of the lock.

43 What is a potentially dangerous practice around locks?
Write your answer on the line.

_____

☞ **Answers and explanations on pages 230-231**

Read the email and answer questions 44 to 50.

A Gift for You

I want to let you all know that John and I have been the victims of credit card fraud this week and I felt I should warn you all about the clever scam. It works like this:

Last Wednesday I had a phone call in the late morning from Express Super Couriers to ask if I was going to be home as he had a delivery for me. He said he would be there in roughly an hour. He turned up with a beautiful basket of flowers and wine. I expressed my great surprise as I wasn't expecting anything like this and said I was intrigued to know who was sending me such a lovely gift. He said he was only delivering the gift and the card was being sent separately (the card has never arrived). There was a consignment note with the gift.

He went on to explain that because the gift contained alcohol he has to charge the recipient $3.50 as proof that he has actually delivered to an adult, and not left it on a doorstep if the recipient is out, to be stolen or taken by children. This seemed logical and I offered to get the cash. He then said that the company required the payment to be by Eftpos so he's not handling cash and everything is properly accounted for. My husband, John, was there and got his credit card and 'John' swiped the card on this small mobile machine that also had a small screen upon which Ray entered in his pin number. A receipt was printed out and given to us.

Between last Thursday and Monday $4000 was withdrawn from our credit account at ATM machines in the North Shore area. It appears a dummy credit card was made using the details in the machine and, of course, they had John's pin number.

The bank has stopped our cards and I've been to the police this morning, where they confirmed that it is a definite scam and many households were hit during the first three days of October.

So PLEASE be wary of accepting a gift you're not expecting, especially if the card is not with it. We've all received gifts like this and would never dream that it could be such a despicable act. Please also let other female friends and relatives know. Hopefully these fraudsters have ceased this activity by now but you never know. I wanted to warn all my friends.

Carrie

P.S. I don't think I'll ever drink the wine—I'd probably choke on it!

Permission given to reproduce email: names have been changed

44 What surprised Carrie about the gift?
   A It was from a long-lost friend.
   B It included a bottle of her favourite wine.
   C Its delivery fee was less than $4.
   D It was unexpected.

45 What reason did the courier give for not leaving the 'gift' on the doorstep?
   A The flowers would have wilted.
   B There was no card attached to the gift.
   C Children might have taken the wine.
   D They were required to print a receipt.

46 The real reason the 'courier' had to visit was to
   A collect the $3.50 delivery charge.
   B get John's or Carrie's credit card details.
   C explain when the card would arrive.
   D warn of scams run by fraudulent couriers.

47 What reason could Carrie have for vowing not to drink the delivered wine?
   A It would remind her of the $4000 scam.
   B She could no longer afford to buy any wine at all.
   C The gift wine was poor quality.
   D She thought a friend had sent her the wine.

48 How would Carrie describe the 'courier' as he conducted his operation? Circle **two** answers.
   A intimidating and coarse   B friendly and reasonable   C strange and suspicious
   D helpful and smug   E flustered and diffident   F competent and amenable

49 How did Carrie feel after learning the truth?
   A withdrawn   B depressed   C helpless
   D disillusioned   E patronising   F complacent

50 What reason would Carrie have for sending this email? Circle **two** answers.
   A to cover her feelings of embarrassment
   B to assist police with enquiries
   C to expose the scam to her friends
   D to warn the scammer she knew about his method
   E because she was angry
   F because she was humble

☞ **Answers and explanations on page 231**

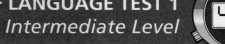

1 Which of the following correctly completes this sentence?

Kelly had been awake and ░░░░░░ the alarm go off.

had heard	has heard	heared	hears
A	**B**	**C**	**D**

2 Which of the following correctly completes this sentence?

We both had haircuts but mine was different ░░░░░ Roy's.

to	at	too	from
A	**B**	**C**	**D**

3 Shade two bubbles to show where the missing question marks (?) should go.

You don't understand, do you ⓐ The total is 'ten' ⓑ but you said 'six' ⓒ Why is that so hard ⓓ

Read the text *Stress*. The text has some gaps. Choose the correct word to fill each gap.

Stress

Things never work as planned. We need a good night's rest. The whole team ░░░░░░ the importance of a win tomorrow. It's our last match. We have a chance of winning the trophy for the first time. Late in the afternoon Pippa and I heard music coming from across the street. Over there they have parties, ░░░░░ go most of the night. We weren't going to get much rest!

We had to escape for a while at least. The local cinema seemed a good distraction. A mistake. The film was quite silly ░░░░░░ I got up and left. This upset my sister, Pippa.

'My nails ░░░░░ been broken,' she complained as she examined her hands on the walk home. I know she had really been biting them!

4
know	knowing	knows	knew
A	**B**	**C**	**D**

5
when	who	what	which
A	**B**	**C**	**D**

6
but	so	except	instead
A	**B**	**C**	**D**

7
having	have	has	had
A	**B**	**C**	**D**

8 Shade a bubble to show where the missing comma (,) should go.

Sandra ⓐ have you finished ⓑ any of your ⓒ reading ⓓ or Maths?

9 List in the boxes any adverbs used in the sentence. You may choose more than one.

The explorers arrived soon after sunrise and moved quickly and silently across the river.

☞ **Answers and explanations on page 232**

10 Write a word from this sentence in each empty box to match the given parts of speech.

Brightly coloured junks floated in the harbour.

verb		preposition	

adverb		adjective	

Read the text *Sign Up*. The text has some gaps. Chose the correct word to fill each gap.

Sign Up

1 Being late for class is forgivable once—or even twice.

2 Kim was never ⬚ time for the start of a lesson.

3 Her English teacher has drawn up an agreement. **4** It states exactly what time her lessons start and which room they are in. **5** As if Kim doesn't know! **6** The teacher insists the agreement should be signed as soon ⬚ possible.

11
at	for	on	about
A	B	C	D

12
is	are	if	as
A	B	C	D

13 In sentence 5 the exclamation mark is included to
A let the reader know that Kim is about to shout.
B indicate that Kim is being told something that is all too obvious to her.
C show that Kim is aghast at her teacher's suggestion.
D highlight the importance of the agreement to the teacher.

14 In which sentence is the word *check* used as a noun?
A Our team has a T-shirt with a blue check border.
B You need to check in your bags before you get a boarding pass.
C Mothers often check the temperature of food for babies.
D The police are calling for a regular check on underage drivers.

15 Which of the following correctly completes this sentence?

Di's bruise is ⬚ than yours.

more dark	darkerer	darker	more darkest
A	B	C	D

16 Which of the following correctly completes this sentence?

As the sun had ⬚ it was time to head for home.

rised	risen	rose	rosed
A	B	C	D

17 Read this text and identify the parts of speech of the underlined words.
<u>Lately</u> Mia had been <u>late</u> for class but today she was on time!

adverb adjective	adverb verb	conjunction verb	adjective adverb
A	B	C	D

☞ **Answers and explanations on pages 232-233**

18 Which of the following correctly completes this sentence?

In Australia, each ▨▨▨▨ population is recorded in a Commonwealth Year Book.

city's	cities'	citys'	cities	citie's
A	**B**	**C**	**D**	**E**

19 Which of the following correctly completes this sentence?

The latest news now ▨▨▨▨ a report about a world record in yachting.

have	had	haves	has
A	**B**	**C**	**D**

20 Which of the following correctly completes this sentence?

If survivors ▨▨▨▨ to upturned crafts, we should be able to reach them in time.

cling	clings	clung	clinged
A	**B**	**C**	**D**

21 Which of the following correctly completes this sentence?

▨▨▨▨ we act now, all is lost.

Although	Unless	However	Because	Whenever
A	**B**	**C**	**D**	**E**

22 In which sentence is the word *inside* used as an adverb?
A Max knew that what he was looking for was inside the drawer.
B The driver found his licence in an inside coat pocket.
C A radio was playing inside the empty flat.
D We need to wipe the inside of the windscreen.

23 Choose the part of this sentence that is an adjectival clause.

<u>Auntie Cecelia</u> <u>enjoyed the book</u> <u>on birds</u> <u>that she borrowed from the library</u>.
   A   **B**   **C**   **D**

24 Which of the following correctly completes this sentence?

I said hello then realised I had ▨▨▨▨ him for my uncle!

mistaken	mistaked	mistook	mistooken
A	**B**	**C**	**D**

25 Which sentence uses brackets correctly?
A Lenny (thought he could play Scrabble but he) was a drongo slow-witted person when it came to scoring.
B Lenny thought he could play Scrabble but he was a drongo (slow-witted person) when it came to scoring
C Lenny thought he could play Scrabble but he was a drongo slow-witted person (when it came to scoring).
D Lenny thought he could play Scrabble but he was (a drongo) slow-witted person when it came to scoring.

**It would be a good idea to check your answers to questions
1 to 25 before moving on to the other questions.**

☞ **Answers and explanations on pages 233-234**

To the student
Ask your teacher or parent to read the spelling words for you. The words are listed on page 249. Write the spelling words on the lines below.

26 _____   34 _____

27 _____   35 _____

28 _____   36 _____

29 _____   37 _____

30 _____   38 _____

31 _____   39 _____

32 _____   40 _____

33 _____

Each line has one word that is incorrect. Write the correct spelling of the underlined word in the box.

41 He was <u>slightely</u> injured in the accident.

42 The marksman hit the <u>targett</u> at least eight times.

43 The distance covered was quite <u>significent</u>.

44 The man in remand made a statement to the officer in <u>charg</u>.

45 After the sixtieth minute the <u>situeation</u> had not changed.

Each line has one word that is incorrect. Write the correct spelling of word in the box.

46 The sourse of the river system is in an alpine region.

47 Someone has to be resposable for the wreckage.

48 The weather threatend to turn very nasty, very quickly.

49 The police unit captured the criminalls holding the hostages.

50 'Your presence is a hinderance,' muttered the guide.

☞ **Answers and explanations on page 232**

Section 1: Non-calculator questions

1 On average Lara's heart beats 64 times every minute. How many times will it beat in 5 minutes?

A 69   **B** 309   **C** 320   **D** 405

2 Pablo had $7.80. He bought a magazine that cost $6.90. How much money did he have left?

A $0.90   **B** $1.10   **C** $1.90   **D** $14.70

3 Anna recorded the amount she spent on petrol over four weeks.

Week 1: $64.85

Week 2: $49.40

Week 3: $71.80

Week 4: $75.25

To estimate the total cost of petrol over the four weeks Anna rounded each of the weekly amounts to the nearest $10 and added them. How much is Anna's estimate?

A $220   **B** $240   **C** $260   **D** $280

4 What is the value of $3.24 \div 0.4$?

5 A tank is one-third full and currently holds 6000 litres. How much water is in the tank when it is 25% full?

litres

6 The timeline shows the year of birth of four generations of a family.

Frederick   Darcy   Barry   Jackson

1903   1994

Frederick was 25 years old when his son Darcy was born. When Jackson was born, Barry was half the age of Darcy. In what year was Barry born?

7 The cost of five cappuccinos is $24. What is the cost of three cappuccinos?

$

8 $3 + 5 \times (8 - 4 \div 2) =$?

What number does ? represent?

13	16	33	48	58
A	**B**	**C**	**D**	**E**

This is the end of the part where you are not allowed to use a calculator. It would be a good idea to check your answers to the questions in this section before moving on to the other questions.

Section 2: Calculator Allowed questions

9 Four different shapes are drawn on grid paper.

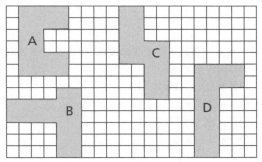

Which of the following is correct?

A All the shapes have the same perimeter and the same area.

B The perimeter of Shape C is less than the perimeter of Shape D.

C The area of Shape A is more than the area of Shape B.

D The perimeter of Shape A is less than the perimeter of Shape C.

☞ **Answers and explanations on pages 234-237**

10 Four students were discussing their ages. Peta is 26 days older than Greg but 11 days younger than Sam. Emily is four days younger than Greg. Label the boxes in the diagram to show the order of students from oldest to youngest.

oldest   **youngest**

Who was the third oldest?

A Emily

B Greg

C Sam

D Peta

11 The diagram shows a composite figure made from two rectangles.

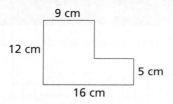

Which of these expressions gives the area of the shape?

A $(12 \times 9) + (16 \times 5)$

B $(16 \times 12) - (9 \times 5)$

C $(12 \times 9) - (16 \times 5)$

D $(16 \times 12) - (7 \times 7)$

12 When Dylan uses his spinner, the chance that it lands on B (black) is unlikely but not impossible. Which of these is Dylan's spinner?

A   B

C   D

13 This shape is rotated a quarter turn in an anticlockwise direction. What does the shape look like after the rotation?

A   B

C   D

14 The grid contains two triangles where Triangle II is an enlargement of Triangle I.

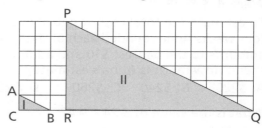

The vertices of the triangles have been named. Which of these statements is correct? Select **all** the correct answers.

A The enlargement factor is 6.

B PQ is 6 times the length of AB.

C The perimeter of triangle II is six times the perimeter of triangle I.

D The area of triangle II is twelve times the area of triangle I.

15 Kim is reading a book. It has 120 pages. On the first night she read one-sixth of the book. On the next night she read one-fifth of the remainder of the book. How many pages does she have left to read?

20	40	72	80	109
A	B	C	D	E

☞ **Answers and explanations on pages 234–237**

16 From a class of 30 Year 7 students, 4 had previously attended McCarthy Public school. The fraction of the class who had attended McCarthy Public School is closest to

A $\frac{1}{8}$ B $\frac{1}{5}$ C $\frac{1}{4}$ D $\frac{1}{3}$

It would be a good idea to check your answers to questions 9–16 before moving on to the other questions.

---

17 Kara made two identical square pyramids. She glued the bases of the pyramids together to form a single solid. Which statement is correct about the new solid?

A It has 8 faces and 8 edges.

B It has 8 faces and 12 edges.

C It has 10 faces and 10 edges.

D It has 10 faces and 12 edges.

18 Here is the map of a small town.

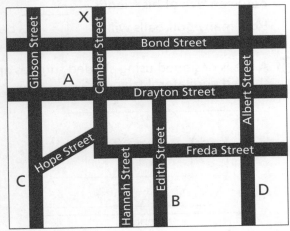

Jerome leaves X and travels along Camber Street. He takes the second street on his left and then the next street on his right. When Jerome travels along this street he passes

A A on his right.   B B on his left.

C C on his right.   D D on his left.

19 4 hours 15 minutes is the same as

A 4.025 hours.   B 4.15 hours.

C 4.2 hours.   D 4.25 hours.

20 These cards are turned over and mixed up.

| 4 | 5 | 6 | 7 | 8 |

A card is chosen at random. What is the probability that it is even?

A $\frac{1}{5}$ B $\frac{2}{5}$ C $\frac{1}{2}$ D $\frac{3}{5}$

21 The Eiffel Tower has a height of 300 metres. A scale drawing of the tower is shown.

What scale has been used in the drawing?

A 1 cm represents 60 m

B 1 cm represents 6 m

C 1 m represents 6 cm

D 1 m represents 60 cm

22 The table shows the travellers from different continents who arrived at an Australian airport.

Continent	Percentage
Asia	32
America	20
Africa	14
Europe	34

If there were 1 million travellers, how many were from America?

☞ **Answers and explanations on pages 234-237**

23 Saasha drew up a Weekly Fitness Program to show the times she spent in different activities.

Weekly Fitness Program			
Activity	Minutes in activity	No. of sessions	Total minutes
Soccer training	60	2	120
Soccer game	80	1	80
Walk dog	30	3	90
Ride bike	12	10	120

What was the total time Saasha spent on the activities in the program?

A 4 hours 10 minutes

B 6 hours 30 minutes

C 6 hours 40 minutes

D 6 hours 50 minutes

24 Alma built this solid from small cubes. What is the view of the solid from the right?

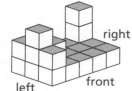

A

B   C   D

25 Darryl is planning a train journey from Sydney to Perth and then a flight to return to Sydney. He used the tables below to find the total cost of the trip.

By train:

$ per person one-way	Gold Service	Red Service	
Sydney–Perth or vice versa		Sleeper Cabin	Daynighter Seat
Adult	1908	1322	676

By plane:

$ per person one-way	Supa Saver	Basic	Corporate	First Class
Sydney–Perth or vice versa	225	630	779	940

Darryl books a Sleeper Cabin from Sydney to Perth and a Corporate booking on the flight from Perth to Sydney.

How much will the entire trip cost?

$ [   ]

26 Isabella makes a dice where the values on opposite faces of a dice add up to 14. Which of the following nets represents her dice?

A   B

C   D

27 Greg has decided to give away his collection of golf balls.

If he gives a dozen balls to each of his four friends he will have seven left over.

Instead, Greg decides to share the balls between five of his friends.

How many golf balls will each of his friends receive? [   ] balls

28 A tile is designed using shaded squares and shaded equilateral triangles.

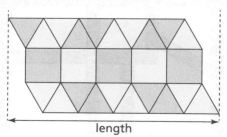

length

The perimeter of each square is 24 cm. What is the length of the shape?

[   ] cm

☞ **Answers and explanations on pages 234-237**

29 A rectangle with side 6 cm has a diagonal of length 10 cm.

6 cm

The rectangle is cut along the diagonal to form two identical triangles.
The perimeter of each triangle is 24 cm.
What is the area of each triangle?

[ ] square centimetres

30 Llanah is overseas and is returning to Australia. Her airline has a restriction on the mass of her baggage. The set of scales shows the mass of her packed suitcase.

20.7 kg

Llanah removed souvenirs which had a total mass of 1200 grams. What is the new mass of her suitcase?

A 19.2 kg   B 19.3 kg
C 19.4 kg   D 19.5 kg

31 A survey was conducted to find a group of students' favourite sports on television and recorded in the graph below.

Favourite sport on television

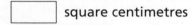

| AFL | NRL | Soccer | Cricket |

The graph shows that 40 students said their favourite television sport was cricket.
How many students chose AFL?

A 35   B 70   C 75   D 80

32 The table shows the cost of hiring a paddle board for different numbers of hours.

Number of hours	$\frac{1}{2}$	1	$1\frac{1}{2}$	2	$2\frac{1}{2}$	3
Cost in dollars	20	25	30	35	40	45

Select the answer that shows the cost of hiring a paddle board.
A $25 for every hour
B $15 for every hour plus an extra $5
C $5 for every hour plus an extra $15
D $10 for every hour plus an extra $15

It would be a good idea to check your answers to questions 17 to 32 before moving on to the other questions.

---

33 If the angle $y°$ is three times the size of the angle $x°$, what is the size of y?

not to scale

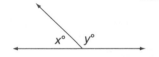

$x°$ $y°$

A 60   B 120   C 135   D 145

34 The table shows the masses of groceries:

Item	Mass
Loaf of bread	680 grams
Carton of eggs	800 grams
Box of washing detergent	2.5 kilograms
Tin of tomatoes	440 grams

What is the mean (average) mass of the groceries?
A 481 gram   B 542.5 grams
C 1100 grams   D 1.105 kilogram

☞ **Answers and explanations on pages 234-237**

35 Fiona draws a number line and locates

$2\frac{2}{3}$ and $3\frac{2}{3}$ on it.

What number is exactly in the middle of 2 and 3?

A 3   B $3\frac{1}{6}$ C $3\frac{1}{3}$ D $3\frac{1}{2}$

36 The diagram shows a plan of a small farm.

Chickens			Storage	Vegetable patch
Horses			Machinery	

The area allocated to the chickens is 40 m². What is the area of the vegetable patch?

☐ m²

37 For their Fruit and Nut Mix packets, the National Natural Food Company combines the mass of fruit and the mass of nuts in the ratio of 3 to 5. What is the mass of nuts in a 480-gram bag?

National Natural Food Company
480 g
Fruit & Nut Mix

A 180 grams
B 240 grams
C 300 gram
D 360 grams

38 Fresh prawns are selling at $24 per kilogram. John bought $18 worth of prawns. What mass of prawns did he buy?

$24/kg

A 250 grams
B 500 grams
C 750 grams
D 800 grams

39 The net of a square pyramid has been drawn on the grid below.

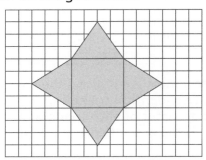

Bridgett uses the net to form the solid. What is the sum of the areas of all the faces of the solid?

A 20 square units
B 24 square units
C 32 square units
D 40 square units

40 A budget is drawn up for the Harvey family's overseas trip. The trip will cost $45 000.

Item	Percentage
Airline tickets	20%
Escorted tour	40%
Additional accommodation	10%
Souvenirs	10%
Other spending money	20%

What is the cost of the airline tickets for the family?

A $9000   B $10 000
C $12 000   D $20 000

41 Craig drove his car for 2 hours and travelled 180 kilometres. At this same speed, how far will Craig travel in 3 hours?

A 90 kilometres
B 200 kilometres
C 210 kilometres
D 270 kilometres

☞ **Answers and explanations on pages 234–237**

42 What is the size of *x*?

43 The shortest distance from Hidden Waters to Outlook is 40 kilometres.

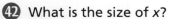

What is the shortest distance from Highland County to Sanctuary?

- **A** 70 kilometres
- **B** 72 kilometres
- **C** 76 kilometres
- **D** 84 kilometres

44 Which solids have the same volume?

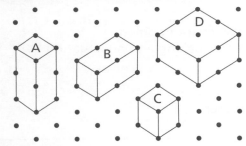

- **A** A and B
- **B** B and C
- **C** C and D
- **D** B and D

45 The mass of an Australian 10-cent coin is 5.65 grams. Selena has saved $30 worth of 10-cent coins. What is the total mass of the coins in kilograms?

_____ kg

46

Which of these statements is correct? Select **all** the correct answers.

- **A** A hexagonal prism has twice as many vertices as faces.
- **B** A cube has twice as many edges as faces.
- **C** A triangular pyramid has four faces.
- **D** A triangular prism has the same number of faces as a square pyramid

47 Sarah is 3 cm shorter than Craig. Which statement is correct?

- **A** Craig's height = Sarah's height – 3
- **B** Sarah's height = Craig's height – 3
- **C** Craig's height = Sarah's height ÷ 3
- **D** Craig's height + Sarah's height = 3

48 Charlotte marks an **X** on the coordinates (2, –1). From **X** she moves 3 units up and 4 units to the left and marks a **Y**.

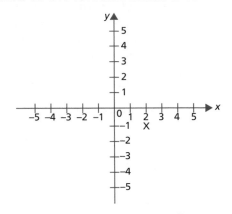

What are the coordinates of **Y**?

(–2, 2)	(2, –2)	(5, –5)	(–5, 5)	(5, –3)
A	**B**	**C**	**D**	**E**

☞ **Answers and explanations on pages 234-237**

You are going to write a narrative or story. Your story will be about THE UNEXPECTED VISITOR. Your writing will be judged on your expression and the structure of your story.

Look at the picture on the right. The visitor might be someone from space. But it could be an old friend, a relative or someone with some unexpected news. It may be an animal. It might be a reporter from a TV station or newspaper.

Think about where your story takes place. It could be at home or at school.

Think about when your story takes place—daytime or night-time, summer or winter. The visitor might arrive at a sporting field when your team is training. Your story might be amusing or it might be serious. Think about how the people in your story react.

Before you start writing, give some thought to:
- where your story takes place
- the characters and what they do in your story
- the events that take place in your story and the problems that have to be resolved
- how your story begins, what happens in your story, and how your story ends.

Don't forget to:
- plan your story before you start writing
- write in correctly formed sentences and take care with paragraphing
- choose your words carefully and pay attention to your spelling and punctuation
- write neatly but don't waste time
- quickly check your story once you have finished.

Start writing here or type in your answer on a tablet or computer.

_____
_____
_____
_____
_____
_____
_____
_____
_____
_____
_____
_____

☞ **Marking guide on page 237**

Read *'Tin Legs' Bader* and answer questions 1 to 8.

'Tin Legs' Bader

Douglas Bader was born in London on 21 February 1910. He was an outstanding sportsman while at school. After a visit to the RAF College, Bader set his sights on becoming a pilot and won a cadetship at the college. He had a reputation as an above-average, if rash, pilot.

Bader became an Officer in the Royal Air Force in 1930. He was a skilled pilot and in 1931 was selected to fly in the RAF's aerobatic display team. He was notorious for low-level aerobatics. In December 1931 he crashed during an unauthorised low-level stunt.

Though he survived the crash, his injuries were severe. Both of his legs were amputated. He was fitted with artificial 'tin' legs. He soon learned to walk without a stick and to drive his car, but he was also flying—unofficially.

Though he passed as perfectly able to fly, he was not allowed to fly for the RAF and was offered a ground commission. Bader resigned.

At the outbreak of the Second World War (1939) Bader applied to rejoin the RAF. Pilots were in short supply. The rules were overlooked. By June 1940 Bader was given command of a Squadron that had suffered high casualties.

In 1941 he was promoted to Wing Commander. Bader led sweeps over Europe aimed at bringing the German fighters into combat. By that summer he had claimed 22 victories, becoming the fifth–highest scoring RAF pilot. On 9 August 1941 Bader failed to return from an operation when his aircraft was downed in France.

The circumstances of Bader's loss are uncertain—Bader thought a German aircraft had collided with him. Other reports say Bader had been shot down by one of his pilots—a victim of 'friendly fire'.

Bader bailed out from his damaged machine and parachuted to the ground but both his artificial legs were badly damaged. Captured by Germans, he was taken to a hospital near St Omer. His damaged legs were patched up. Unaware of the character of the prisoner, hospital staff allowed Bader to keep his clothes. He broke out of the hospital but was later re-arrested. The Germans sent him to a prisoner-of-war camp. Bader remained in captivity despite numerous escape attempts until liberated in 1945.

Back in the UK, Bader was promoted to Group Captain but left the Royal Air Force in 1946.

Paul Brickhill's biography of Bader, *Reach for the Sky*, was published in 1954 and later became a movie. Bader's autobiography, *Fight for the Sky*, appeared in 1973. He was knighted in 1976 for his work on behalf of the disabled.

Douglas Bader died in 1982 but the memory of his heroics is an inspiration to many. The Douglas Bader Foundation, set up after his death, assists those who have lost limbs.

Sources:
http://briarfiles.blogspot.com/2009/03/featured-pipe-smoker-douglas-bader.html
http://www.acesofww2.com/UK/aces/bader.htm

Online-
Style
Sample
Test

READING TEST 2
Advanced level

1 Choose two options. Bader's life story is one of
  A determination.
  B foolhardiness.
  C hostility.
  D disrespect.
  E regret.
  F audacity.

2 Bader is described as being *rash*. This suggests that he
  A was a danger to his fellow pilots.
  B was foolish more than brave.
  C acted quickly with little regard for the consequences.
  D overlooked rules when he felt like it.

3 Why did the RAF allow Bader to fly again even though he had artificial legs?
Write your answer on the lines.

_____

_____

4 What fact indicates that Bader was an exceptional pilot?
  A He was an outstanding sportsman at school.
  B He could drive a car and fly a plane with 'tin legs'.
  C He survived capture by the Germans.
  D He was a member of the aerobatics display team.

5 The term 'tin legs', when applied to Bader, is one of
  A mockery.
  B respect.
  C contempt.
  D jealousy.

6 When did Bader receive his knighthood? Write your answer in the box.

  ☐

7 What was the Douglas Bader Foundation set up to do?
  A teach young people to fly
  B help those who had lost limbs
  C encourage people to join the RAF
  D assist pilots who had survived air crashes

8 The term 'friendly fire' refers to
  A being accidentally shot by members of the same side.
  B shooting without any real target in sight.
  C a training session with firearms.
  D a shooting club competition.

☞ **Answers and explanations on pages 237–241**

Read *Beagle Bay Church* and answer questions 9 to 15.

Beagle Bay Church

The Dampier Peninsula is of special significance to the Catholic Church because it was from here that it began to spread through the rest of the Kimberley region—the north-west corner of Australia.

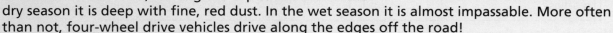

There is an amazing little church at Beagle Bay. It is a timber and brick structure. The 60 000 double clay bricks were shaped and baked in local stone kilns.

The Beagle Bay community is located 120 kilometres north of Broome. You'll have to drive on an unsealed road most of the time, making the trip strenuous. In the dry season it is deep with fine, red dust. In the wet season it is almost impassable. More often than not, four-wheel drive vehicles drive along the edges off the road!

In the centre of the Beagle Bay community there's a beautiful church, built between 1914–1918 for German Pallottine monks, who settled here around 1901.

Plans for Sacred Heart Church were drawn up by Father Thomas Bachmair (Pallottine Order) some time prior to 1908. At that time the construction was beyond the means of the Beagle Bay Mission Community.

However, a committed workforce of locals completed the job using local materials. Day after day parties set off into the bush or to the coast to cut timber, cart sand, dig clay and gather tons of broken shells for lime. In August 1918, on the Feast of the Assumption of Our Lady, the Sacred Heart Church was dedicated to the Sacred Heart of Jesus by Father Creagh, the Apostolic Administrator of the Kimberley Vicariate.

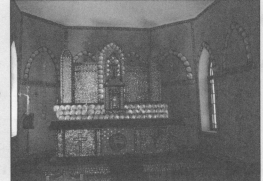

On entering the church you first see a stunning pearl shell altar. The interior of the church is just as stunning. It is decorated with shells, including mother-of-pearl, cowries, volutes and olives from the waters of the nearby Indian Ocean. While the mother-of-pearl has been used to decorate the main altar, the side altars are inlaid with opercula, a rare stone taken from shellfish.

Some of the decoration designs form the tribal symbols of the Njul Njul, the Nimanborr and the Bardi people of the area, while others formed the lamb, the fish and shepherd's crook of the Christian faith. Coloured windows create a special mood in the building.

The community's name was derived from the vessel *The Beagle*, which moored at the bay when the priests were looking for a suitable mission place in 1889. Adjacent to the church grounds are the school grounds and the community store.

Sources:
http://www.broomediocese.org/beaglebay.html;
http://catalogue.nla.gov.au/Record/3550863
Photos by A Horsfield: Road to Beagle Bay (top), Interior of Beagle Bay Church (bottom)

9 When were plans drawn up for the Beagle Bay church?

A around 1901 **B** prior to 1908 **C** during 1914 **D** in 1918

10 The community and bay where the village is located is named after _____.

11 You are going to compare the texts *'Tin Legs' Bader* (page 157) and *Beagle Bay Church* (page 159). What are the main purposes of these texts? Tick **two** options for each text.

	'Tin Legs' Bader	*Beagle Bay Church*
to inspire	☐	☐
to describe	☐	☐
to provide a biography	☐	☐
to advise	☐	☐

12 The Beagle Bay area was originally

A Aboriginal land.

B a brick-making location.

C a mission outpost.

D a bay to moor ships.

13 According to the text which **two** internal features of the Beagle Bay Church did the writer find impressive?

A the use of imported timber **B** the tons of crushed shells

C the mother-of-pearl altar **D** the location of the church

E the designs using tribal and Christian symbols **F** the use of baked clay bricks

14 The church's construction was one of

A frustration. **B** perseverance. **C** revelation. **D** enjoyment.

15 Choose a phrase from each column to best complete this statement.

Using materials available from **(1)** _____, the Beagle Bay Church was

completed with the help of **(2)** _____.

Column 1	Column 2
A the ship *The Beagle*	**D** the Apostolic Administrator, Father Creagh
B the Dampier Peninsula	**E** sailors from the ship *The Beagle*
C the Sacred Heart Church	**F** tribal people from the region
D Pallottine monks	**G** the mission administration

**It would be a good idea to check your answers to questions
1 to 15 before moving on to the other questions.**

☞ **Answers and explanations on page 238**

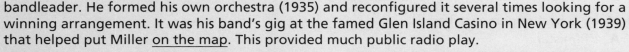

Read *The Glenn Miller story* and answer questions 16 to 22.

The Glenn Miller story

Born in Iowa (USA) in 1904, bandleader and musician Glenn Miller played the mandolin as a child, before switching to the trombone. His family moved several times—first to Missouri, then Nebraska and finally to Colorado (1918). Here Miller played in his high school band. After graduating (1921) he joined an orchestra as a professional.

Miller quit the orchestra (1932) and spent a year at university before returning to the music business. Moving to Los Angeles, California, Miller worked briefly with Ben Pollack's band. He then went to New York, where he freelanced as a trombonist and an arranger. In 1934, Miller became the musical director for the Dorsey Brothers' Big Band.

Although he had recorded under his own name for several years, Miller struggled to establish himself as a musician and bandleader. He formed his own orchestra (1935) and reconfigured it several times looking for a winning arrangement. It was his band's gig at the famed Glen Island Casino in New York (1939) that helped put Miller on the map. This provided much public radio play.

Miller's first hit was 'Wishing' (1939). He penned a more successful single, 'Moonlight Serenade', which also climbed the 1939 charts. Between 1939 and 1942 the Glenn Miller Orchestra enjoyed amazing popularity and commercial success. They dominated the music charts with over 60 top hits, including Miller's signature song 'In the Mood' in 1940. With their distinctive swing-jazz style, Miller's orchestra became the country's top dance band.

Miller's first film (1941), *Sun Valley Serenade*, featured the popular song 'Chattanooga Choo Choo'. In 1942 he appeared in *Orchestra Wives*.

With the American involvement in World War II (1942) Miller willingly left his successful musical career to serve his country. He was inducted into the US Army.

Miller led the Army Air Force Band, which entertained the troops during World War II. He was stationed in England in 1944 when told his band was to go to Paris. On 15 December, Miller boarded a transport plane headed to the newly liberated French capital. He had plans for a new series of concerts but he never arrived.

What happened to Miller's plane is a mystery. Neither the plane nor Miller's body was ever recovered. Miller's military band continued to play for months after his death, and the Glenn Miller Orchestra was revived after the war to honour his legacy. The 1954 film *The Glenn Miller Story* was based on Miller's life.

The melodies inspired the World War II generation and boosted morale. Collections of his greatest hits did well on the charts for many years after his passing. The Big Band era may have passed but Miller's music is still popular today.

Adapted from http://www.biography.com/people/glenn-miller-37990 and http://www.glennmiller.com/about/bio2.htm

16 In which US state did Glenn Miller join a school band? Write your answer in the box.

> [   ]

17 Tick **two** boxes. The text *The Glenn Miller Story* is an example of

A a journal. ☐   B an autobiography. ☐   C a summary. ☐
D a biography. ☐   E a factual recount. ☐   F a report. ☐

18 The term *on the map* as used in paragraph 3 refers to

A becoming famous or popular.
B having one's origin recognised.
C getting accepted in New York.
D travelling between performance venues.

19 Which of the options best describes Glenn Miller's career?

A It suffered after he joined the army.
B It developed greater impetus after 1944.
C It was unexpectedly cut short.
D It was advanced by going to university.

20 Miller is best remembered as

A a film star.
B a professional orchestral trombonist.
C the leader of a swing-jazz band.
D an entertainer of American troops.

21 According to the text, which of Miller's songs is he best remembered for?
Write your answer on the line.

_____

22 Which event gave a boost to Miller's musical career?

A his first film, *Sun Valley Serenade*
B his band's gig at the Glen Island Casino
C leading the US Army Air Force Band
D becoming musical director for the Dorsey Brothers' Big Band

☞ **Answers and explanations on pages 238-239**

Read *Sudoku* and answer questions 23 to 29.

Sudoku

Sudoku is a modern craze that doesn't require any special maths skills. It is a simple and enjoyable game of logic—all that's needed is brains and concentration. It could just as easily have nine different symbols or even nine different letters. Numbers are easier to recognise and remember.

The Challenges

A completed puzzle contains the numbers 1 through 9 in every row, column, and 3 x 3 box.
Fill in the grid so that the numbers 1 through 9 appear in each row.
Fill in the grid so that the numbers 1 through 9 appear in each column.
Fill in the grid so that the numbers 1 through 9 appear in each 3 x 3 box

How To Solve Sudoku Puzzles

Don't try to complete a row, column or box first. Solving techniques are divided into two categories: standard and advanced. Many puzzles can be solved using just the standard technique, including some puzzles labelled 'Advanced' or 'Challenge'.

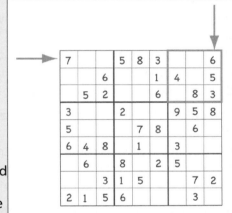

Standard Technique

Here are the basic steps:

1 First, for each blank cell on the grid, determine all the possible values the cell can have. This can be done by looking at the numbers in all other cells of the associated groups (row, column and 3 x 3 square).

2 Whenever the value of a cell is known, that value can be eliminated from the list of possible values for all other cells of the associated groups.

3 Look for an empty cell that has just one possible value. That becomes the value of the cell. Then apply rule 1.

4 Look through all the unsolved cells of a group looking for a possible value that exists only in one cell. That value now becomes the value of that cell. Then apply rule 1. Repeat steps 1, 2 and 3 until either all cells are solved or you reach an impasse. If the puzzle is not yet completely solved, you need to use the advanced techniques.

Players with a bit of practice don't actually write down all possibilities for the unsolved cells. When starting to solve a puzzle, they often spot several cells where the value is obvious. For some puzzles it is possible to start writing solutions without making notes. But for many puzzles, at least some annotation is needed to keep track of possibilities. Learn to distinguish between 'possible' and 'definite' solutions. Don't be scared to take a risk.

Advanced Techniques

In the standard technique, look at just one cell or one possible value at a time. In the advanced techniques, look at several cells or possible values. Using an advanced technique, players don't actually determine a cells value—they eliminate possibilities allowing them to continue solving using the standard technique.

23 List two strategies players require to complete a Sudoku grid. Write your answer on the lines.

_____

_____

24 How many times will the number nine (9) appear in a correctly completed game of Sudoku?

Write your answer in the box. ☐

25 To begin solving a Sudoku puzzle it is best to
  A complete the top left-hand 3 x 3 square first.
  B determine which number is least shown in the grid.
  C look for an unsolved cell that has just one possible value.
  D list all possibilities for every blank cell in the grid.

26 After some practice, puzzle solvers will find they
  A have improved maths skills.
  B can ignore steps 1 and 2 in the Standard Technique instructions.
  C can begin solving, starting with the top 3 x 3 square.
  D won't need to write down all possibilities for every blank cell.

27 The value of using numbers to solve a Sudoku grid is that
  A everyone can count.
  B they are easier to remember than other symbols.
  C calculations are kept to a minimum.
  D there are nine number symbols that have a positive value.

28 In the advanced technique for solving a Sudoku puzzle, the solver
  A writes down all possibilities for every blank cell in the grid.
  B looks at several cells or possible values to eliminate possibilities.
  C concentrates on rows and columns rather than 3 x 3 grids.
  D works randomly through the grid.

29 Choose a statement from each column that relates to strategies for solving a Sudoku grid using Standard and Advanced techniques.

Standard strategies		Advanced strategies	
A	Start with filling in all the nines.	D	Eliminate possible cell values.
B	Begin by filling the corner cells.	E	Count the number-filled cells.
C	Write in the value of an easily known cell.	F	Look for patterns and repetitions.
D	Write numbers to 9 beside the puzzle.	G	Check using guesswork.

**It would be a good idea to check your answers to questions
16 to 29 before moving on to the other questions.**

☞ **Answers and explanations on page 239**

Read *Escapees from the Garden* and answer questions 30 to 36.

Escapees from the Garden

Some of the most destructive and dangerous 'weeds' in the bush were once prized garden plants. These plants have adapted to Australian bush conditions to the detriment of local flora and fauna. Many of these plants are still for sale in nurseries!

Included in the top 10 most serious invasive garden plants for sale are: Asparagus Fern, Broom, Glory Lily, Japanese Honeysuckle, Pepper Tree, Periwinkle and Sweet Pittosporum. Sixty-five per cent of Australia's environmental weeds originated in, and have escaped from, home gardens.

Of these, Glory Lily (*Gloriosa Superba*), also known as Flame Lily, is a major problem. It is a declared noxious weed by the Minister for Agriculture. Once a plant has been declared noxious it is the landholder's responsibility to rid his or her property of the plant.

Glory Lily is a climber with subterranean, perennial tubers (fleshy roots), and red and yellow flowers. They are widely cultivated as ornamental garden plants and have become naturalised in parts of Australia. They are grown commercially in some countries for a chemical to treat gout. In parts of India, it has been harvested so heavily for the pharmaceutical trade that it is now threatened.

All parts of the lily are highly toxic if eaten. The weed has been responsible for the poisoning of both humans and livestock, and can cause death. The roots are more toxic than other parts of the plant. Glory Lily seeds may remain dormant for up to nine months.

In the Australian bush, Glory Lily can form dense understorey carpets smothering other plants. In dunes along the coast, it competes strongly with native flora. It was identified as naturalised in South-East Queensland in 1950. It has since been recorded in North Queensland and Central Queensland. It is now a serious weed on Moreton Island and along the North Coast of New South Wales.

Photos by Andrew Storrie, NSW Department of Primary Industries

30 What must a landowner do if a noxious weed is discovered on his property?

A report its presence to the Minister for Agriculture

B remove all livestock from the property

C eradicate the plant from his or her property

D warn nearby landowners of the problem

31 Which part of the Golden Lily is the most toxic?

A seeds   B roots   C leaves

D flowers   E buds   F stem

32 The word *naturalise* implies that a plant

A would never be as successful as those native to an environment.

B had to be a garden plant before becoming established in the bush.

C had been taken from a plant nursery and relocated to a bush environment.

D came from another area and successfully established itself in a new area.

33 What is the main reason that the Glory Lily became a garden plant?

A It could be used as a treatment for gout.

B It had become endangered in India.

C It was in short supply for pharmaceutical purposes.

D It was an attractive, easy-to-grow ornamental plant.

E It was a cheap source of food.

34 Glory Lily is a threat to native plants because

A it poisons the soil.

B it deprives native plants of air and sunlight.

C it's a fast-growing, water-thirsty plant.

D its seeds remain dormant for many months.

35 The importance of the photographs is to

A assist in the identification of a noxious weed.

B make people aware of the powers of the Minister for Agriculture.

C create a feeling a sympathy for growers of Glory Lilies.

D present a case for the return of the Glory Lily to the garden.

36 You are going to compare the texts *Sudoku* (page 163) and *Escapees from the Garden* (page 165). For what purposes were these texts written? Tick **two** options for each text.

	Sudoku	*Escapees from the Garden*
to entertain	☐	☐
to explain	☐	☐
to describe	☐	☐
to advise	☐	☐

☞ **Answers and explanations on pages 239–240**

Read *Types of Extinguishers* and answer questions 37 to 43.

Types of Extinguishers

The three most common types of fire extinguishers are:
>   Water,
>   Dry Chemical Powder (DC) and
>   Carbon Dioxide (CO_2).

Other less common extinguisher types are:
>   Foam and Wet Chemical.

Three things must be present at the same time to produce fire. These three things make up the fire triangle: fuel (any combustible material), oxygen and heat.

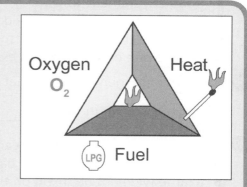

1 Water Extinguisher

Water Extinguishers are large red extinguishers, filled about two-thirds with ordinary tap water and then pressurised with air.

When the extinguisher is activated, a stream of water is forced out of the nozzle. This type of extinguisher removes the 'heat' element of the fire triangle. Water Extinguishers are designed for flammable material (wood, clothing, furniture, drapery, etc.) fires only.

Never use water to extinguish flammable liquid fires. The burning liquid may float and spread out on the water surface, thus spreading the fire.

Never use water to extinguish an electrical fire. Water is a good conductor, and there is a high risk that users may receive a severe electric shock if water is used on an electrical fire. Electrical equipment must be unplugged before using a water extinguisher.

2 Dry Chemical Powder Extinguisher

These extinguishers are filled with a fine powder and pressurised by nitrogen. They extinguish a fire by coating the fuel with a thin layer of powder, which separates the fuel from the oxygen in the air, and the powder also interrupts the chemical reaction of fire. They are extremely effective at extinguishing fires. Dry Chemical powder extinguishers are identified by a white band on a red body.

Dry Chemical Extinguishers come in two types. They are labelled:

AB(E) indicating that they are for use on ordinary combustible material and flammable liquid fires, or

B(E) indicating that they are for use on electrical fires.

Either one may be used for a flammable gas fire after the source of gas is turned off and for a cooking oil (or fat) fire.

3 Carbon Dioxide (CO_2) extinguishers

These are filled with non-flammable carbon dioxide gas under extreme pressure. The pressure in the cylinder is so great that when you use one of these extinguishers, bits of dry ice may shoot out of the nozzle. They extinguish the fire by displacing the air and thus removing the Oxygen. They also provide some cooling of the fire. A CO_2 extinguisher has a black band on a red body and a large wide nozzle shield (horn) on the end of a flexible hose. They are often used in laboratories and other areas where flammable liquids or sensitive electrical instruments are stored or used.

Sources:
http://ehs.okstate.edu/modules/exting/Triangle.htm http://en.wikipedia.org/wiki/Fire_extinguisher
http://www.officezone.com/fire-extinguisher-guide.htm

37 The basic principle behind all extinguishers is to
  A flood any flame with water.
  B ensure they are all painted red.
  C control all three elements of the fire 'triangle'.
  D remove one of the elements essential for fire to burn.

38 Other than oxygen and fuel what must also be present to produce fire?

Write your answer in the box. [   ]

39 A dry chemical extinguisher is readily recognised by
  A the absence of any coloured band around the cylinder.
  B a large wide nozzle shield on the end of a flexible hose.
  C the white band around a red cylinder.
  D a fire 'triangle' on the front of the cylinder.

40 Water should not be used on liquid fires because
  A many flammable liquids float on water.
  B water does not reduce the supply of oxygen.
  C the water many come in contact with electrical wiring.
  D water increases the chances of an explosion.

41 Before using a water extinguisher on an electrical fire the user should
  A stand well back from the fire.
  B wait until the fire has cooled down.
  C direct water at the source of the fire.
  D ensure the power supply has been disconnected.

42 Draw a line to match the type of fire with the most suitable extinguisher.

A house curtains	1 carbon dioxide extinguisher
B electrical fires	2 water extinguisher
C laboratory liquids	3 dry chemical extinguisher

43 Dry chemical extinguishers work by inhibiting burning by
  A separating the fuel from the oxygen supply.
  B replacing the amount of oxygen available.
  C reducing the amount of heat available.
  D cooling the fuel that may become combustible.

☞ **Answers and explanations on page 240**

Read *How the Eye Works* and answer questions 44 to 50.

How the Eye Works

There are things in your eyes called cones and rods that help you to see. They are minute parts of the eye and are very important.

Rods

Rods are the receptor cells in the retina, which are sensitive to varying amounts of light and help you see in dim light. Rods detect light and dark. The retina has about 150 million rods. They tell how much grey can be seen.

When you 'see' at night, since there is no colour, you see only shades of black and white (greys). Without rods, when the light goes out you would see nothing.

Cones

Cones are small nerve endings at the back of the eye. When you look at something, they determine how much red, green and blue is in what you see. These three colours can mix in different ways to get all other colours! Some people and animals (including dogs) don't have cones, just rods, and see everything in grey tones. They are commonly called colourblind. They don't see colours.

Other important pasts of the eye

Cornea: the transparent multi-layered front part of the eye that covers the pupil and iris. It provides most of the eye's optical power.

Pupil: the dark circle in the centre of the eye which changes size to control how much light is entering the eye. In dark places, the pupil enlarges, letting more light into your eye. In a bright place it becomes smaller, letting less light into your eye. It protects the workings of the eye.

Sclera: the white of the eye, composed of fibrous tissue that covers and protects the inner workings of the eye.

Iris: the coloured part of the eye that controls the size of the pupil.

Optic Nerve: a bundle of nerve fibres that transmits the image from the eyes to the brain.

Retina: changes the image to a message for your brain. It interprets what the rods and cones see.

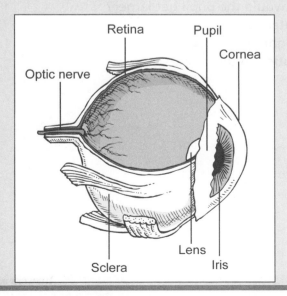

44 What is the main function of the eye's rod cells? Write your answer on the line.

_____

45 What part of the eye changes the image to a message?

Write your answer in the box. [   ]

46 Draw a line to match the eye part with its colour.

A cornea	1 white
B sclera	2 transparent
C pupil	3 black

47 Without cones in the eye a person or animal would
A be sensitive to bright light.
B not see shades of grey.
C be colourblind.
D have no protection for the cones.

48 What is the function of the iris?
A It adjusts the size of the pupils.
B It transmits the image from the eyes to the brain.
C It adds colour to the eye.
D It controls the workings of rods and cones.

49 How does a dog's eyesight differ from the eyesight of most humans?
Write your answer on the line.

_____

50 Under what circumstances would the pupil get larger?
A when the eye needs protection
B when there is a bright light on the eye
C when there is little variation in the colours seen
D when the light is dim

☞ **Answers and explanations on pages 240-241**

1 Which is the correct punctuation to complete this sentence?

The inscription on the soldier's grave read ▢▢▢▢ 'He completed his tour of duty with honour.'

A exclamation mark (!)   **B** semicolon (;)
C colon (:)   **D** question mark (?)

2 Read this text.

As Raymond stepped off the bus he spied the pen that he had lost when his mobile phone sudddenly rang. He took his eyes off the pen for a moment, then trod on it.

The first thing that happened was

A Raymond stepped off the bus.
B Raymond lost his pen.
C Raymond's phone rang.
D Raymond saw his pen.

Read the text *Fishy Tale*. The text has some gaps.
Chose the correct word or words to fill each gap.

Fishy Tale

1 Sally and I have a small, square fish tank. One day Sally decided she'd prefer a large fish bowl. I wasn't so sure. A new fishbowl will be costly. We will need ▢▢▢▢ of money.

3   alot   a lot   allot   all lot
       A   B   C   D

2 Sally has a simple plan. She will divide the cost ▢▢▢▢ the two of us! I don't get a say so it seems.

4   between   among   with   to
       A   B   C   D

3 We also need two new ornaments to go in the bottom of the bowl. At the pet shop Sally said, 'I chose the treasure chest. Now you ▢▢▢▢ something different.'

5   chose   choice   choose   chosen
       A   B   C   D

4 Lucky me!

5 Now she wants me to go swimming with her. She's a great swimmer and she dives ▢▢▢▢ . Just hope she doesn't want me to catch fish for the fish bowl with my bare hands.

6   good   best   all right   well
       A   B   C   D

7 In paragraph 5 of the text *Fishy Tale* the narrator refers to her friend as *she* rather than *Sally*. This indicates that the narrator

A has forgotten her friend's name.
B is embarrassed to go swimming with Sally.
C is attempting to distance herself from Sally and the project.
D has lost interest in the fish bowl project.

☞ **Answers and explanations on pages 241-243**

8 Choose the words that complete this text.

I know Mathematics ⬚⬚⬚⬚ difficult for you, but nothing else ⬚⬚⬚⬚ available.

is is	is are	are are	are is
A	**B**	**C**	**D**

9 Which sentence has the correct punctuation?
  A The agent inquired if, 'We needed speakers for the band.'
  B The agent inquired if we needed speakers for the band.
  C The agent inquired if we needed speakers for the band?
  D The agent inquired, 'If we needed speakers for the band?'

10 Which of the following correctly completes the sentence?

The tree Jim planted was so well looked after that its trunk was quite ⬚⬚⬚⬚.

plump	chubby	fat	thick
A	**B**	**C**	**D**

11 Read these sentences and choose the option that best assembles the ideas in a single sentence.

Lance ordered a tub of fries. He also ordered a beef burger. He planned to eat them before school.
  A Lance ordered a tub of fries and he also ordered a beef burger, which he planned to eat before school.
  B Lance ordered a tub of fries and a beef burger, which he planned to eat before school.
  C Before school Lance ordered a tub of fries and a beef burger.
  D After ordering Lance planned to eat the tub of fries and then the beef burger he had ordered.

12 Shade two bubbles to show where the missing commas (,) should go.

No ⬆ you shouldn't have done that Roger ⬆ old friend ⬆ You ⬆ must save your money.
    Ⓐ   Ⓑ   Ⓒ Ⓓ

13 Which sentence has the correct punctuation?
  A 'Ingrid, I don't care,' she said. 'What you think about it.'
  B Ingrid, I don't care. She said, 'what you think about it?'
  C 'Ingrid, I don't care,' she said, 'what you think about it.'
  D 'Ingrid, I don't care,' she said, 'What you think about it.'

14 List any nouns used in the sentence in the boxes. You may choose more than one.

The love of fine poetry was a result of Gavin knowing what he most enjoyed.

15 Which sentence has the correct punctuation?
  A Adelaide, South Australia, is often called 'The Garden City'.
  B Adelaide, South Australia is often called 'The Garden City'.
  C Adelaide South Australia is often called 'The Garden City'.
  D Adelaide South Australia, is often called 'The Garden City'.

☞ **Answers and explanations on pages 241-243**

16 Which of the following correctly completes this sentence?

That birthday cake is the [_____] I've ever seen!

most prettier	more pretty	so prettiest	prettiest	more prettiest
A	**B**	**C**	**D**	**E**

Read the text *Law Firm*. The text has some gaps. Choose the correct word to fill each gap.

Law Firm

Last week our class had an excursion for Legal Studies to a law office in our town. Then we went to the nearby courthouse to see a court in session. The next day the class [_____] a report on their visit to the law firm. I know a lot of people in our town. I don't, however, know all the lawyers in the law firm, [_____] you?

17
writ	write	wrote	wrid
A	**B**	**C**	**D**

18
don't	do	did	does
A	**B**	**C**	**D**

19 Which of the following correctly completes this sentence?

Reading a book [_____] his brother mowed the lawns made James feel guilty.

which	while	why	where	however
A	**B**	**C**	**D**	**E**

20 Which of the following correctly completes this sentence?

By Tuesday, my report [_____] completed.

would been	will being	will be	would be
A	**B**	**C**	**D**

21 Which word or words are unnecessary in this sentence?

It's been raining for eight consecutive days in a row and the football ovals are awash.

consecutive	in a row	football	are awash
A	**B**	**C**	**D**

22 The sentence below is incomplete. Choose the option that correctly completes the sentence.

Dad never invested foolishly, [_____]

A but only used the services of a wise advisor.

B although only used the services of a wise advisor.

C yet only used the services of a wise advisor.

D or only used the services of a wise advisor.

23 In which sentence is the word *black* used as an adjective?

A Only two of the mourners were in black.

B The censors will black out any profanities in the text.

C The only thing visible in the black was the flare of a match.

D The walls were black with the soot from steam trains.

☞ **Answers and explanations on pages 241-243**

24 Write a word from this sentence in each empty box to match the given part of speech.

Ahab maintained a collection of ancient coins and notes on his desk.

verb		adjective	
pronoun		conjunction	

25 Which part of this text is the adverbial phrase?

<u>Without looking back,</u> <u>he turned</u> <u>down the road</u> and <u>headed for the gate</u>.

   A   **B**   **C**   **D**

**It would be a good idea to check your answers to questions 1 to 25
before moving on to the other questions.**

To the student
Ask your teacher or parent to read the spelling words for you. The words are listed on
page 249. Write the spelling words on the lines below.

26 _____ **34** _____

27 _____ **35** _____

28 _____ **36** _____

29 _____ **37** _____

30 _____ **38** _____

31 _____ **39** _____

32 _____ **40** _____

33 _____

Each line has one word that is incorrect. Write the correct spelling of the underlined word in the box.

41 The premier said the <u>faileur</u> was due to an unexpected visitor.

42 I met a <u>reveler</u> going home from the celebration.

43 The desert valleys were <u>stiffling</u> hot.

44 I am truly sorry about your <u>rescent</u> accident.

45 Many teenagers <u>mispell</u> the word *awful*.

☞ **Answers on pages 241-243**

Each line has one word that is incorrect.
Write the correct spelling of the word in the box.

46 Penny had a caddy and an ancient golf buggie.

47 Is the documentation compleat?

48 'My generation knows nothing about vidoes', Dad said.

49 There was an imediate response from the technical staff.

50 We live in a democractic society and have to vote!

☞ **Answers on pages 241-243**

65 MIN

Section 1: Non-calculator questions

1 The heights of two trees in the playground were measured. One tree was 6.7 metres taller than the other tree. If the height of the smaller tree was 9.8 metres, what was the height of the taller tree?

A 2.1 metres

B 2.9 metres

C 15.5 metres

D 15.9 metres

E 16.5 metres

2 Every schoolday Jordan spends $3.60 on lunch at the canteen. What is the total amount he spends in five days?

A $3.65

B $15.60

C $17.00

D $18.00

E $20.00

3 There are 836 students at our school and they are to be divided evenly into these four sports houses: Boomalli, Jindabyne, Mulgabirra and Tingira. How many students are allocated to Mulgabirra?

A 209   B 210   C 240   D 290

4 The table shows the extremes of temperature for Australia.

Date	Location	Temperature
3 Jan 1960	Oodnadatta	50.7°
29 Jun 1994	Charlottes Pass	−23°

What is the difference between the two temperatures?

[ ] degrees

5 Which of these expressions is equal to 24? Select **all** the correct answers.

A $32 - 10 - 2$

B $\dfrac{32}{2 + 2} \times 3$

C $8 + 4 \times 2$

D $50 \div 5 \times 2 + 2^2$

E $\dfrac{16 + 16}{2}$

6 Which of these has a 3 in the hundredths place?

A 2389

B 7.283

C 11.300 87

D 14.931

7 The average of 6 numbers is 8. If the average of the first 4 numbers is 5, what is the average of the last 2 numbers?

[ ]

8 A jug is three-fifths full of juice. If it takes another 360 mL of juice to completely fill the jug, how much juice does the jug contain when it is half-full?

[ ] mL

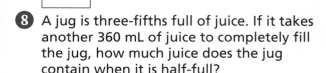

This is the end of the part where you are not allowed to use a calculator. It would be a good idea to check your answers to the questions in this section before moving on to the other questions.

☞ **Answers and explanations on pages 243-246**

Section 2: Calculator Allowed questions

9 A bag contains 12 blue, 6 green, 4 black and 8 red balls. Mia closes her eyes and takes a ball from the bag. What is the probability that the ball is green?

A $\frac{1}{6}$　　B $\frac{1}{5}$　　C $\frac{1}{4}$　　D $\frac{1}{3}$

10 A jug of milk contains 1.4 litres of milk. What quantity needs to be added to make 2 litres?

A 6 mL
B 60 mL
C 600 mL
D 1600 mL

11

The number line shows three fractions as X, Y and Z. X = $\frac{1}{4}$ and Y = $\frac{1}{2}$.

If Z is in the middle of X and Y, write the fraction for Z.

A $\frac{1}{3}$　　B $\frac{3}{5}$　　C $\frac{2}{7}$　　D $\frac{3}{8}$

12

On the number line, what is the number represented by the number X?

4.45	4.65	4.68	4.72	4.75
A	B	C	D	E

13 The chart shows the times, in 24-hour time, of the high tides and the low tides at Port Stephens.

Port Stephens Tides				
	High Tides		Low Tides	
	Time	Height (m)	Time	Height (m)
Tues.	0541	1.70	1229	0.40
	1818	1.26	2355	0.45
Wed.	0632	1.82	1320	0.28
	1913	1.30		
Thu.			0047	0.41
	0724	1.93	1411	0.18

According to the table, what is the difference, in metres, between the highest and lowest tides over the three days?

Difference = ☐ metres

14 Both of these scales are evenly balanced.

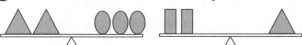

What is the correct arrangement from lightest to heaviest?

A

B

C

D

15 Neicia makes a spinner using three different colours. She records her results in a table.

Colour	Number of times
Red	4
Blue	12
Green	8

Which diagram is most likely to show her spinner?

A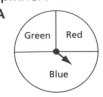

B

C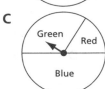

D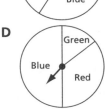

☞ **Answers and explanations on pages 243-246**

16 Maree poured water into four different measuring containers.

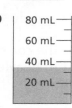

Arrange the containers from smallest amount of water to largest.

smallest   **largest**

It would be a good idea to check your answers to questions 9–16 before moving on to the other questions.

---

17 The pattern of triangles is made with sticks.

1 triangle   2 triangles   3 triangles   4 triangles

How many triangles could be made using 37 sticks?

12	17	18	19	111
A	B	C	D	E

18 A group of footballers compared the number of goals they had scored in their season. The table shows the number of goals scored in the games that were played.

Name	Number of goals	Number of games
Jamie	18	8
Luke	16	5
Jesse	21	7
Brodie	20	10

Which person has the highest average of goals scored per game?

A Jamie   B Luke
C Jesse   D Brodie

19 The clock shows the time Bianca finished her practice NAPLAN Test.

She took 55 minutes to complete the test. At what time did Bianca commence the test?

A 9:20   B 9:25
C 9:10   D 10:10

20 The Australian Bureau of Statistics reported that on 30 June 2016 the population of Darwin was 145 916. On the same day, the population of Hobart was 224 462. What is the difference between the two cities' populations, to the nearest thousand?

21 A rectangle has an area of 60 cm². If the width of the rectangle is 6 cm, what is the perimeter of the rectangle?

	cm

22 Rachel makes a three-dimensional solid using small cubes that are joined together. She draws the top view and the side view of the solid.

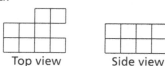

Top view   Side view

Which of these views could be the front view?

A   B

C   D

☞ **Answers and explanations on pages 243–246**

23 When Kevin checked his inbox he had 50 emails. He replied to 20% of the emails and deleted the remainder. How many emails did Kevin delete?

A 10 **B** 30 **C** 40 **D** 45

24 This net is used to make a cube.

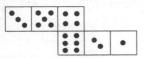

Which number is missing from the top face of the cube?

A [·] **B** [::] **C** [:·:] **D** [:::]

25 A cube is made from lengths of wire. The total length of the wire is 24 cm. What is the volume of the cube?

[____] cm³

26 The time on the clock below is 8 o'clock.

What is the size of the reflex angle between the two hands?

[____] degrees

27 A cube is to be made from two objects. Which of these will form a cube? Select **all** the correct answers.

A

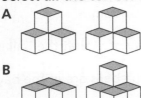

B

C

D

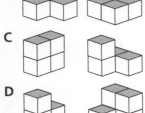

28 $18 \div \triangle = 12$

What is the value of the $\triangle$?

A $\frac{2}{3}$ **B** $\frac{1}{3}$ **C** $\frac{3}{4}$ **D** $\frac{3}{2}$

29 [ ] = 3   ◯ + [ ] = 7

This means ◯ + ◯ + [ ] =

A 8 **B** 10 **C** 11 **D** 14

30 Part of the price list for the school canteen is detailed below.

Item	Cost
Sandwich	$1.40
Roll	$1.50
Wrap	?
Milk	$1.80
Juice	$1.50
Water	$1.00

Kyle bought 2 wraps and a bottle of water. The cost was $4.40. How much will Jackie pay for a wrap and 2 bottles of water?

A $2.20 **B** $3.40 **C** $3.70 **D** $4.70

31 The mass of a pumpkin is 2.5 kg and the mass of a carrot is 150 grams. What is the difference in the masses of the two vegetables?

A 1.1 kg **B** 2.235 kg
C 2.25 kg **D** 2.35 kg

32 Ayrton left his home at 10:00 am and travelled for 180 kilometres. If he arrived at his destination at 12:30 pm the same day, what was his average speed in kilometres per hour?

A 72 **B** 90 **C** 120 **D** 135

It would be a good idea to check your answers to questions 17–32 before moving on to the other questions.

☞ **Answers and explanations on pages 243-246**

33 A map is drawn using a scale of 1 cm = 8 km. The distance between Ackley and Brindaburg is 4.6 cm on the map. What is the distance between the places in kilometres?

34 Ian uses matches to form a pattern of squares.

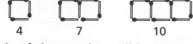

4   7   10

Which of these rules will he use to find the number of squares that he can make using any number of matches?

A number of squares + 3

B 2 × number of squares + 3

C 3 × number of squares + 1

D 3 × number of squares + 4

35 The tibia is the larger of the two bones that connect the knee to the ankle in humans. The length of the bone can be used to determine the height of a person. The formula used is different for males and females:

(Note: the measurements are in cm.)

Males:

height = 75.79 + length of tibia × 2.52

Females:

height = 59.24 + length of tibia × 2.90

The length of students' tibias have been measured and recorded in the table:

Student name	Gender	Length of tibia (cm)
Emily	Female	32
Madison	Female	30
Ethan	Male	36
Ryan	Male	32

What is the difference in the heights of Emily and Ryan?

[   ] cm

36 A teacher wrote this number game on the whiteboard.

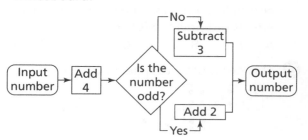

The output number is 7.
What are the two possible input numbers?

A 1 and 3

B 2 and 3

C 1 and 6

D 5 and 6

37 The diagram shows a line drawn across a triangle.

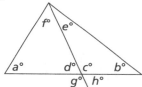

Which of these statements is true?
Select **all** the correct answers.

A $a + b + e + f = 180$

B $c + b = 180$

C $a + d + f = 180$

D $c + d + g + h = 360$

38 A bag contains 24 balls.
The balls are either red or blue.
A ball is chosen at random.

There is a probability of $\frac{3}{8}$ that the ball is red.
How many more blue balls are in the bag than red balls?

A 4   B 5

C 6   D 8

☞ **Answers and explanations on pages 243–246**

39 A shape is made from 4 identical rectangular planks.

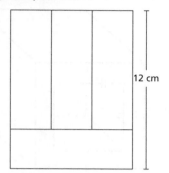

12 cm

What is the area of each of the planks?

 cm²

40 A shop sells packets of toilet paper in two sizes:
- 12 rolls for $3.50
- 8 rolls for $3.00

Jack bought **exactly** 100 rolls.
What is the least amount he spent?

$ [____]

41 Pim has earned $560. If Jack earns another $45 he would have earned three-quarters of what Pim has earned. How much has Jack earned?

A $375   B $385
C $455   D $465

42 Grant cuts out a square with a perimeter of 26 cm. By matching lengths of sides, Grant joins the square to a triangle to form a pentagon, as shown in the diagram.

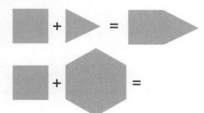

If Grant joins the same square to a hexagon, what will be the perimeter of the new shape?

A 40 cm   B 45.5 cm
C 52 cm   D 58.5 cm

43 A random sample group of students were asked for the number of movies they had watched during the vacation. The results are shown in the table.

Movies	Students
0	6
1	11
2	8
3	7
4	5
5	3

Using the data from the survey, predict the number of students who had watched 2 movies, if a random group of 75 students were surveyed.

[____]

44 Gordon is driving 245 kilometres from Fremantle to Dunsborough. His car uses 7.8 litres of fuel per 100 kilometres. How much fuel will Gordon need to travel the distance. Round your answer to the nearest litre.

[____] L

45 Marg reads some of her novel every night. After reading on Wednesday night, Marg calculated that she had read 65% of the novel. On Thursday night she read 60 pages which meant that she had read a total of 80% of the novel. How many pages are in Marg's novel?

[____]

46 Leno and Eddie own a landscaping business. They are charging a customer $11 400 for building a retaining wall. To complete the job they will employ 2 labourers for 8 hours work each day for 5 days paying them $60 per hour. They also need to pay $1650 for material to use in the building of the wall. The remaining money is to be divided evenly between Leno and Eddie. How much will Leno receive?

$ [____]

☞ **Answers and explanations on pages 243-246**

47 Donna wants to buy a pair of running shoes and has found that four stores have the shoes on sale. The table shows the original price and the amount of discount.

Shop	Original Price	Discount
A	$200	15%
B	$195	$30
C	$240	$\frac{1}{3}$
D	$180	10%

Which shop has the lowest sale price for the shoes?

48 From a cube of side length 12 cm, a square-based prism is removed.

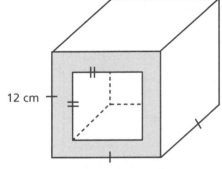

12 cm

If the area of the shaded region is 80 cm², what is the volume of the prism that has been removed?

 cm³

WEEK 1

NUMBER AND ALGEBRA (Test Your Skills)
Whole numbers   Page 2

1 4307 = 4 thousands + 3 hundreds + …
Place value is 3 hundreds.

2 three hundred and seven thousand and
forty = 307 040

3 In ascending order: 99   907   2001   3416
Smallest number is 99.

4 As $3^2 = 9$ and $5^2 = 25$, the number between
9 and 25 is 10.

5 18 is not greater than 19. The number
sentence that is not true is 18 > 19.

6 753 is closer to 750 than 760.

7 2873 is closer to 2900 than 2800.

8 191 is closer to 200 than 100, 326 is closer to
300 than 400, 708 is closer to 700 than 800.
This means the answer is 200 + 300 + 700.

9 The arrow is pointing to –3.

10 Halfway between –8 and –6 is –7.

11 As $2 \times 8 = 16$, then 16 is a multiple of 8.

12 Multiples of 8 are 8, 16, 24, 32, 40, … and
multiples of 10 are 10, 20, 30, 40, …
The LCM is 40.

13 The factors of 20 are 1, 2, 4, 5, 10, 20.
This means 8 is not a factor.

14 The factors of 30: 1, 2, 3, 5, 6, 10, 15, 30.
This means there are 8 factors.

15 The prime number is 31 as it has factors
1 and 31.

16 Factors of 10 are 1, 2, 5, 10 and factors of 16
are 1, 2, 4, 8, 16. The HCF is 2.

17 The composite number is 15 as factors are
1, 3, 5, 15.

18 63 is not a square number.

19 100 000 000 means 8 zeros.

NUMBER AND ALGEBRA (Real Test)
Whole numbers   Page 4

1 C **2** A **3** D **4** B **5** D **6** A, E, C, B, D **7** 3498
8 A **9** B, C **10** B **11** C **12** D **13** A **14** D **15** C
16 B, C, D

EXPLANATIONS

1 160 million = 160 000 000

2 $3^2 = 3 \times 3$

3 610 > 602 (610 is greater than 602)

4 6000 + 400 + 8 = 6408

5 237 509 is closer to 240 000 than 230 000.

6 $1^5 = 1 \times 1 \times 1 \times 1 \times 1 = 1$
$3^2 = 3 \times 3 = 9$
$2^3 = 2 \times 2 \times 2 = 8$
$4^2 = 4 \times 4 = 16$
$2^2 = 2 \times 2 = 4$
The order from smallest to largest is 1^5, 2^2,
2^3, 3^2, 4^2.

7 Smallest even is 3498.

8 –5 is between –6 and –4. This means it is A.

9 The factors of 18 are 1, 2, 3, 6, 9, 18.
This means that 4 and 8 are not factors.

10 Halfway between 42 and 46 is 44.

11 36 709 = thirty-six thousand, seven hundred
and nine

12 In ascending order: 276   326   __545__   830

13 38 is closer to 40 than 30, 73 is closer to 70
than 80. This means the closest estimate is
40×70.

14 $9^2 = 9 \times 9 = 81$
This means it is between 80 and 90.

15 452 becomes 4520. This means the new
number is 10 times larger than 452.

16 Use the calculator to divide each of the
options by 9. The numbers that are
multiples of 9 are 45, 108 and 378.

NUMBER AND ALGEBRA (Test Your Skills)
Addition and subtraction   Page 5

1 $57 + 4 = 57 + 3 + 1$
           $= 60 + 1$
           $= 61$

2 $95 + 12 = 95 + 5 + 7$
            $= 100 + 7$
            $= 107$

3 $620 + 68 = 620 + 60 + 8$
              $= 688$

4 $42 - 16 = 42 - 10 - 6$
            $= 32 - 6$
            $= 26$

5 $100 - 45 = 100 - 40 - 5$
             $= 60 - 5$
             $= 55$

6
$$\begin{array}{r} {}^2{}^15\ 3 \\ 8\ 3 \\ +\ 1\ 7\ 5 \\ \hline 3\ 1\ 1 \end{array}$$

7
$$\begin{array}{r} 1^12\ 9 \\ 2\ 0\ 9 \\ 2\ 1 \\ +\ 1\ 0\ 0 \\ \hline 4\ 5\ 9 \end{array}$$

8 $20 - \_\_ = 13$ means $20 - 13 = 7$

9 $50 - 19 = 50 - 20 + 1$
            $= 31$
This means $31.

10 ${}^17\ {}^16\ {}^13\ 9$ This means 12 935.
$$\begin{array}{r} 1\ 3\ 8\ 6 \\ +\ \ 3\ 9\ 1\ 0 \\ \hline 1\ 2\ 9\ 3\ 5 \end{array}$$

11
$$\begin{array}{r} 3\ {}^3\cancel4\ {}^10 \\ -\ 1\ 2\ 9 \\ \hline 2\ 1\ 1 \end{array}$$

13 $100 - 78 = 100 - 80 + 2$
            $= 20 + 2$
            $= 22$

---

13 $88 - 32 = 56$

14
$$\begin{array}{r} \cancel1\ {}^9\cancel0\ {}^10\ 0 \\ -\ \ 4\ 4\ 0 \\ \hline 5\ 6\ 0 \end{array}$$

15 $73 + \_\_ = 100$ means $100 - 73 = 27$

16
$$\begin{array}{r} \cancel1\ {}^9\cancel0\ {}^9\cancel0\ {}^10 \\ -\ \ 3\ 2\ 7 \\ \hline 6\ 7\ 3 \end{array}$$

17
$$\begin{array}{r} \cancel1\ {}^9\cancel0\ {}^9\cancel0\ {}^10 \\ -\ \ 8\ 1\ 1 \\ \hline 1\ 8\ 9 \end{array}$$

18 $48 - 17 = 48 - 10 - 7$
            $= 38 - 7$
            $= 31$

19
$$\begin{array}{r} {}^2\cancel3\ {}^9\cancel0\ {}^9\cancel0\ {}^10 \\ -\ 1\ 2\ 8\ 3 \\ \hline 1\ 7\ 1\ 7 \end{array}$$

20 $25 - 3 - 5 - 2 - 6 - 2 = 7$

NUMBER AND ALGEBRA (Real Test)
Multiplication and division   Page 7

1 B   **2** 82   **3** B   **4** C   **5** B   **6** C   **7** D   **8** A   **9** C   **10** A
11 864   **12** B   **13** D   **14** B   **15** 91   **16** 1420

EXPLANATIONS

1 $100 - 79 = 100 - 80 + 1$
            $= 20 + 1$
            $= 21$ This means $21.

2 $67 + 15 = 67 + 10 + 5$
            $= 77 + 5$
            $= 82$

3 $15 + 33 = 15 + 30 + 3$
            $= 45 + 3$
            $= 48$

4 $47 - 18 = 47 - 20 + 2$
            $= 27 + 2$
            $= 29$

5 $53 + 20 - 17 = 73 - 17$
                 $= 73 - 20 + 3$
                 $= 53 + 3$
                 $= 56$

6

$$
\begin{array}{r}
{}^{2}{}^{1}5\;3 \\
8\;3 \\
+\;1\;7\;5 \\
\hline
3\;1\;1
\end{array}
$$

7 $11 + 11 + 11 + 11 + 11 + 11 = 6 \times 11$
$$= 66$$

66 is between 60 and 70.

8 Cost $= 19 + 7$
$$= 26$$
Change $= 40 - 26$
$$= 40 - 20 - 6$$
$$= 20 - 6$$
$$= 14 \qquad \text{Change is \$14.}$$

9 $1^2 + 2^2 + 3^2 + 4^2 = 1 + 4 + 9 + 16$
$$= 1 + 9 + 4 + 16$$
$$= 10 + 20$$
$$= 30$$

10 Numbers are 8421 and 1248.

$$
\begin{array}{r}
8\;{}^{3}4\;{}^{11}2\;{}^{1}1 \\
-\;1\;2\;4\;8 \\
\hline
7\;1\;7\;3
\end{array}
$$

11

$$
\begin{array}{r}
987 \\
-\;123 \\
\hline
864
\end{array}
$$

12 $1 + 4 + 9 = 14$

13

$$
\begin{array}{r}
6\;2\;{}^{1}7\;8 \\
+\;3\;7\;0\;9 \\
\hline
9\;9\;8\;7
\end{array}
$$

14 $\$10.00 - \$5.20 = \$4.80$
Coins are $2, $2, 50c, 20c, 10c.
This means 5 coins.

15

$$
\begin{array}{r}
{}^{2}1\;3 \\
2\;1 \\
1\;8 \\
1\;8 \\
+\;2\;1 \\
\hline
9\;1
\end{array}
$$

Total distance is 91 km.

16 $5420 - 2000 + 1000 - 3000$
$$= 3420 + 1000 - 3000$$
$$= 4420 - 3000$$
$$= 1420$$

NUMBER AND ALGEBRA (Test Your Skills)
Multiplication and division   Page 8

1 $40 \times 8 = 320$

2 $16 \times 3 = 48$

3 As $4 \times 6 = 24$, $4 \times 8 = 32 \neq 24$.

4 $8 \times 6 = 48$

5 As $63 \times 2 = 126$, $63 \times 200 = 12\,600$.
The answer is 12 600.

6

$$
\begin{array}{r}
275 \\
\times\;{}_{6\,4}8 \\
\hline
2200
\end{array}
$$

7 11, 22, 33, 44
The fourth multiple is 44.

8 As $90 = 9 \times 10$, $108 = 9 \times 12$, $900 = 9 \times 100$,
then 901 is not a multiple of 9.

9

$$
\begin{array}{r}
725 \\
\times\;{}_{1}30 \\
\hline
21\,750
\end{array}
$$
This means 21 750.

10 $20 \times 30 \times 10 = 6000$

11

$$
\begin{array}{r}
327 \\
\times\;35 \\
\hline
1635 \\
9810 \\
\hline
11\,445
\end{array}
$$
The answer is 11 445.

12 As $30 = 4 \times 7 + 2$, the remainder is 2.

13 Half of 24 times twice $3 = 12 \times 2 \times 3$
$$= 12 \times 6$$
$$= 72$$

14

$$
\begin{array}{r}
151 \\
5\overline{)7\,{}^{2}5\,5}
\end{array}
$$

15

$$
88\tfrac{1}{4}
$$
$$
4\overline{)35\,{}^{3}3}
$$

16 $23\,900 \div 100 = 239$

17

$$
\begin{array}{r}
141 \\
3\overline{)4\,{}^{1}2\,3}
\end{array}
$$

18 Average $= \dfrac{14 + 15 + 22 + 21}{4}$

$= \dfrac{72}{4}$

$= 18$

19
```
    1 2 9. 4
5 )6¹4⁴7.²0
```

20 $20 \div 5 + 5 \times 2 = 4 + 10$
$= 14$

21 $5 + 6 \times 2 = 5 + 12$
$= 17$

NUMBER AND ALGEBRA (Real Test)
Multiplication and division — Page 10

1 A **2** B **3** 72 **4** D **5** B **6** D **7** C **8** C **9** B **10** A
11 B **12** B **13** A **14** 237 **15** C **16** C

EXPLANATIONS

1 Cakes $= 6 \times 4 + 2$
$= 26$
New arrangements $= 7 \times 4$
$= 28$
As $28 - 26 = 2$, she needs another 2 cakes.

2 Average $= \dfrac{14 + 9 + 22 + 16 + 14}{5}$

$= \dfrac{75}{5}$

$= 15$

3 Number $= 12 \times 6 = 72$

4 First, change the cost of each fruit to dollars: 65c = $0.65, 75c = $0.75, 85c = $0.85
$3 \times 0.65 + 2 \times 0.75 + 5 \times 0.85$

5
```
    1 2 8 1
5 )6¹4⁴0 5
```

6 $34 \times 200 = 6800$

7 $600 \div 50 = 60 \div 5$
$= 12$
The school needs 12 buses.

8 $20 \times 76 = 76 \times 20$
$= 1520$

9 Average of 3 numbers = 10
Sum of 3 numbers = 30
Extra number $= 30 - (4 + 14)$
$= 30 - 18$
$= 12$
The other number is 12.

10 Work backwards from Jane's answer using inverse operations:
10 times by 4 = 40, then divide by 5 is 8
Jane's starting number is 8 (check the answer by putting it back into the question).

11 Number $= 8 \times 12 + 4$
$= 96 + 4$
$= 100$
There were 100 apples in the box.

12 As $6 + 6 + 8 = 20$, the cost is
$3.50 + $3.50 + $4.50 = $11.50

13 Total slices $= 3 \times 8$
$= 24$
Slices per person $= 24 \div 6$
$= 4$
This means 4 slices per person.

14
```
     79
  × ₂3
   237
```

15 As 399 is close to 400 and 21 is close to 20, the answer will be close to $400 \div 20 = 20$. Considering the 4 choices, the correct answer would be 19.

16 As $16 - 4 \times 2 = 16 - 8$
$= 8$
Now $8 = 4 + 20 \div ?$
$4 = 20 \div ?$
This means the missing number is 5.
(We could have checked each of the choices by substitution.)

SPELLING (Real Test)
Common misspellings — Pages 12–13

1 leisure

2 symptoms

3 afford

4 particular

5 stretching

6 burglar

7 shining

8 separated

9 ascend

10 changeable

11 destroyed

12 propeller

13 dyeing

14 quarrelling

15 whiteness

16 balance

17 welcomes

18 purchase

19 beginning

20 cupboard

21 fourth

22 surprise

23 regularly

24 except

25 jealousy

GRAMMAR AND PUNCTUATION (Real Test)
Types of sentences and articles   Pages 15–17

1 B **2** A **3** or **4** D **5** B **6** C **7** A **8** D **9** B **10** C
11 The twins and I **12** D **13** C **14** house, honest,
friendly **15** D **16** D **17** A **18** B **19** B **20** A **21** a
22 A **23** A **24** A **25** D

EXPLANATIONS

1 This is a grammar question. The correct word is *an*.
Tip: *An* is an article and precedes words that begin with vowels. *Honest* has a silent *h*.

2 The correct word is the adverb *fast*.
Tip: 'Fastly' is not a word. *Quick* and *quicker* are comparative adjectives.

3 This is a grammar question. The word is the conjunction *or*.
Tip: In English it is a convention to use *or* with *either*. Remember: *either—or* and *neither—nor*.

4 This is a grammar question. The correct word is the adjective *high*.
Tip: *High* implies extending a long way from the bottom to the top, especially when viewed from the bottom. *Tall* generally refers to something growing or reaching above average height.

5 This is a grammar question. The correct word is the preposition *at*.
Tip: In English it is common practice to use certain prepositions with certain verbs. We usually say *looking at*.

6 This is a grammar question. The correct sentence is: *I know they are your pens, but are you sure you're being fair?*
Tip: *Your* is a possessive pronoun showing ownership. *You* is a relative pronoun used to refer to a person being addressed. *You're* is a contraction of *you are*. The apostrophe indicates that a letter (*a*) has been omitted.

7 This is a punctuation question. The correct sentence is: *The speaker quietly asked us to sit, so we did.*
Tip: This is an example of indirect or reported speech. No question is actually asked. There is no need for a question mark. The tone of the sentence suggests strongly that it is not an exclamation.

8 This is a punctuation question. The correct sentence is: *When buying breakfast cereal I always buy Farmer's Choice brand.*
Tip: Only the sentence beginning and the product name (*Farmer's Choice*) require capital letters. The brand name is a proper noun. All other nouns are common nouns.

9 This is a grammar question. The correct word is the pronoun *which*.
Tip: *Which* is a common pronoun used to refer to animals or things, in this case the rose bush. *Who* is used to refer to people. *What* is most often used to ask a question.

10 This is a grammar question. The correct word is the verb *left*.

Tip: *Leave* is an irregular verb. Most verbs in English form their past tenses by adding *ed* (e.g. *he called*). There are a number of irregular verbs when this doesn't happen. We say *left* instead of 'leaved'.

11 This is a grammar question. The correct sentence is: *The twins and I were last to arrive.*

Tip: Think of the sentence as two separate sentences (*The twins were last to arrive. I was last to arrive.*) You should not say: *Me was last to arrive. Were* is the correct plural verb as it has to agree with a subject that is greater than one.

12 This is a grammar question. The correct sentence is: *The team and the coach are on the bus before the driver arrives.*

Tip: Singular subjects (nouns) need singular verbs; plural subjects (nouns) need plural verbs. In this case *were* is used because there are more than two people on the bus—the team and the coach. There is only one driver. The correct verb is *arrives*. *Arrives* is the correct tense.

13 This is a punctuation question. The correct sentence is: *Dad shouted at the top of his voice, "Get out now!"*

Tip: Only the actual words spoken are enclosed in quotation marks (inverted commas). The exclamation mark is also included inside the quotation marks.

14 This is a grammar question. The adjectives are *house*, *honest* and *friendly*.

Tip: Simply stated, adjectives are describing words that often describe nouns. These adjectives describe *painter*, *face* and *smile*.

15 This is a grammar question. The correct word is the conjunction *however*.

Tip: In this sentence *however* implies a result of a particular action. *In spite of being late Zara still saw some events.*

16 This is a punctuation question. The correct sentence is: *Marcus left his glasses on the stairs at his friend's place.*

Tip: *Marcus* is a proper noun without any direct ownership. *Glasses* and *stairs* are the plural form of nouns. His friend has possession of place—*friend's place.*

17 This is a punctuation question. The correct sentence is: *The liner, at Pier Seven, won't be leaving before next Wednesday.*

Tip: Commas are added to show a pause. The words *at Pier Seven* explain where the liner is. Commas are used to separate parts of the sentence and to make the meaning clear.

18 This is a punctuation question. The words *see Map 4* should be in brackets.

Tip: Brackets are used to include additional information that may be useful. A reader can quickly find relevant information on a map. This could be helpful for the reader who wants more precise details. Bracketed information does not interrupt the flow of basic data.

19 This is a punctuation question. The correct sentence is: *Mark my words, you won't see a view like that for a while.*

Tip: A comma is required after *Mark my words*. The comma indicates a pause and this helps to make the meaning clear.

20 This is a punctuation question. The correct sentence is: *Every town north of Port Allen has a town mayor except for Ibis Lake.*

Tip: The only words with capitals are the proper names (other than sentence beginnings) of places (*Port Allen* and *Ibis Lake*). Be careful with common nouns that have become proper place-name nouns (e.g. *port*, *lake* and *ibis*).

21 This is a grammar question. The correct word is the indefinie article *a*.

Tip: The indefinite article *a* is used in this sentence because it refers to any towel, not some particular to special towel. *An* would only be used if the noun began with a vowel.

22 This is a punctuation question. The correct sentence is: *During June, we began weekly walks, camping by creeks along the way.*

Tip: Commas are used to indicate pauses and to make the meaning clear.

23 This is a punctuation question. The correct sentence is: *'How is your knee?' my friend asked. 'If it is improving, you should start walking.'*
Tip: The speaker says two short sentences—a question (*How is your knee?*) and a statement (*If it is improving, you should start walking.*) The capital *I* (*If*) indicates the beginning of the statement.

24 This is a grammar question. The correct word is *belief.*
Tip: *Belief* is an abstract noun. An abstract noun is a noun that you cannot sense; it is the name we give to an emotion, ideal or idea. It has no physical existence. You can't see, hear, touch, smell or taste it.

25 This is a grammar question. The correct words are *very quietly.*
Tip: *Quietly* is an adverb. It tells how Tracy sat. Many adverbs end with *ly. Very* is used to emphasise the meaning. *Quiet* is most often used as an adjective.

READING (Real Test)
Understanding narratives   **Pages 20–21**

Bosley's French Café

1 B **2** D **3** A **4** C **5** C **6** B **7** 4, 2, 1, 3 **8** D **9** C, E

EXPLANATIONS

1 Bosley has eating expectations that are very choosy. Although hungry, he rejects a number of options to eat because he doesn't like the food or the food available is not up to his expectations: 'Hamburgers weren't his scene. Commonplace, and so unrefined. He moved on. The Indian Curry Palace. Too spicy for a delicate stomach. Thai-Raid served half-cooked vegetables. Definitely not for a sophisticated cat'.

2 Bosley passed the hamburger café then the Indian Curry Palace. The third place he passed was the Thai-Raid café.

3 Bosley's discovery in the French café was treated with disbelief. The waiter was so shocked to see a cat he dropped his cloth: ' "Oh! It's a cat!" the waiter exclaimed, dropping the cloth.'

4 Bosley's attitude can be described as disdainful. He acts as if he is so superior. He exhibits contempt, which is obvious in his reaction to various types of ethnic food.

5 Bosley rejected the hamburger café because: 'Hamburgers weren't his scene. Commonplace, and so unrefined'. They were not up to the expectations of a cat of his calibre.

6 The waiters in the French café were quick to act. They weren't about to tolerate a cat in their café. When they realised there was a cat under the table they put plans into place to capture it or get rid of it.

7 This is a sequencing question. The order in which the action occurs is: **1** Bosley rejects the thought of eating a hamburger; **2** Bosley passes by the Indian Curry Palace; **3** Bosley ventures into a restaurant with French cuisine; **4** Bosley is discovered under a table.

8 Such phrases are not meant to be taken literally. Bosley was so surprised (astonished beyond belief) that he couldn't progress any further. He wasn't prepared for such a smell.

9 Bosley was not upset at being discovered under the table. It's as if that was a place you expect to find a cat. He was unruffled and complacent. He actually thought the waiter was somewhat dumb when he recognised Bosley as a cat.

READING (Real Test)
Understanding narratives   **Pages 22–23**

Perfect Timing

1 A **2** B **3** D **4** 1B, 1D; 2A, 2C **5** A **6** B
7 1D, 2A, 3C, 4B **8** D

EXPLANATIONS

1 You have to read between the lines. The students, Andrew and Amanda, are dropped off at the school's assembly hall. The hall is decorated and the stage is set for a band. The function is a school disco.

2 Andrew and Amanda arrived before the function had started. The players in the band are not on stage. Other students are still arriving.

3 Andrew has checked himself in the mirror several times. This suggests that Andrew wanted to look his best—nothing out of place.

4 The streamers made from scraps that Andrew had found. Andrew 'was pleased that the junk material they had gathered up and recycled had turned out looking so sharp'. You also read that the 'streamers were in profusion'.

5 The students arriving at the function are excited. They are all dressed up. They are talking excitedly and noisily about their clothes, their hair ... and, of course, the band. They are not misbehaving but are very orderly (peaceful).

6 Jackets were not necessary for a rock and roll formal.

7 Reading the text carefully you will see that: **1** Andrew made streamers; **2** Amanda sat in the back seat of the car; **3** Andrew's father commented on Andrew's appearance; **4** Andrew's mother drove the car.

8 To select a good title you have to understand what the whole passage is about. The best title from the selection would be Big Night Out. This is implied by the way the parents are treating the children, as well as the behaviour and dress of other children attending the function.

READING (Real Test)
Understanding narratives   Pages 24–25

Dad, Mum, the Circus and me

1 put Annette to bed; read to Annette **2** C **3** A
4 D **5** B **6** written response **7** A **8** C

EXPLANATIONS

1 Each night Eddy's mother read to Annette: 'Mum organised Annette into getting ready for bed (and) re-reading Annette's favourite story'.

2 You have to read the whole paragraph and interpret Eddy's actions. He had just wiped the image of his father from his mind and brought himself back to reality and finished cleaning his teeth.

3 You need to interpret the saying. Clouds are often considered to be storm clouds. They bring troubles. However, one often sees a silver outline around storm clouds—even the gloomiest outlook contains some hopeful or consoling aspect. This is consistent with the way the father is remembered: 'all I could remember was Dad's laugh and the way his eyes slid and rolled whenever Mum presented him with a new problem'.

4 Grandad's teeth were lost on the beach. It was recorded in the photo album.

5 You have to make a judgement to answer the question. Read the whole passage and work out how the family reacted. Dad was a worker and a provider for the family and a man who shared his life with his family.

6 You have to read between the lines and interpret the actions of the family. Carol and Eddy did the washing-up. Mum continued reading to Annette. Eddy's father is remembered fondly but life has to go on.

7 The death of the dog upset Eddy's father, but he found it hard that a doctor could be more worried about his car than the life of the dog. Eddy remembers the doctor's voice rising and falling after the accident. The doctor's reaction didn't seem consistent with his profession.

8 The implication of this saying is that Eddie was so like his father that they were almost the same person. Eddie sees this in the mirror when he cleans his teeth. When the father dies, people will see the father in the son's looks and behaviour.

Tick each correct point.
Read the student's work through once to get an overall view of their response.

Focus on general points

☐ Did it make sense?
☐ Did it flow? Were the arguments logical and relevant?
☐ Did the opinions expressed arouse any feelings/reactions?
☐ Was the body of the writing mainly in the third person?
☐ Did you want to read on to understand/ appreciate the writer's point of view?
☐ Were the arguments convincing?
☐ Has the writer been assertive (e.g. the use of is rather than a less definite term)?
☐ Was the handwriting readable?
☐ Was the writing style suitable for a persuasive text (objective; not casual or dismissive)?

Now focus on the detail. Read each of the following points and find out whether the student's work has these features.

Focus on content

☐ Did the opening sentence(s) focus on the topic?
☐ Was the writer's point of view established early in the writing?
☐ Did the writer include any evidence to support his or her opinion?
☐ Did the writer include information relevant to his or her experiences?
☐ Were the points/arguments raised by the writer easy to follow?
☐ Did the writing follow the format with an introduction, the body of the text and a conclusion?
☐ Were personal opinions included?
☐ Was the concluding paragraph relevant to the topic?

Focus on structure, vocabulary, grammar, spelling, punctuation

☐ Was there a variety of sentence lengths, types and beginnings?

☐ Was a new paragraph started for each additional argument or point?
☐ Has the writer used any similes (e.g. as clear as crystal) to stress a point raised?
☐ Did the writer avoid approximations such as probably, perhaps and maybe?
☐ Did the writer use such phrases as I know … and It is important to …?
☐ Did the writer refer to the question in the points raised (A good way to do this is to use the key words from the question or the introduction.)?
☐ Has the writer used any less common words correctly?
☐ Was indirect speech used correctly?
☐ Were adjectives used to improve descriptions (e.g. expensive buildings)?
☐ Were adverbs used effectively (e.g. firstly)?
☐ Were capital letters used correctly?
☐ Was punctuation used correctly?
☐ Was the spelling of words correct?

Marker's suggestions (optional)

Tick each correct point.
Read the student's work through once to get an overall view of their response.

Focus on general points

☐ Did it make sense?
☐ Did it flow? Were the arguments logical and relevant?
☐ Did the opinions expressed arouse any feelings/reactions?
☐ Was the body of the writing mainly in the third person?
☐ Did you want to read on to understand/ appreciate the writer's point of view?
☐ Were the arguments convincing?
☐ Has the writer been assertive (e.g. the use of *is* rather than a less definite term)?

☐ Was the handwriting readable?
☐ Was the writing style suitable for a persuasive text (objective; not casual or dismissive)?

Now focus on the detail. Read each of the following points and find out whether the student's work has these features.

Focus on content
☐ Did the opening sentence(s) focus on the topic?
☐ Was the writer's point of view established early in the writing?
☐ Did the writer include any evidence to support his or her opinion?
☐ Did the writer include information relevant to his or her experiences?
☐ Were the points/arguments raised by the writer easy to follow?
☐ Did the writing follow the format with an introduction, the body of the text and a conclusion?
☐ Were personal opinions included?
☐ Was the concluding paragraph relevant to the topic?

Focus on structure, vocabulary, grammar, spelling, punctuation
☐ Was there a variety of sentence lengths, types and beginnings?
☐ Was a new paragraph started for each additional argument or point?
☐ Has the writer used any similes (e.g. as clear as crystal) to stress a point raised?
☐ Did the writer avoid approximations such as probably, perhaps and maybe?
☐ Did the writer use such phrases as I know … and It is important to …?
☐ Did the writer refer to the question in the points raised (A good way to do this is to use the key words from the question or the introduction.)?
☐ Has the writer used any less common words correctly?
☐ Was indirect speech used correctly?
☐ Were adjectives used to improve descriptions (e.g. expensive buildings)?
☐ Were adverbs used effectively (e.g. firstly)?
☐ Were capital letters used correctly?

☐ Was punctuation used correctly?
☐ Was the spelling of words correct?

Marker's suggestions (optional)

WRITING (Real Test)
Recount 1   Page 33

Tick each correct point.
Read the student's work through once to get an overall view of their response.

Focus on general points
☐ Did it make sense?
☐ Did it flow?
☐ Did the story arouse any feeling?
☐ Did you want to read on? Did the story create any suspense?
☐ Was the handwriting readable?

Now focus on the detail. Read the following points and find out whether the student's work has these features.

Focus on content
☐ Did the opening sentence(s) introduce the subject of the recount?
☐ Was the setting established (i.e. when and where the action took place)?
☐ Was it apparent who the main character(s) is?
☐ Have personal pronouns been used (e.g. *I, we, our*)?
☐ Were the events recorded in chronological (time) order?
☐ Was the recount in the past tense?
☐ Did the writing include some personal comments on the events (e.g. *surprised, thrilled*)?
☐ Did descriptions make reference to any of the senses (e.g. *wet rocks, salty air*)?
☐ Were interesting details included?
☐ Did the conclusion have a satisfactory summing-up comment?

Focus on structure, vocabulary, grammar, spelling and punctuation
- ☐ Was there a variation in sentence length and beginnings?
- ☐ Was a new paragraph started for changes in time, place or action?
- ☐ Were subheadings used? (optional)
- ☐ Were adjectives used to improve descriptions (e.g. *smelly bait*)?
- ☐ Were adverbs used to make 'actions' more interesting (e.g. *yelled loudly*)?
- ☐ Are time words used for time changes (e.g. *later, soon, then*)?
- ☐ Were capital letters used where they should have been?
- ☐ Was punctuation correct?
- ☐ Was the spelling of words correct?

Marker's suggestions (optional)

WRITING (Real Test)
Recount 2   Page 34

Tick each correct point.

Read the student's work through once to get an overall view of their response.

Focus on general points
- ☐ Did it make sense?
- ☐ Did it flow?
- ☐ Did the events arouse any feeling?
- ☐ Did you want to read on? (Were the events interesting?)
- ☐ Was the handwriting readable?

Now focus on the detail. Read the following points and find out whether the student's work has these features.

Focus on content
- ☐ Did the opening sentence(s) introduce the subject of the recount?
- ☐ Was the setting established (i.e. when and where the action took place)?

- ☐ Was it apparent who the main character(s) is?
- ☐ Have personal pronouns been used (e.g. *I, we, our*)?
- ☐ Were the events recorded in chronological (time) order?
- ☐ Was the recount in the past tense?
- ☐ Did the writing include some personal comments on the events (e.g. *feeling hot, disappointed*)?
- ☐ Did descriptions make reference to any of the senses (e.g. *loud commentary, blue water*)?
- ☐ Were interesting details included?
- ☐ Did the conclusion have a satisfactory summing-up comment?

Focus on structure, vocabulary, grammar, spelling and punctuation
- ☐ Was there variation in sentence length and beginnings?
- ☐ Was a new paragraph started for changes in time, place or action?
- ☐ Were subheadings used? (optional)
- ☐ Were adjectives used to improve descriptions (e.g. *neat dive*)?
- ☐ Were adverbs used to make 'actions' more interesting (e.g. *swam bravely*)?
- ☐ Are time words used for time changes (e.g. *later, soon, then*)?
- ☐ Were capital letters where they should have been?
- ☐ Was punctuation correct?
- ☐ Was the spelling of words correct?

Marker's suggestions (optional)

WEEK 2

NUMBER AND ALGEBRA/STATISTICS AND PROBABILITY (Test Your Skills)
Fractions, decimals, percentages and probability   Page 36

1 As 3 into 17 goes 5 times and 2 left over,
$$\frac{17}{3} = 5\frac{2}{3}$$

2 As $\frac{8}{12} = \frac{2}{3}$ consider each of the choices
$$\frac{4}{6} = \frac{2}{3}, \frac{2}{3}, \frac{20}{30} = \frac{2}{3} \text{ and } \frac{1}{2} \neq \frac{2}{3}$$

3 There are 5 shaded 'stripes' out of 10 stripes. This means $\frac{5}{10} = \frac{1}{2}$ shaded.

4 $\frac{1}{2} + \frac{1}{4} = \frac{2}{4} + \frac{1}{4}$
$$= \frac{3}{4}$$

5 $2 - \frac{3}{4} = 1\frac{1}{4}$

6 $\frac{3}{4} + \frac{1}{2} = \frac{3}{4} + \frac{2}{4}$
$$= \frac{5}{4}$$
$$= 1\frac{1}{4}$$

7 $\frac{3}{4} \times \frac{2}{5} = \frac{6}{20}$
$$= \frac{3}{10}$$

8 $\frac{2}{5} \times \frac{20}{1} = \frac{40}{5} = 8$

The answer is $8.

9 The value of 8 in 21.978 is 8 thousandths.

10 $30.06 = 3 \times 10 + 6 \times \frac{1}{100}$

11 The nearest hundredth is 2 decimal places: 9.326 is closer to 9.33 than 9.32

12 As 0.2 = 0.20, there are 20 hundredths

13
$$\begin{array}{r} 3.10 \\ 0.42 \\ + 6.00 \\ \hline 9.52 \end{array}$$

14
$$\begin{array}{r} \cancel{1}.\overset{9}{\cancel{0}}\overset{1}{0} \\ - 0.72 \\ \hline 0.28 \end{array}$$

15 $15 \times 3 = 45$, then $1.5 \times 0.3 = 0.45$

16
$$5\overline{)3.1^15} \quad \begin{array}{c}0.63\end{array}$$

17 $0.913 \times 100 = 91.3$

18 $3.6 \div 0.6 = 36 \div 6 = 6$

19 As $\frac{6}{10} = \frac{60}{100} = 60\%$

20 As $15 - (3 + 7) = 15 - 10$
$$= 5$$
This means 5 out of 15 are green.
The chance is $\frac{5}{15} = \frac{1}{3}$.

NUMBER AND ALGEBRA/STATISTICS AND PROBABILITY (Real Test)
Fractions, decimals, percentages and probability   Page 38

1 B   2 A   3 C   4 D   5 D   6 D   7 D   8 C   9 B   10 D
11 A   12 D   13 B   14 C   15 A   16 5.4

EXPLANATIONS

1

The arrow is in the middle of $1\frac{1}{2}$ and 2.

This means it is pointing to $1\frac{3}{4}$.

2 Change $2 to 200 cents. Firstly rewrite as a fraction: $\frac{20}{200} = \frac{10}{100} = 10\%$

3

$$\begin{array}{r} 9\,.\,9\,7 \\ \times \quad _2\,_2\,3 \\ \hline 2\,9\,.\,9\,1 \end{array}$$

This means the books cost $29.91.

4 As $75\% = \dfrac{3}{4}$, we need $\dfrac{3}{4}$ of 120:

$$\dfrac{3}{4} \times \dfrac{120}{1} = \dfrac{360}{4} = 90$$

90 houses were damaged.

5 As $10\% = \dfrac{1}{10}$, we need $\dfrac{1}{10}$ of 125 000, or $125\,000 \div 10 = 12\,500$.
This means new profit is
$125\,000 + 12\,500 = 137\,500$

6 $6.4 \div 0.4 = 64 \div 4 = 16$

7 6 purple out of a total of 16 balls.
This means $\dfrac{6}{16} = \dfrac{3}{8}$

8 As there are 3 black, there must be 13 not black. This means the chance is $\dfrac{13}{16}$.

9 If two-thirds watched, then one-third did not watch. As $\dfrac{1}{3}$ of 21 = 7, this means 7 million did not watch the game.

10 Decrease = $160 - 40 = 120$; $\dfrac{120}{160} = \dfrac{3}{4}$

Decrease % = $\dfrac{3}{4} \times \dfrac{100}{1}\% = 75\%$

11 As $25\% = \dfrac{1}{4}$, this means $\dfrac{1}{4}$ of 12 are cracked, or $12 \div 4 = 3$. 3 are cracked.

12 As $\dfrac{5}{10} = \dfrac{1}{2}$, then $4\dfrac{1}{2} = 4\dfrac{5}{10}$

13 $2.3 \times 100 = 230$

14 As 18.4 is close to 20 and 16.30 is close to 15, then the estimate is $20 \times 15 = 300$. The answer close to $300 is $299.92.

15 Firstly add $\dfrac{1}{2}$ and $\dfrac{1}{3}$: $\dfrac{1}{2} + \dfrac{1}{3} = \dfrac{3}{6} + \dfrac{2}{6}$
$$= \dfrac{5}{6}$$

As $1 - \dfrac{5}{6} = \dfrac{1}{6}$, this means $\dfrac{1}{6}$ travelled by car.

16 Average = $\dfrac{4.5 + 9.3 + 1.7 + 6.1}{4}$

$$= \dfrac{21.6}{4}$$

$$= 5.4$$

The average is 5.4 m

MEASUREMENT AND GEOMETRY
(Test Your Skills)
Length, time and mass   Page 39

1 As $7390 \div 100 = 73.9$, there are 73.9 m

2 First change to cm: 410 cm and 392 cm
Difference = $410 - 392$
$\qquad\qquad = 18$
Difference is 18 cm

$$\begin{array}{r} ^3\!4\,^{10}\!1\,^1\!0 \\ -\quad 3\,9\,2 \\ \hline 1\,8 \end{array}$$

3 Count the lengths of each side:
Perimeter = $5 + 3 + 3 + 1 + 5 + 2 + 3 + 2$
$\qquad\qquad = 24$
The perimeter is 24 units.

4 Perimeter = 4.8×4
$\qquad\qquad = 19.2$
The perimeter is 19.2 cm.

$$\begin{array}{r} 4.8 \\ \times\,_3\,4 \\ \hline 19.2 \end{array}$$

5 Length = $10.8 \div 3$
$\qquad\quad = 3.6$
The length is 3.6 metres.

$$3\overline{)10.^18}\;\;3.6$$

6 As 20 m = 1 cm, 60 m = 3 cm,
so that 70 m = $3\dfrac{1}{2}$ cm

7 As 5 cm = 120 km,
we divide 120 by 5: $120 \div 5 = 24$
This means 1 cm = 24 km.

$$5\overline{)12^20}\;\;24$$

8 Speed = Distance ÷ Time
$\qquad\quad = 450 \div 5$
$\qquad\quad = 90$
This means 90 km/h.

9 Time = Distance ÷ Speed
$\qquad\; = 240 \div 60$
$\qquad\; = 4$
This means 4 hours.

10 As 70 km was travelled in one hour,
then 35 km in $\frac{1}{2}$ h

As 70 + 35 = 105, then Ronaldo will travel 105 km.

11 20 to midnight = 23:40 (or 11:40 pm)

12 The clock is showing a time of 6:40.
The next screening is at 19:05 or 7:05 pm.
From 6:40 to 7:05 is 25 minutes.

13 As 52 weeks in a year, we need to multiply:
Amount = 52 × 2000
= 104 000
Mario is paid $104 000 per year.

14 Hobart is 2 hours behind. This means it is 9:30 am in Hobart.

15 48.62 × 1000 = 48 620
This means 48 620 grams.

16 Subtract 225 from 1000
The remaining flour has
a mass of 775 g.

$$\begin{array}{r} \cancel{1}\,{}^9\cancel{0}\,{}^9\cancel{0}\,{}^1 0 \\ -\quad 2\ 2\ 5 \\ \hline 7\ 7\ 5 \end{array}$$

17 As 1 L = 1000 mL has mass 1000 grams,
then 600 mL has mass 600 grams.

MEASUREMENT AND GEOMETRY (Real Test)
Length, time and mass   Page 41

1 C 2 B 3 C 4 1.21 5 A 6 D 7 B 8 C 9 D
10 D 11 B 12 A 13 B 14 B 15 100 16 0.006

EXPLANATIONS

1 17:45 is in the afternoon: 5:45 pm.

2 Using a ruler, length of rectangle is 3 cm.
As 3 cm = 120 m, then 1 cm = 40 m.

3 Perimeter = 3 + 2 + 3 + 2
= 10
The perimeter is 10 cm.

4 Add 440 and 770
The total mass is 1210 grams
= 1.21 kg.

$$\begin{array}{r} {}^1 4\ 4\ 0 \\ +\ 7\ 7\ 0 \\ \hline 1\ 2\ 1\ 0 \end{array}$$

5 As 30 minutes = $\frac{1}{2}$ hour, and

Distance = Speed × Time
$$= 14 \times \frac{1}{2}$$
$$= 7$$

Trudi ran 7 km.

6 As $\frac{6}{24} = \frac{1}{4}$, then Alma bought $\frac{1}{4}$ kg,
or 250 grams.

7 From 10:15 am to 10:00 pm is only
15 minutes short of 12 hours.
This means 11 hours 45 minutes.

8 As 80 grams = 0.080 kg,
so 1 kg 80 g = 1.080 or 1.08 kg.

9 By counting the units, 8 units = 160 km.
This means 1 unit = 20 km.
As the distance from Frypan Flat to Clifford Hill is 4 units, the distance is 80 km.

10 As   100 metres = 120 paces, then
25 metres = 30 paces, and
75 metres = 90 paces
Ali uses 90 paces to walk 75 metres.

11 Firstly add 5 h 10 min on to 10:40 am:
This means 15:50 (in 24 h time)

Now as Sydney is 2 hours ahead of Perth, add another 2 h on to 15:50, which gives 17:50.
Graeme arrives at 17:50, 5:50 pm.

12 From 11 am to 3 pm is 4 hours.
Speed = Distance ÷ Time
= 240 ÷ 4
= 60
This means 60 km/h.

13 As 25 m 30 s + 8 m 30 s = 33 m 60 s
= 34 min

Walk = 45 min − 34 min
= 11 min
Bailey walked for 11 minutes.

14 As 150 km/h means 150 km in 60 minutes,
or 25 km in 10 minutes
This means 100 km in 40 minutes.

15 As 10 years = one decade
10 decades in a century
10 centuries in a millennium
This means there are 100 decades in a millennium.

16 6 ÷ 1000 = 0.006
This means 6 mm = 0.006 m

MEASUREMENT AND GEOMETRY
(Test Your Skills)
Area, volume and capacity   Page 42

1 Area = 14 × 8
$\quad$ = 2 × 7 × 8
$\quad$ = 2 × 56
$\quad$ = 112
The area is 112 cm².

2 As 12 × 9 = 108
Area = 1.2 × 0.9
$\quad$ = 1.08
The area is 1.08 cm².

3 As 20 × ___ = 340, then
340 ÷ 20 = 34 ÷ 2 = 17
This means the breadth is 17 cm.

4 As 4.8 is close to 5, the area is close to
5² = 25. The best estimate is 25 cm².

5 As $\frac{1}{2} \times \frac{1}{2} = \frac{1}{4}$, the area is $\frac{1}{4}$ cm².

6 Area = $\frac{1}{2}$ × base × height
$\quad = \frac{1}{2} \times 8 \times 6$
$\quad = 24$
The area is 24 cm².

7 Area = $\frac{1}{2}$ × base × height
$\quad = \frac{1}{2} \times 17 \times 10$
$\quad = \frac{1}{2} \times 170$
$\quad = 85$ The area is 85 cm².

8 Volume = 7 × 5 × 6
$\quad$ = 210
The volume is 210 cm³.

9 As 1000 kg = 1 t, 39.05 × 1000 = 39 050
This means 39.05 t is 39 050 kg.

10 Volume = 12 × 5 × 10 = 600
The volume is 600 cm³.

11 Area = 320 × 300
$\quad$ = 96 000
Hectares = 96 000 ÷ 10 000
$\quad$ = 9.6
The area is 9.6 hectares.

12 By counting the area of the front face,
which is 16 units²
Total area = 16 × 6
$\quad$ = 96
The area is 96 units².

13 As 1000 mL in 1 L, 3.07 × 1000 = 3070
This means 3070 millilitres in 3.07 litres.

14 Mass = 625 − 175
$\quad$ = 450
The mass of jam is 450 grams.

$$\begin{array}{r} {}^5 6\,{}^1 2\,5 \\ -\ 1\,7\,5 \\ \hline 4\,5\,0 \end{array}$$

15 As 1 cm³ = 1 mL,
5000 cm³ = 5000 mL = 5 L
This means 5 L in 5000 cm³.

16 10 × 5 × ___ = 200, the missing number is 4
This means the height is 4 cm.

17 Consider each of the volumes:
4 × 3 × 2 = 24
5 × 2 × 3 = 30
8 × 2 × 1 = 16
6 × 3 × 1 = 18
As the largest value is 30, the dimensions
giving the greatest volume are 5 × 2 × 3.

MEASUREMENT AND GEOMETRY (Real Test)
Area, volume and capacity   Page 44

1 B **2** A **3** C **4** 200 **5** D **6** 420 **7** 0.01 **8** 16 **9** 24
10 C **11** B **12** C **13** A **14** D **15** B **16** D

EXPLANATIONS

1 750 − 300 = 450
This means that 450 mL remain in the jug.

2 As 8 × 100 = 800, we need to multiply 15 by 8:
Fuel = 15 × 8
$\quad$ = 120
The truck uses 120 litres.

3 On the grid the rectangular rug covers 6 units^2.
This means the scale is 6 units^2 = 12 m^2
1 unit^2 = 2 m^2
By counting there are 32 − 6 = 26 square units uncovered. As 26 × 2 = 52, there are 52 m^2 uncovered.

4 12 litres every 60 seconds means
1 litre every 5 seconds or
1000 mL every 5 seconds or
200 mL every 1 second.
The rate is 200 mL/second.

5 As 12 × 2 = 24; 6 × 4 = 24; 8 × 3 = 24;
20 × 4 = 80 ≠ 24.
Jake's rectangle is not 20 cm × 4 cm.

6 Volume = 10 × 7 × 6
= 10 × 42
= 420
The volume is 420 cm^3.

7 Area = 0.1 × 0.1
= 0.01
The area is 0.01 cm^2.

8 Volume = 40 × 20 × 20
= 16 000
The volume is 16 000 cm^3.
As 1 cm^3 = 1 mL, the capacity is 16 000 mL or 16 L.

9 By counting the squares, you get 24 units^2.

10 Volume = 3 × 2 × 4
= 24
The volume is 24 cm^3.
Mass = 24 × 3
= 72
The mass is 72 g.

11 Area = $\frac{1}{2}$ × base × height
= $\frac{1}{2}$ × 12 × 10
= 60
The area is 60 cm^2.

12 Area = 10 × 6
= 60
Amount = 60 × 200
= 12 000
This means 12 000 grams, or 12 kg needed.

13 As 4 + 4 + 1 + 1 = 10,
Cost = 70 + 70 + 28 + 28
= 140 + 56
= 196
The cost of the paint is $196.

14 As there are 6.5 lots of 10 in 65, we need to multiply 6.5, or $6\frac{1}{2}$ by 12:
Time = $6\frac{1}{2}$ × 12
= 6 × 12 + $\frac{1}{2}$ × 12
= 72 + 6
= 78
It would take 78 seconds.

15 As 1 kg = 1000 g, need to find how many 25s in 1000?
As there are four 25s in 100, there are 40 in 1000.
This means 40 m^2 will be covered.

16 2 × 1000 gives number of mL, and then divide by 7 for the 7 glasses: 2 × 1000 ÷ 7.

SPELLING (Real Test)
Common misspellings   Pages 46–47

1 umbrellas

2 truly

3 writing

4 receipt

5 opposing

6 marriage

7 travelling

8 becoming

9 similar

10 doctored

11 anchored

12 awful

13 business

14 cotton

15 ancestor

16 invisible

17 persuading

18 accommodation

19 admittance

20 addressing

21 disappeared

22 hottest

23 shepherds

24 supposing

25 woollen

GRAMMAR AND PUNCTUATION (Real Test)
Tenses, contractions and
punctuation   Pages 49–51

1 A 2 C 3 B 4 A 5 D 6 B 7 C 8 D 9 A 10 C
11 B 12 D 13 A 14 C 15 B 16 B 17 D 18 A
19 always, brilliantly 20 A, B 21 D 22 D 23 A
24 C 25 verb: *bounded*, adverb: *effortlessly*,
conjunction: *and*, adjective: *sleek*

EXPLANATIONS

1 This is a grammar question. The correct
word is *a*.
Tip: *A* is an article and precedes words that
begin with vowel sounds. *Union* starts with
a vowel but the sound is a consonant sound
(*y* as in *yawn*).

2 The correct word is the adverb *most
comfortable*.
Tip: Adverbs are words that help verbs.
Short adverbs usually end with *ly* (e.g.
quickly).Longer words take *more* (when
comparing two items) or *most* (when
comparing more than two items). The
article *the* indicates there are more than
two chairs.

3 This is a grammar question. The correct
word is the collective noun *fleet*.
Tip: It is normal practice to refer to a
number of naval ships as a *fleet*.

4 This is a grammar question. The correct
word is the noun *advice*.

Tip: Uncountable nouns (e.g. *advice*) only
have a singular form but you cannot put *a*
or *an* in front of them.

5 This is a grammar question. The correct
word is the verb *is*.
Tip: *Billiards* is an uncountable noun that
has an s ending. It is singular. Singular
subjects (nouns) need singular verbs; plural
subjects (nouns) need plural verbs. In this
case *is* must be used because it refers to a
single sport (*billiards*).

6 This is a grammar question. *Welsh* is an
adjective.
Tip: Adjectives are describing words. They
provide information about nouns and
pronouns. Proper adjectives are formed
from proper nouns, e.g. *Wales—Welsh*.

7 This is a punctuation question. The correct
sentence is: *The judge asked the foreman of
the jury for their verdict.*
Tip: This is an example of indirect speech.
The actual words the judge said are not
recorded. There is a report of what he said.
There is no requirement for quotation
marks. The word *judge* in this sentence is
not a title but a common noun.

8 This is a grammar question. The correct
sentence is: *The British team out-played the
Fijians on their home ground in Suva.*
Tip: The proper noun *Suva*, and the proper
adjectives *British* and *Fijian*, require capital
letters. *Team, home* and *ground* are
common nouns.

9 This is a grammar question. The correct
word is the conjunction *and*.
Tip: Conjunctions join ideas in sentences.
In this sentence the conjunction *and* joins
together things that are similar—*incorrect
and distressing*.

10 This is a grammar question. The correct
sentence is: *The pony is fit and I know its
age is important to you, but it's not my rule.*
Tip: *It's* is a contraction of *it is*. The apostrophe
indicates that a letter (*i*) has been omitted.
Its is a possessive pronoun showing ownership
and does not need an apostrophe.

⑪ This is a punctuation and grammar question. The correct sentence is: *Yesterday, when the bell rang, the children were still working.* Tip: Commas are required for the phrase *when the bell rang*. Commas are used to indicate a pause and to separate parts of the sentence to make the meaning clear. *Were* is the correct plural verb as it has to agree with a subject that is greater than one. *Children* means more than one child.

⑫ This is a grammar question. The correct sentence is: *For lunch, Dana had an apple, a banana and a plum.* Tip: *Items* in a list must be treated the same way. An article precedes all the items. In this sentence the article is *a* or *an* (for words that begin with a vowel sound).

⑬ This is a punctuation question. The correct sentence is: *We have an old newspaper, a magazine, a comic and a book to read.* Tip: A comma is used to separate the items in a series—three or more things. There is no comma where and is used in the series: *an old newspaper, a magazine, a comic and a book to read.*

⑭ This is a punctuation question. The correct punctuation is: *I'm the group's leader and this dog is its mascot!* Tip: No apostrophe is required for its as it is a possessive pronoun and not a shortened form of *it is*. I'm is the shortened form of *I am*. As there is only one group with a leader, the apostrophe goes before the *s*: *group's*.

⑮ This is a grammar question. The correct word is the verb *had given*. Tip: *Had given* is past tense. *Given* is part of a verb and needs a 'helper'. The helping verb is always close to the verb it is helping. *Given* is an irregular verb. Most verbs in English form their past tenses by adding *ed* (e.g. *he called*). There are a number of irregular verbs when this doesn't happen. We say *given* instead of 'gived', which is not a word. *Began* is the simple past tense form of *begin*. It does not need any helping or auxiliary verb, such as *had*.

⑯ This is a punctuation question. The correct sentence is: *Marilyn said it was hers but Mum's suspicions were based on past experience.* Tip: The only possessive noun is *Mum's*: *Mum has suspicions. Hers* is a possessive pronoun and does nor require an apostrophe. *Suspicions* is the plural of *suspicion*. *Past* is not a shortened word.

⑰ This is a punctuation question. The correct sentence is: *Rusty, our friendly red setter, barked all through the night.* Tip: Commas are added to show a pause. The commas separate an interruption to the main flow of the sentence. It is part of the sentence that can be removed without changing the meaning of the sentence. The words *our friendly red setter* explain what Rusty is.

⑱ This is a grammar question. The correct word is the verb *were*. Tip: Singular subjects (nouns) need singular verbs; plural subjects (nouns) need plural verbs. In this case *were* must be used because it refers to a singular, personal pronoun (*you*). *Were* is past tense.

⑲ This is a grammar question. The adverbs are *always* and *brilliantly*. Tip: Simply stated, adverbs add meaning to verbs. They modify the verbs. The adverbs *always* and *brilliantly* tell how the moon rises.

⑳ This is a punctuation question. The correct sentence is: *"Sit on the seat," Judy directed, "and I will read you a story. It will be my favourite."* Tip: The actual words spoken are *Sit on the seat, and I will read you a story. It will be my favourite.* The spoken words are interrupted by *Judy directed*. The quotation marks are closed after *seat* and reopened before *and*.

㉑ This is a grammar question. The correct clause is: *when he was in Year 1*. Tip: Complex sentences have a principal clause (independent clause) and a subordinate clause (dependent clause). The subordinate clause cannot stand on its own and doesn't make much sense when in isolation.

㉒ This is a punctuation question. The correct sentence is: *We found the pepper and salt, the bread and butter and the honey, but only one knife.*
Tip: In this series there are groups of pairs of items (e.g. *pepper and salt*). Each group is treated as a single unit or item. There is a comma after *honey* as it is followed by the conjunction *but* which introduces a new idea. *But* is used to connect two ideas with the meaning of 'with the exception of'. Commas are used to indicate pauses and to make the meaning clear.

㉓ This is a punctuation question. The correct sentence is: *I can't believe it! You have the $5 that Dad gave you. I think you should find that enough.*
Tip: Exclamation marks are used after exclamatory sentences and to express ridicule: *I can't believe it!*

㉔ This is a grammar question. The correct sentence is: *The bands were so exciting I could've danced all night.*
Tip: The correct word is *could've* which is short for *could have*. Learn to pronounce words correctly. 'Could of' is incorrect. It is a common error.

㉕ This is a grammar question. Simply put, verbs are action or doing words, adverbs modify verbs, conjunctions join words and adjectives describe nouns and pronouns.

> **READING (Real Test)**
> *Understanding poetry* Pages 54–55

Some Families of my Acquaintance

1 A **2** *The Teams*: to portray an ordeal/to evoke respect; *Families of My Acquaintance*: to entertain/to indulge in nonsense **3** D **4** B **5** D **6** C **7** Wiggle-wags **8** A

EXPLANATIONS

1 The names of the families are nonsense (Rummy-jums, Viddipocks and Wiggle-wags). These names are almost certainly created to contribute to the amusement of the verse.

2 Read the poems carefully (almost to yourself). You will feel the respect for the ordeal of the bullock driver and his team. It has a slow 'plodding' rhythm. The second poem jingles along as if it's meant to be read aloud.

3 The Rummy-jum family climb steeples: 'They run as hard as they can go, / And clamber up the steeple'.

4 People who don't know their mind are considered unsure of their actions and their thoughts. They are not definite or assertive.

5 The Wiggle-wags family fasten their frocks at the back (and sometimes at the front).

6 The Rummy-jum family discover that when they climb a steeple they also have to find a way down: 'They say, "Good gracious, we must stop!"/ And turn about with grief and pain, / And clamber-climber down again'.

7 The Wiggle-wags family wear their frocks inside out some of the time: 'And first they turn them inside out'.

8 The families, as mentioned in the poem's title, are 'acquaintances' of the poet. *Acquaintance* implies someone who is known slightly and not a close friend.

> **READING (Real Test)**
> *Interpreting posters* Pages 56–57

Ladder poster

1 A **2** C **3** B **4** A **5** D **6** C **7** B **8** D **9** A

EXPLANATIONS

1 The main intention of the poster is to promote sensible ladder use. Even when buying a ladder, buyers have to be aware of the qualities of a safe ladder.

2 This question requires a value judgement. The poster would be unsuitable at a bus stop as bus commuters are too varied and their attention is on catching a bus. Ladders are not common at sports grounds. The poster may have limited value at a doctor's surgery. Hardware stores are where builders (both professional and handypersons) would most likely go to get a ladder. It would be good public relations.

3 It is implied by the graphics and the warnings that ladders can be dangerous to work from. This being the case, a fall from a ladder is a possibility. Someone to offer assistance is an important precaution. You don't have to fall far to be seriously injured. The text spells out: 'Do not use a ladder if you are alone'.

4 The triangle is a warning sign. The exclamation mark creates the idea of urgency and surprise.

5 You have to make a value judgement based on your observations and your experience. Read the text and look at the picture. Standing on the top of the ladder offers no support for the climber. It could make the ladder unstable. The 'safe style of home ladder' has supports higher than the top step.

6 Most people weigh less than 100 kg. This difference in the climber's weight and the ladder's capacity adds a safety margin to the use of a ladder.

7 The first requirement before using a ladder is a precaution. Climbers should check the ladder before use. The poster advises this practice.

8 This is an instance of knowing a word's meaning and applying it to the text. *Domestic* in this case means for use in and around the home. The ladder is not intended for use by professional builders. The graphics indicate this assertion.

9 The safe home ladder's special feature is the safety rail round the top. The colour and number of steps (within reason) are irrelevant. The width of the steps would be an option decided by the buyer.

READING (Real Test)
Understanding narratives   Pages 58–59

The Sylvia Mystery
1 A 2 D 3 C **4** written response 5 D 6 C 7 A, F
8 B

EXPLANATIONS

1 Sylvia's intention was to take turns to ride the trolley down the driveway. She considered putting a pillow in it to make it more comfortable to ride.

2 Sylvia was concerned about the wheels, especially if they ran true, meaning they didn't suddenly change the direction of the trolley. They discovered this as they wheeled the trolley from the shed: 'The wheels did, indeed, still run true, if squeakily'.

3 Sylvia suggests that she could stop Kat from feeling bored if they had something to do. It becomes apparent, later in the passage, that Sylvia is using the reason as an excuse to carry out a scheme of her own.

4 Sylvia thought that they could tie a piece of rope attached to the gatepost and the person in the trolley could grab it as he or she rolled past. This would swing the trolley up the road rather than across the street.

5 Kat felt guilty about having the trolley, not because her family had taken it, but because it was in the shed when they had bought the house and it hadn't been returned to the shop. She defended having the trolley in the shed.

6 You can get the meaning of the word from the context in which it is used and from the sound of the word. Kat expected the trolley to 'wham' into a wall with a loud forceful blow.

7 When you read the complete text you will discover that Kat is not only apprehensive about the plan but has some practical points she wants considered. Where will the runaway trolley stop? What will happen to the hands holding the rope?

8 To get a suitable title for the passage you need to read the whole passage and get the main idea behind the passage. Do not be distracted by irrelevant detail. Sylvia's idea can best be described as a crazy idea. It is riddled with problems and dangers.

☐ Were capital letters where they should have been?
☐ Was punctuation correct?
☐ Was the spelling of words correct?

Marker's suggestions (optional)

WRITING (Real Test)
Narrative text 1   Page 61

Tick each correct point.
Read the student's work through once to get an overall view of their response.

Focus on general points
☐ Did it make sense?
☐ Did it flow?
☐ Did the story arouse any feeling?
☐ Did you want to read on? Did the story create any suspense?
☐ Was the handwriting readable?

Now focus on the detail. Read the following points and find out whether the student's work has these features.

Focus on content
☐ Did the opening sentence(s) 'grab' your interest?
☐ Was the setting established (i.e. when and where the action took place)?
☐ Was it apparent who the main character(s) is? (It can be the narrator, using *I*.)
☐ Was there a problem to be solved early in the writing?
☐ Was a complication or unusual event introduced?
☐ Did descriptions make reference to any of the senses (e.g. *pink sky, cool breeze*)?
☐ Was there a climax (a more exciting part near the end)?
☐ Was there a conclusion (resolution of the problem) and was it believable?

Focus on structure, vocabulary, grammar, spelling, punctuation
☐ Was there variation in sentence length and beginnings?
☐ Was a new paragraph started for changes in time, place or action?
☐ In conversations or speaking were there separate paragraphs for each change of speaker?
☐ Were adjectives used to improve descriptions (e.g. *hollow sound*)?
☐ Were adverbs used to make 'actions' more interesting (e.g. *listened carefully*)?

WRITING (Real Test)
Narrative text 2   Page 62

Tick each correct point.
Read the student's work through once to get an overall view of their response.

Focus on general points
☐ Did it make sense?
☐ Did it flow?
☐ Did the story arouse any feeling?
☐ Did you want to read on? Did the story create any suspense?
☐ Was the handwriting readable?

Now focus on the detail. Read the following points and find out whether the student's work has these features.

Focus on content
☐ Did the opening sentence(s) 'grab' your interest?
☐ Was the setting established (i.e. when and where the action took place)?
☐ Was it apparent who the main character(s) is? (It can be the narrator, using *I*.)
☐ Was there a problem to be solved early in the writing?
☐ Was a complication or unusual event introduced?
☐ Did descriptions make reference to any of the senses (e.g. *pink sky, cool breeze*)?
☐ Was there a climax (a more exciting part near the end)?
☐ Was there a conclusion (resolution of the problem) and was it believable?

Focus on structure, vocabulary, grammar, spelling, punctuation
- ☐ Was there variation in sentence length and beginnings?
- ☐ Was a new paragraph started for changes in time, place or action?
- ☐ In conversations or speaking were there separate paragraphs for each change of speaker?
- ☐ Were adjectives used to improve descriptions (e.g. *hollow sound*)?
- ☐ Were adverbs used to make 'actions' more interesting (e.g. *listened carefully*)?
- ☐ Were capital letters where they should have been?
- ☐ Was punctuation correct?
- ☐ Was the spelling of words correct?

Marker's suggestions (optional)

WRITING (Real Test)
Procedure 1   Page 64

Tick each correct point.
Read the student's work through once to get an overall view of their response.

Focus on general points
- ☐ Did it make sense?
- ☐ Did it flow?
- ☐ Did the procedure seem clear?
- ☐ Was the handwriting readable?

Now focus on the detail. Read the following points and find out whether the student's work has these features.

Focus on content
- ☐ Does the title clearly advise the reader of the topic?
- ☐ Is the goal/aim of the writing clearly presented in the first sentences?
- ☐ Is the equipment to be used listed and/or briefly described?

- ☐ Is there some advice on what NOT to do? (optional)
- ☐ Is there some advice on the topic chosen?
- ☐ Are the steps listed in sequence (can be numbered) and each one on a new line?
- ☐ Is the instruction in each step clear?
- ☐ Are the main sections readily defined or spaced and do any headings stand out?
- ☐ Have helpful tips or suggestions been included?
- ☐ Has a last comment or suggestion been included?
- ☐ Were interesting details included?
- ☐ Did the conclusion have a satisfactory summing-up comment?

Focus on structure, vocabulary, grammar, spelling, punctuation
- ☐ Are sentences short and clear?
- ☐ Were subheadings used? (optional)
- ☐ Are action verbs used to start most steps (e.g. *make, lift, speak*)?
- ☐ Were adverbs used to describe how to carry out actions (e.g. *talk clearly*)?
- ☐ Were capital letters where they should have been?
- ☐ Was punctuation correct?
- ☐ Was the spelling of words correct?

Practical suggestion: follow the steps as written and see if the explanation really works.

Marker's suggestions (optional)

WRITING (Real Test)
Procedure 2   Page 65

Tick each correct point.
Read the student's work through once to get an overall view of their response.

Focus on general points
- ☐ Did it make sense?
- ☐ Did it flow?
- ☐ Did the procedure seem clear?
- ☐ Was the handwriting readable?

Now focus on the detail. Read the following points and find out whether the student's work has these features.

Focus on content
☐ Does the title clearly advise the reader of the topic?
☐ Is the goal/aim of the writing clearly presented in the first sentences?
☐ Is the equipment to be used listed and/or briefly described?
☐ Is there some advice on what NOT to do? (optional)
☐ Is there some advice on the topic chosen?
☐ Are the steps listed in sequence (can be numbered) and each one on a new line?
☐ Is the instruction in each step clear?
☐ Are the main sections readily defined or spaced and do any headings stand out?
☐ Have helpful tips or suggestions been included?
☐ Has a last comment or suggestion been included?
☐ Were interesting details included?
☐ Did the conclusion have a satisfactory summing-up comment?

Focus on structure, vocabulary, grammar, spelling, punctuation
☐ Are sentences short and clear?
☐ Were subheadings used? (optional)
☐ Are action verbs used to start most steps (e.g. *make, lift, speak*)?
☐ Were adverbs used to describe how to carry out actions (e.g. *talk clearly*)?
☐ Were capital letters where they should have been?
☐ Was punctuation correct?
☐ Was the spelling of words correct?

Practical suggestion: follow the steps as written and see if the explanation really works.

Marker's suggestions (optional)

WEEK 3

STATISTICS AND PROBABILITY
(Test Your Skills)
Mean, graphs and tables   Page 68

1 Mean $= \dfrac{11 + 19 + 33 + 17}{4}$

$= \dfrac{80}{4}$

$= 20$

The mean is 20.

2 Mean $= \dfrac{125 + 135 + 145}{3}$

$= \dfrac{405}{3}$

$= 135$

The mean height is 135 cm.

3 Total mass of 4 watermelons $= 23.68$
Mean mass $= 23.68 \div 4$
$= 5.92$
The mean mass is 5.92 kg.

$$4\overline{)23.^368}$$
$$5.\ 92$$

4 As $1\frac{1}{2} = 1.5$ and $2\frac{1}{2} = 2.5$,

Mean $= \dfrac{1.5 + 2.5}{2}$

$= \dfrac{4}{2}$

$= 2$

The mean is 2.

5 From the graph: 4 students out of 24 scored 8. As $\dfrac{4}{24} = \dfrac{1}{6}$, or one in six.

6 1 student scored 6 and 5 students scored 7. This means 6 out of 24 scored less than 8.
As $\dfrac{6}{24} = \dfrac{1}{4}$, or one quarter.

7 The largest section represents the bird. This means the most popular pet is a bird.

8 A cat is represented as 2 out of 10. The cat is the pet of $\dfrac{2}{10}$ of 100, or 20 people.

9 A dog is represented as 3 out of 10 or 30%.

10 The population is increasing at the fastest rate where the line segment is increasing most steeply. This occurs between 1950 and 1960.

11 From the graph, the population reaches 10 000 in 1957.

12 From the graph, 60° out of 360° represents between 2 km and 5 km.

This means $\frac{60}{360} = \frac{1}{6}$ of 120 students,

or 20 students live between 2 km and 5 km.

13 From the graph: 90° out of 360° represents within 2 kilometres. This means $\frac{90}{360} = \frac{1}{4}$ or 25%.

14 The line with the smallest slope represents the cyclist who took the greatest time. This means that Don was the slowest.

15 Speed = Distance ÷ Time
= 48 ÷ 4
= 12
Chris' average speed is 12 km/h.

STATISTICS AND PROBABILITY (Real Test)
Mean, graphs and tables   Pages 71–72

1 C 2 B 3 D 4 C 5 12 6 A 7 C 8 C 9 20 10 B
11 B 12 A 13 8 14 50 15 180 16 19

EXPLANATIONS

1 As total is 50, there must be 5 vans. This means vans = $\frac{5}{50}$ or $\frac{1}{10}$ which is 10%.

2 Motor bike is $\frac{3}{50}$ or $\frac{6}{100}$ which is 0.06.

3 From graph, 60 US $ is 75 Australian $.

4 From graph, 100 Australian $ is 80 US $. This means 1000 Australian $ is 800 US $.

5 Average = $\frac{12 + 15 + 15 + 10 + 8}{5}$
= $\frac{60}{5}$
= 12

6 As a whole circle is 360°,

Fraction = $\frac{60}{360} = \frac{1}{6}$

7 School = $\frac{90}{360} = \frac{1}{4}$ = 25%
Mitchell spent 25% of the day at school.

8 Sleeping = $\frac{8}{24} = \frac{1}{3}$

Angle for sleeping = $\frac{1}{3}$ of 360°
= 120°

9 From the graph, heights were 1.4 m and 1.6 m.
Difference = 1.6 – 1.4
= 0.2
The difference is 0.2 m or 20 cm.

10 From the graph, Kim was 1.5 metres when she was 12 years old.

11 From the graph, there were 7 viewers of channel P.

12 The columns in the graph show 10, 7, 14, ?, 4. As 10 + 7 + 14 + 4 = 35, and total viewers is 40, there must be 5 viewers of Channel T.

13 From the graph, food = $\frac{2}{6} = \frac{1}{3}$
As $\frac{1}{3}$ of $24 = $8, Sonia spends $8 on food.

14 Savings = $\frac{3}{6} = \frac{1}{2}$ = 50%

15 As $\frac{1}{2}$ of 360 is 180, the angle for savings is 180°.

16 Fastest trip is the 0817 from Jeffersen arriving in Bradley at 0836.
This is a trip time of 36 – 17 = 19 min.

NUMBER AND ALGEBRA (Test Your Skills)
Patterns and algebra   Page 73

1 The pattern is counting forward by 13:
91 + 13 = 104
The missing value is 104.

2 The pattern is counting forward by $\frac{2}{5}$:
$\frac{4}{5} + \frac{2}{5} = \frac{6}{5}$
= $1\frac{1}{5}$

The missing value is $1\frac{1}{5}$.

3 The pattern is counting forward by 0.7:
1.6 + 0.7 = 2.3
The missing value is 2.3.

4 Continue the pattern: 16, 12, 8, 4, 0, –4, …
The sixth number is –4.

5 The rule: 'bottom number = double the top number and then add 7'
= 2 × 3 + 7
= 6 + 7
= 13
The value of X is 13.

6 Pattern of matches: 3, 5, 7, 9, ___
The next number is 11.
This means 11 matches for 5 triangles.

7 Continuing the pattern:, … 9, 11, 13, 15, 17
The value of X is 17.
[Also, the rule is Matches = 2 × triangles + 1]

8 Top row is counting forward by 5, and the bottom row is counting backward by 5.
This means X = 27 and Y = 33.

9 The pattern is 1, 3, 6, 10, …
The differences are 2, 3, 4, etc.
The next number is 10 + 5 = 15.

10 The pattern of dots is 1, 3, 6, 10, 15, 21, …
The number X is 21.

11 As 295 – ___ = 86,
then 295 – 86 = ___
The missing number is 209.

$$\begin{array}{r} 2\,{}^8\!9\,{}^1\!5 \\ -\quad 8\,6 \\ \hline 2\,0\,9 \end{array}$$

12 As 4 × __ – 2 = 18 then 4 × __ = 20
then the missing number is 5.

13 Work backwards from Jack's answer by using the inverse operations:
24 – 6 is 18, then halve which is 9.
Jack started with 9; check by substituting.

14 10 – third of a number = 6
This means that a third of the number is 4.
The number must be 12.
Check by substitution:
10 – third of 12 is 6 … correct.

15 48 ÷ __ + 5 = 13 means 48 ÷ ___ = 8
This means the missing number is 6,
as 48 ÷ 6 = 8.

16 93, 98, 103, 108, 113, …
This means the missing number is 113.

17 The number of dots is 1, 5, 9, …
The pattern is counting forward by 4
The next number is 13.

18 The pattern is 1, 5, 9, 13, 17, 21, …
As 21 is the 6th term, there are 21 dots in Fig. 6.

NUMBER AND ALGEBRA (Real Test)
Patterns and algebra   Page 75

1 C 2 B 3 D 4 102 5 A 6 D 7 D 8 B, D 9 B
10 A 11 C 12 B 13 B 14 A 15 B 16 B, E

EXPLANATIONS

1 Matches = 2 × triangles + 1
This means 2 × 6 + 1 = 13.
[We could have extended the pattern:
3, 5, 7, 9, 11, 13.]

2 From question 1, Matches = 2 × triangles + 1
then 2 × 10 + 1 = 21
You need 21 matches to make 10 triangles.

3 Again, from question 1,
Matches = 2 × triangles + 1
then 2 × 50 + 1 = 101

4 7 × Δ = 714, means
Δ = 714 ÷ 7
= 102
The missing number is 102.

5 Work backwards from Suzie's answer:
32 subtract 8 is 24, then divide by 4 is 6
Suzie's number was 6.
[We can check this answer by substituting 6 back into the question.]
We could also have tried each of the choices to find the number.

6 Pattern is counting forwards by 8.
This means 25, 33, 41, 49, 57, 65, …
The missing number is 65.

7 Using inverse operations, Amaya's number will be found by the rule: 'Add 5 to 17 and then divide by 2.'

8 The pattern is counting forward by 6.
This means 21, 27, 33, 39, 45, 51.
The missing numbers are 33 and 45.

9 Sean uses the rule 'multiply top number by 3 and add 2'. Check some of the numbers: $6 \times 3 + 2 = 20$; $11 \times 3 + 2 = 35$, etc.

10 If $\triangle = 6$, then $6 + 6 + \bigcirc = 15$, or $12 + \bigcirc = 15$ means $\bigcirc = 3$

11 Use inverse operations: 3 times 8 is 24, then divide by 6 is 4.
Gavin started with the number 4.

12 The sequence is the square numbers:
1, 4, 9, 16, 25, 36, 49
This means the missing numbers are 9 and 16.

13 As $45 = 2 \times \_\_ + 5$ means $40 = 2 \times \_\_$
The missing number is 20.

14 From 64, subtract 8 gives 56 and then divide by 8 which is 7.
Shari started with the number 7.

15 The pattern is 0.3, 0.8, 1.3, 1.8, …

16 Using the rule: 'bottom number = 30 minus 2 times top number' means
First missing number $= 30 - 2 \times 5$
$= 30 - 10$
$= 20$
Second missing number $= 30 - 2 \times 11$
$= 30 - 22$
$= 8$
The missing numbers are 8 and 20.

MEASUREMENT AND GEOMETRY
(Test Your Skills)
2D and 3D shapes and position Page 76

1 The angle is obviously more than a right angle (90°) and less than a straight angle (180°). The angle is about 120°.

2 $x = 180 - 50$ (straight angle = 180°)
$= 130$

3 $x = 180 - (100 + 30)$ (angles in $\triangle$ = 180°)
$= 180 - 130$
$= 50$

4 With angles of 100°, 30° and 50°, the triangle is scalene.

5 All angles equal and therefore equal to 60°.

6 A rhombus has all sides equal and the diagonals are of different lengths.

7 A quadrant is not shown on the diagram.

8 An isosceles triangle has 1 axis of symmetry.

9 An equilateral triangle has an order of rotational symmetry of 3.

10 The sides have been doubled in size. This means $x = 2.3 \times 2$
$= 4.6$

11 As $3 \times 15 = 45$, diameter is 45 cm.

12 With 5 faces, 9 edges and 6 vertices, the shape is a triangular prism.

13 The cross-section would be a rectangle.

14

15 The net consists of 2 triangles and 3 rectangles.

16 R is south-east of J.

MEASUREMENT AND GEOMETRY (Real Test)
2D and 3D shapes and position Page 78

1 C **2** C **3** D **4** D **5** E **6** B **7** C **8** A **9** B **10** B
11 B, C, D **12** B **13** A **14** A **15** C **16** D

EXPLANATIONS

1

2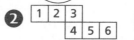
As 5 on front and 6 on right side, the 3 is missing from the top.

3 The protractor measures 140°.

4

5 The cube will be 3 by 3 by 3. This means that it will contain $3 \times 3 \times 3 = 27$ cubes. By counting, the solid contains 8, so another 19 cubes are needed.

6

7
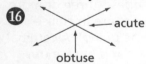

8 As 180 − (40 + 70) = 180 − 110 = 70, the triangle has angles 40°, 70° and 70°.
This means the triangle has 2 angles equal and is an isosceles triangle.

9 The pentagonal prism contains 2 pentagons and 5 rectangles.

10

11 The hexagonal pyramid does not have 8 faces—it has 7 faces. All the other options are correct.

12

N

east

135°

south-west

13 x = 180 − (120 + 35)
= 180 − 155 = 25

14 An arc is a section of the circumference of a circle.

15 An equilateral triangle has a rotational symmetry of order 3.

16

acute

obtuse

The angles are acute and obtuse.

SPELLING (Real Test)
Common misspellings   Pages 80–81

1 deceitful

2 definite

3 lightning

4 superstition

5 opportunity

6 adhesive

7 immediate

8 applicator

9 familiar

10 reviewing

11 neighbourly

12 fulfilled

13 financially

14 fierce

15 illegal

16 professor

17 scientific

18 guarantee

19 possession

20 really

21 brochure

22 hoping

23 junior

24 niece

25 capsizes

GRAMMAR AND PUNCTUATION (Real Test)
Verbs and commas   Pages 83–85

1 1 an, 2 a, 3 a **2** D **3** B **4** C **5** D **6** A **7** B **8** D
9 B **10** C **11** D **12** A **13** B **14** C **15** A **16** B **17** D
18 C **19** A **20** A, D **21** B **22** A **23** A **24** C **25** D

EXPLANATIONS

1 This is a grammar question. The correct articles are: *an* (elm), *a* (eucalypt), *a* (banksia).
Tip: *An* is an article and precedes words that begin with vowel sounds. *Eucalypt* starts with a vowel but the sound is a consonant sound (*y* as in *yawn*). *A* precedes words that begin with a consonant sound.

2 The correct word is the adverb *superbly*.
Tip: In English it is more appropriate to refer to a speech as being *superbly delivered* rather than *attractively, stunningly* or *gorgeously delivered*, which have more to do with appearance.

3 This is a grammar question. The correct word is the verb *done*.

Tip: With the verb *done* you need a 'helper' —another verb to 'help' it. *Have*, *has* and *had* can be helping verbs: *The new boys have done ...* The helping verb is always close to the verb it is helping. Because there are a number of boys (plural noun) the correct plural verb is *have done*. For one boy the verb would be *has done*.

4 This is a grammar question. The correct word is the noun *practice*.
Tip: *Practice* is an uncountable noun (Remember: it ends with *ice* which is also a noun). Uncountable nouns only have singular form. The *ise* ending is a verb. There is no requirement for an apostrophe.

5 This is a grammar question. The correct word is the verb *is*.
Tip: Singular subjects (nouns) need singular verbs; plural subjects (nouns) need plural verbs. In this case *is* must be used because it refers to a single group (*of everybody*).

6 This is a grammar question. The correct sentence is: *Sentences 5 and 6 contain information about when something took place.*
Tip: Both *now* (adverb) and *during* (preposition) are used to introduce text that has to do with time.

7 This is a punctuation question. The correct sentence is: *Kelly, the class captain, asked for permission to speak to Inspector Sartor.*
Tip: Only the proper nouns (*Kelly* and *Sartor* with his official title, *Inspector*) require capital letters. Commas are required for the phrase. Commas are used to indicate a pause and to separate parts of the sentence to make the meaning clear..

8 This is a grammar question. The correct sentence is: *I have made the perfect sauce for the meat.*
Tip: *Perfect* is a word that doesn't take any modifiers. Something is either perfect or it isn't. There are no degrees of being perfect. It is an absolute.

9 This is a grammar question. The correct word is the conjunction *although*.

Tip: Conjunctions join ideas in sentences. In this sentence, *although* makes it known that the race was won in spite of having a blistered foot.

10 This is a grammar question. The correct word is the possessive pronoun *whose*.
Tip: *Who* is used to refer to people. When that person owns something (a name) then *whose* is the correct word. *Who's* is the shortened form of *who is*.

11 This is a grammar question. The correct sentence is: *'I remember you two used the sink after I had finished,' protested Ryan.*
Tip: 'Youse' is not the plural of *you* (*you* is both singular and plural). The sentence is in the past tense. *Had* (*finished*) is the correct verb.

12 This is a grammar question. The correct sentence is: *On her long plane trip, Mum took a book, a crossword and an old diary.*
Tip: Items in a list must be treated the same way. An article precedes all the items. In this sentence the article is *a* or *an* (for words that begin with a vowel sound).

13 This is a punctuation question. The correct sentence is: *At the fete Jan, my sister, played the violin, Kerry played the piano and I sang the songs.*
Tip: A comma is used to indicate pauses and separate the items in a series—three or more things. The items in this list are in clause form (e.g. *Kerry played the piano*). A comma is added to separate the noun phrase (*my sister*) from the rest of the sentence. There is no need for a comma where *and* is used to complete the series: *Kerry played the piano and I sang the songs.*

14 This is a punctuation question. The correct punctuation is: *He's the children's idol but Matt's songs are more memorable.*
Tip: *He's* is the shortened form of *He is*. As *Matt* is an individual, the apostrophe goes before the *s*: *Matt's songs*.

15 This is a grammar question. The correct word is the verb *spun*.
Tip: *Spin* is an irregular verb. *Spun* is past tense. Most verbs in English form their past tenses by adding *ed* (e.g. *he called*). There

are a number of irregular verbs when this doesn't happen. We say *spun* instead of 'spinned', which is not a word.

16 This is a punctuation question. The correct sentence is: *Both teams' mascots were plastered on billboards down all major roads!*
Tip: The only possessive noun is *teams*: *teams' mascots*. As there is more than one team (both), the apostrophe goes after the *s*. *Mascots* and *billboards* do not require apostrophes as they are both plural nouns.

17 This is a punctuation question. The correct sentence is: *The lonely, old, bent pensioner was given a handout of fruit, milk and tea.*
Tip: Commas are added to show a pause and separate items in a list. The list describing the old man contains adjectives: *lonely, old, bent pensioner*. The items in the list of things he was given require one comma: *fruit, milk and tea*. No comma is required with *and*.

18 This is a grammar question. The correct word is the verb *was*.
Tip: Singular subjects (nouns) need singular verbs; plural subjects (nouns) need plural verbs. In this case, *was* must be used because *sums*, such as *ten dollars*, take a singular verb. *Was* and *donated* are both verbs in the past tense.

19 This is a punctuation question. The correct sentence is: *'That can't be right, can it?' Lindy asked.*
Tip: The actual words spoken and the question mark are all enclosed in inverted commas (quotation marks). The question Lindy asks is actually a statement with a question tag. Question tags have the opposite verb to the introductory statement (*can't, can*).

20 This is a punctuation question. The correct sentence is: *'Take off your cap,' suggested the diver, 'and bow to the guide. It's good manners.'*
Tip: The actual words spoken are *Take off your cap and bow to the guide. It's good manners*. The spoken words are interrupted by *suggested the diver*. The quotation marks are closed after *cap* and reopened before *and*. The quotation marks always

come after the comma at the end of units of direct speech.

21 This is a grammar question. The correct word is the adverb *easily*.
Tip: *Easily* is an adverb. Many adverbs end with *ly*. *Easily* tells the reader how Warren could see (verb). *Easy* is an adjective. 'More easy' is not English.

22 This is a punctuation question. The correct sentence is: *'If two plus two is not four, then what is it?' questioned the examiner.*
Tip: Quotation marks enclose the actual words spoken, including the question mark. The comma is included to indicate a pause.

23 This is a punctuation question. The correct sentence is: *'Stand by Hugh,' Father O'Brien said to the new boy in the choir.*
Tip: The quotation marks are closed after *Hugh*. The quotation marks always come after the comma (and other punctuation marks) at the end of direct speech.

24 This is a grammar question. The correct word is *recognise*.
Tip: A verb is a part of speech (or word class) that describes an action (often called a 'doing' word) or occurrence, or indicates a state of being. The word *recognise* shows that an action has taken place.

25 This is a grammar question. The correct word is the conjunction *neither*.
Tip: In English *neither* and *nor* make a pair (as do *either* and *or*). *Neither* and *nor* join two parts of a sentence to make a negative statement.

READING (Real Test)
Understanding recounts **Pages 88–89**

Wreck of the 'Sanko Harvest'

1 A **2** C **3** Friday 15 February 1991 **4** D **5** A **6** C **7** A **8** B **9** D **10** C

EXPLANATIONS

1 The State Emergency Service was the first to be informed of the difficulties aboard the *Sanko Harvest*. Salvage operators would have been contacted by the SES. Later, the

insurance company was made aware of the problem. Inflatable bags from New Zealand were considered as the situation deteriorated.

2 The *Sanko Harvest* was sailing in 'dangerous waters'. The storm came up as it was passing through the waters.

3 This is a straight fact-finding question. The diary records show that on Friday 15 February 'At 5 pm the ship was abandoned'.

4 A dispersant is a liquid that helps the break down of a mass of a substance (oil).

5 You have to make a value judgement. The writer is trying to impress upon the reader just how bad the oil spill was. The accident happened at sea. It not only affected marine life: 'Even kangaroos on coastal beaches suffered'.

6 The SES abandoned salvage attempts when the insurance company decided that because the weather had deteriorated dramatically it was too risky to attempt a salvage operation. A salvage operation could have resulted in greater loss of ships as well as the loss of life. (This would increase the insurance company's payouts.)

7 The vessel sank onto rocks, then slipped off the rocks, splitting into two. The hatch lifted off after the vessel had split.

8 This is a factual account. It gives names, times, dates and places. The events are in chronological sequence.

9 The writer found it ironic that the outcome of an environmental disaster, which destroyed much marine life, was the opposite to what one would expect: 'Some good came of the disaster. The wreck site was declared a marine sanctuary and wildlife within 500 m of the wreck protected from spear fishing'.

10 Locals were concerned about the wellbeing of marine life, including seal pups. To protect marine life and limit the amount of pollution, they wanted to physically remove as much oil as possible.

READING (Real Test)
Understanding recounts   Pages 90–91

Ben Hall

1 D **2** A **3** B **4** His funeral was well attended.
5 Billy Dargin **6** B, E **7** D **8** A

EXPLANATIONS

1 Ben Hall was almost forced into becoming a bushranger. He did not become a criminal until he 'was wrongly arrested for being an accomplice in a hold-up'. After his release he found that a number of disasters had struck. His wife ran off with a policeman and his property was vandalised.

2 The term 'he took to the gun' is a metaphor. It means that Hall used a gun to solve his problems. This involved taking up a life of crime.

3 Hall had no time for the police. His need for revenge was often directed at the police. One way of 'getting back' at the police was to embarrass them whenever possible. Hall stole Pottinger's horse. Pottinger was a trooper—a mounted policeman. He also stole their uniforms.

4 You need to make a judgement to answer this question. Reading through the whole passage, you will note that there was some public sympathy for Hall and his deeds. He directed his anger at the authorities, rather than at the common people. A funeral attended by a crowd indicates that Hall was respected, liked and 'well regarded'.

5 When wounded in a gunfight Hall 'appealed to tracker Billy Dargin to finish him off'. Whether or not Dargin would have obeyed we do not know. A hail of bullets fired by the police killed Hall.

6 You have to read the whole passage to get an understanding of what sort of person Ben Hall was. 'Brash' is the best description. He was assertive in an aggressive way. He taunted the police with his bold exploits. He is described as audacious (brash) in the

passage. This means he was bold, daring and fearless when challenging the established authority.

7 This is an historical recount. It gives a brief recount of Hall's life from when he was first arrested in 1862 until his death in 1865. The recount provides names, dates and places.

8 Knowing what made Hall turn to a life of crime provides some understanding of his behaviour and actions. He wasn't merciless. He didn't kill the police when he had the opportunity but he did embarrass them. His actions weren't irrational: there was a reason for them. From the huge attendance at his funeral it can be assumed that many could understand the reasons for Hall's exploits.

READING (Real Test)
Following procedures   Pages 92–93

Egg Decorating

1 B, E **2** D **3** A **4** C **5** B **6** C **7** written response

EXPLANATIONS

1 Egg decorating is a traditional craft. In the article it is reported as being popular in Australia in the 19th Century with both Indigenous and European Australians.

2 The answer is found in food safety tips. It is advised that the egg be kept in the fridge until you are ready to eat it.

3 Sculpting removes layers of the shell, often revealing different colours as the artist cuts deeper into the egg. This implies that the thicker shells from emus or ostriches are more suitable for sculpting.

4 If you intend to keep a decorated egg for any length of time you can protect the design with a 'coating of thinned white glue, clear nail polish or craft finish'.

5 Using the word *you* makes the writing more personal for the reader. The reader will feel that the information is pertinent to him or her specifically. This is a literacy technique used to engage with the reader.

6 Eggs that still contain the yolk and white go bad. Removing the contents of the shell means that the shell will last for a long time: 'Emptied eggshells have nothing inside to spoil, so you can keep them on display for years'.

7 The term 'faint-hearted' means lacking courage or boldness—not bold or daring. A faint-hearted person would be scared of breaking the eggs shells.

WRITING (Real Test)
Description of a scene   Page 95

Tick each correct point.
Read the student's work through once to get an overall view of their response.

Focus on general points
☐ Did it make sense?
☐ Did it flow?
☐ Did it arouse your interest?
☐ Did you want to read on to understand more about the scene?
☐ Was the handwriting readable?

Now focus on the detail. Read the following points and find out whether the student's work has these features.

Focus on content
☐ Is the general scene and basic location clearly stated?
☐ Has the writer provided some physical general description of scene or landscape?
☐ Is the description broken up into parts (e.g. house, tree, pond)?
☐ Does the writer try to put the scene in a time frame (e.g. late autumn day)? (optional)
☐ Is relevant detail included (e.g. long verandah)?
☐ Does the language create clear pictures?
☐ Does the writer make reference to reactions to the scene through several senses (e.g. *cool water*)?
☐ Does the writer convey any feelings created by the scene?
☐ Is there a concluding comment, opinion or reaction to the scene?

Focus on structure, vocabulary, grammar, spelling, punctuation
- ☐ Is the description in the present tense?
- ☐ Was there variation in sentence length and beginnings?
- ☐ Are there paragraphs separating different aspects of the scene?
- ☐ Has the writer used any similes (e.g. *reflected as if in a mirror*)?
- ☐ Is there a generous use of adjectives to enhance the writing (e.g. *cool, shady lawns*)?
- ☐ Are adverbs used effectively (e.g. *sitting snugly by ...*)?
- ☐ Were capital letters where they should have been?
- ☐ Was punctuation correct?
- ☐ Was the spelling of words correct?

Practical suggestion: ask yourself if you can visualise the scene.

Marker's suggestions (optional)

WRITING (Real Test)
Description of a person — Page 96

Tick each correct point.
Read the student's work through once to get an overall view of their response.

Focus on general points
- ☐ Did it make sense?
- ☐ Did it flow?
- ☐ Did it arouse your interest?
- ☐ Did you want to read on to understand more about the person?
- ☐ Was the handwriting readable?

Now focus on the detail. Read the following points and find out whether the student's work has these features.

Focus on content
- ☐ Has the character to be described been established?
- ☐ Has the writer provided some general physical description of the person?

- ☐ Is the description broken up into parts (e.g. appearance, mannerisms, age, interests)?
- ☐ Is relevant detail included (e.g. hair colour)?
- ☐ Does the language create clear pictures?
- ☐ Does the writer make reference to reactions to the person through several senses (e.g. *wiry hair, soft skin*)?
- ☐ Does the writer convey any feelings towards the character?
- ☐ Is there a concluding comment, opinion or reaction to the person? (It can be reflective.)

Focus on structure, vocabulary, grammar, spelling, punctuation
- ☐ Is the description in the present tense?
- ☐ Was there variation in sentence length and beginnings?
- ☐ Are there paragraphs separating different aspects of the character?
- ☐ Has the writer used any similes (e.g. *bent like an old stick*)?
- ☐ Is there a generous use of adjectives to enhance the writing (e.g. *long, bony fingers*)?
- ☐ Are adverbs used effectively (e.g. *smiled happily*)?
- ☐ Were capital letters where they should have been?
- ☐ Was punctuation correct?
- ☐ Was the spelling of words correct?

Practical suggestion: ask yourself if you can visualise the person described.

Marker's suggestions (optional)

WRITING (Real Test)
Book review — Page 97

Tick each correct point.
Read the student's work through once to get an overall view of their response.

Focus on general points
- ☐ Did it make sense?
- ☐ Did it flow?
- ☐ Did the review arouse your interest?

☐ Did you want to read on to understand more about the book?
☐ Was the handwriting readable?

Now focus on the detail. Read the following points and find out whether the student's work has these features.

Focus on content
☐ Has the title been stated correctly?
☐ Do the introductory sentences identify book and author? (Giving cost is optional.)
☐ What is the type of book described (e.g. fantasy, comedy)?
☐ Do you have some idea what the book is about?
☐ Is there a short description of the main characters and events (e.g. evil stepmother)?
☐ Does the writer suggest who would like the book?
☐ Are there short statements of the book's strengths?
☐ Are there short statements of the book's weaknesses (if any)?
☐ Is there information on where the book is available? (optional)
☐ Does the writer comment on the author's style (e.g. *lively paced story full of humorous incidents*)?
☐ Does the writer give a concluding comment, opinion or personal judgement of the book?

Focus on structure, vocabulary, grammar, spelling, punctuation
☐ Is the review in the past tense?
☐ Was there variation in sentence length and beginnings?
☐ Are the review sections broken up into clear paragraphs?
☐ Are adjectives used to enhance the writing (e.g. *long descriptions)*?
☐ Were capital letters where they should have been?
☐ Was punctuation correct?
☐ Was the spelling of words correct?

Practical suggestion: ask yourself if this review provides enough information for you to make a decision on whether or not to read the book.

Marker's suggestions (optional)

WRITING (Real Test)
Review of a production   Page 98

Tick each correct point.
Read the student's work through once to get an overall view of their response.

Focus on general points
☐ Did it make sense?
☐ Did it flow?
☐ Did the review arouse your interest?
☐ Did you want to read on to understand more about the show?
☐ Was the handwriting readable?

Now focus on the detail. Read the following points and find out whether the student's work has these features.

Focus on content
☐ Has the show's title been stated correctly?
☐ Do the introductory sentences identify the show and performers? (Giving the cost is optional.)
☐ Is the type of show described (e.g. concert, play)?
☐ Do you have some idea what the show is about?
☐ Is there a short description of the show's main features (e.g. acting, singing)?
☐ Does the writer suggest who would enjoy the show?
☐ Are there short statements of the show's strengths?
☐ Are there short statements of the show's weaknesses (if any)?
☐ Is there information on where the show can be seen? (optional)
☐ Does the writer comment on the show's style (e.g. *lively paced, amateur)*?
☐ Does the writer give a concluding comment, opinion or personal judgement of the show?

Focus on structure, vocabulary, grammar, spelling, punctuation
☐ Is the review in the past tense?
☐ Was there variation in sentence length and beginnings?
☐ Are the review sections broken up into clear paragraphs?

☐ Are adjectives used to enhance the writing (e.g. *colourful costumes*)?

☐ Were capital letters where they should have been?

☐ Was punctuation correct?

☐ Was the spelling of words correct?

Practical suggestion: ask yourself if this review provides enough information for you to make a decision on whether or not to see the show.

Marker's suggestions (optional)

WEEK 4

NUMBER AND ALGEBRA (Test Your Skills)
Calculator allowed   Page 100

1 153 + 786 + 987 + 11 = 1937

2 8007 − 2398 = 5609

3 Missing number = 986 − 235
                    = 751

4 Missing number = 896 ÷ 7
                    = 128

5 Use inverse operations:
Original number = 42 × 5
                  = 210
Margaret's number was 210.

6 As 1000 ÷ 7 = 142 with remainder. Now as 142 × 7 = 994, the remainder was 6.

7 Consider each of the choices:
51 ÷ 4 = 12 with remainder 3
This is the correct answer. (Checking others: 62 has remainder 2; 76 has no remainder; 85 has remainder 1 when divided by 4)

8 $\frac{3}{4}$ of 600 = 3 [a b/c] 4 × 600
                  = 450

9 For $9\frac{1}{6}$, multiply 6 by 9 and then add 1.
This means $9\frac{1}{6} = \frac{55}{6}$ and so $x = 55$.

10 As $2\frac{1}{5} = \frac{11}{5}$ and $3\frac{4}{5} = \frac{19}{5}$, we can find the middle of 11 and 19 which is 15.
As $\frac{15}{5} = 3$, the middle of the numbers is 3.
Also, 3 is $\frac{4}{5}$ more than $2\frac{1}{5}$ and $\frac{4}{5}$ less than $3\frac{4}{5}$.

11 $\frac{3}{4} \times \frac{1}{2}$ = 3 [a b/c] 4 × 1 [a b/c] 2
            = $\frac{3}{8}$

12 $1\frac{1}{4} - ? = \frac{3}{4}$, means ? = $1\frac{1}{4} - \frac{3}{4}$
            = 1 [a b/c] 1 [a b/c] 4 − 3 [a b/c] 4
            = $\frac{1}{2}$

13 $\frac{15}{35} = \frac{5 \times 3}{5 \times 7} = \frac{3}{7}$, or 15 [a b/c] 35 = $\frac{3}{7}$

14 As $\frac{12}{48} = \frac{12 \times 1}{12 \times 4} = \frac{1}{4}$, which is 25%

15 3 [a b/c] 4 × 60 = 45, which means $45.

16 Page numbers are 2, 12, 20, 21, 22, 23, 24, 25, 26, 27, 28, 29, 32, 42, …, 92.
This means 20 2s (as 22 uses 2 twos).

17 As 20% = $\frac{1}{5}$,
Students = $\frac{1}{5} \times 740$
           = 1 [a b/c] 5 × 740
           = 148
148 students purchase lunch.

18 As 10% = $\frac{1}{10}$,
Discount = $\frac{1}{10} \times 79$
            = 7.90
New price = $79 − $7.90
                = $71.10
The new price is $71.10.

19 As $3.75 \times 1.07 = 4.0125$
$= 4.01$ (to nearest hundredth)

20 $37^2 = 1369$
$= 1400$ (to nearest hundred)

21 As $25\% = \dfrac{1}{4}$, then $\dfrac{1}{4}$ of crowd $= 60$

Total crowd $= 4 \times 60$
$= 240$
There are 240 spectators at the game.

NUMBER AND ALGEBRA (Real Test)
Calculator allowed   Page 102

1 A **2** A **3** C **4** C **5** C **6** B **7** C **8** B **9** C **10** A
11 D **12** D **13** A **14** A **15** A **16** 509

EXPLANATIONS

1 $2.304 + 23.04 = 25.344$

2 $18.76 + ? = 51.27$ means $? = 51.27 - 18.76$
$= 32.51$

3 $26.513 \times \underline{\quad} = 26\,513$
The decimal point has moved 3 places to the right. This means it has been multiplied by 1000.

4 $100 \div 6 = 16$ with a remainder.
As $6 \times 16 = 96$, and $100 - 96 = 4$, the remainder was 4. He has 4 cards left.

5 As $96 \times 2 = 192$,
the question is $12 \times \underline{\quad} = 192$
Missing number $= 192 \div 12$
$= 16$
The missing number is 16.

6 As $9 \times 7 + 5 = 63 + 5$
$= 68$ then $7\dfrac{5}{9} = \dfrac{68}{9}$

7 $9.009 \div 0.03 = 300.3$

8 Number of cows $= 16 \times 5 + 7$
$= 80 + 7$
$= 87$
The farmer has 87 cows.

9 For $\dfrac{100}{3}$, 3 into 100 is 33 with a remainder
of 1. This means $\dfrac{100}{3} = 33\dfrac{1}{3}$.

10 $\dfrac{2}{3} = \dfrac{12}{18} = \dfrac{48}{X}$
To find the value of X, firstly consider the numerators: From 2 to 48 we multiply by 24. Now as $3 \times 24 = 72$, then $X = 72$.

11 Number divided by $8 = 5$ and remainder 6
This means the number $= 5 \times 8 + 6$
$= 40 + 6$
$= 46$
Ruby's number is 46.

12 As $20\% = \dfrac{1}{5}$, then $\dfrac{1}{5}$ of full tank $= 800$

Full tank $= 800 \times 5$
$= 4000$
This means the tank will hold 4000 L when full.

13 If Jacob is half Brianna's age and they total 24, it means that Jacob's age is $\dfrac{1}{3}$ of 24.
Jacob is 8 and Brianna is 16. In 5 years Brianna will be 21 and Jacob 13.

14 Total for first 2 months $= 9 + 17$
$= 26$
Total for final 2 months $= 21 + 4$
$= 25$
Difference $= 26 - 25$
$= 1$
The difference is $1.

15 Swimming $= \dfrac{1}{4}$
Fraction remaining after swimming $= \dfrac{3}{4}$
Fraction of course running $= \dfrac{2}{3} \times \dfrac{3}{4}$
$= \dfrac{1}{2}$

This means $\dfrac{1}{4}$ were swimming; $\dfrac{1}{2}$ cycling; so $\dfrac{1}{4}$ will be running.

16 Number $- 298 = 211$
This means number $= 211 + 298$
$= 509$.

MEASUREMENT AND GEOMETRY
(Test Your Skills)
Calculator allowed Page 103

1 1 m equals 100 cm.
As $5 \div 100 = 0.05$, so 5 cm = 0.05 m,
then 2 m 5 cm = 2.05 m.

2 There are 10 mm in 1 cm.
As $0.04 \times 10 = 0.4$, then 0.04 cm = 0.4 mm.

3 There are 60 minutes in 1 hour.
As $6 \times 60 = 360$, and $360 + 27 = 387$,
then 6 h 27 min = 387 minutes.

4 There are 60 minutes in 1 hour.
As $72 \times 60 = 4320$, then Maria's heart
beats 4320 times.

5 As $56 + 52 = 108$ and 60 minutes in 1 hour,
the total is 1 hour 48 minutes.

6 Total $= 8 + 8.5 + 7.5 + 4 + 10.5$
$= 38.5$
Gordon worked 38.5 hours.

7 Total mass $= 871 + 739$
$= 1610$
The total mass is 1610 grams.

8 10 L minus 7 L 200 mL $= 3$ L minus 200 mL
$= 2$ L 800 mL
There is 2 L 800 mL remaining.

9 Area $= 200 \times 100$
$= 20\,000$
Hectares $= 20\,000 \div 10\,000$
$= 2$
The area is 2 hectares.

10 Area $= \dfrac{1}{2} \times 9 \times 7$
$= 31.5$
The area is 31.5 cm².

11 Volume $= 12 \times 10 \times 9$
$= 1080$
Volume is 1080 cm³.

12 Length $\times 18 = 360$
Length $= 360 \div 18$
$= 20$
The length is 20 cm.

13 There are 4.5 100s in 450.
This means we multiply 4.5 by 9:
Petrol $= 4.5 \times 9$
$= 40.5$
Uses 40.5 litres.

14 There are 1.5 100s in 150.
This means we multiply 1.5 by 14:
Payment $= 1.5 \times 14$
$= 21$
Jo is paid $21.

15 There are 60 seconds in 1 minute.
Distance $= 12 \times 60$
$= 720$
Goran travels 720 metres in one minute.

16 The ratio is 3 to 2.
This means 2 parts $= 60$ so
1 part $= 30$, and
3 parts $= 90$
This means 90 bus travellers.

17 Runs $= 6.8 \times 20$
$= 136$
136 runs required.

18 Distance $= 66 \times 3$
$= 198$
Gerard will travel for 198 km.

19 First, change 100 cm to 1 m
Area $= 1 \times 1$
$= 1$
The area is 1 m².

MEASUREMENT AND GEOMETRY (Real Test)
Calculator allowed Page 105

1 D **2** C **3** 56 **4** D **5** A **6** A **7** B **8** B **9** D **10** 21
11 B **12** B **13** 165 **14** C **15** 105 **16** 6.2

EXPLANATIONS

1 Distance $=$ Speed $\times$ Time
$= 18 \times 2$
$= 36$
Jack travelled 36 km.

2 As 9 into 54 is 6, then we multiply 6 by 100
Distance $= 6 \times 100$
$= 600$
The car travels 600 km.

3 By counting, the area of the shape is 14 squares. As each square is 4 cm²,
Sum of areas = 14 × 4
= 56
The area is 56 cm².

4 Mass = 4.5 × 500
= 2250
The mass is 2250 grams, or 2.25 kg.

5 There are five 8 litres in a 40-litre container.
We multiply 5 by 12:
Time = 5 × 12
= 60
It takes 60 seconds, or 1 minute.

6 Area of each face = 5² = 25
As there are 6 faces,
Total area = 25 × 6
= 150
The total area is 150 cm².

7 1 h 21 min = 81 min
Total = 81 + 49
= 130
This means 130 minutes, or 2 h 10 min.

8 Area = 64 cm².
Side will be 8 cm, as 8² = 64.

9 If ratio is 4 to 3, there is a total of 7 'parts'.
As 4 parts out of 7 parts is red then $\frac{4}{7}$ of 21 is 12. This means 12 red balls.

10 Time from 6:30 to 10:00 is 3.5 hours.
Payment = 3.5 × 6
= 21
Jan is paid $21 for babysitting.

11 From the grid Whitebridge to Hamilton is 3 units.
As 3 units = 6 km, then 1 unit = 2 km
Now Whitebridge to Glendale is 8.5 units means 8.5 × 2 = 17 km.

12 As 15 mm = 1.5 cm, and using 1 cm = 2 m, then 1.5 × 2 m = 3 m
Length is 3 m.

13 Remove 250 from 415 = 415 − 250
= 165
Kahlia has to remove 165 g.

14 As 600 grams = 0.6 kg,
Price = 6.99 × 0.6
= 4.194
The price is $4.194, which is closest to $4.20.

15 Number of US dollars = 150 × 0.70
= 105
Mitchell receives 105 US dollars.

16 There are 10 000 m² in 1 hectare.
Number of hectares = 62 000 ÷ 10 000
= 6.2
This means 6.2 hectares.

NUMBER AND ALGEBRA/MEASUREMENT AND GEOMETRY/STATISTICS AND PROBABILITY (Test Your Skills)
Calculator allowed   Page 106

1 Mean = $\frac{14 + 17 + 45 + 16}{4}$
= (14 + 17 + 45 + 16) ÷ 4
= 23

2 Mean = $\frac{2.5 + 4.5 + 5.5 + 6.5 + 8.5}{5}$
= (2.5 + 4.5 + 5.5 + 6.5 + 8.5) ÷ 5
= 5.5

3 Mean = $1\frac{1}{2}$ + 3 + $2\frac{1}{4}$ + $1\frac{1}{4}$ ÷ 4
= 8 ÷ 4
= 2

4 Change 2 kg 40 g to 2040 g.
Mean = (2040 + 810 + 245 + 110 + 270) ÷ 5
= 3475 ÷ 5
= 695
The mean is 695 g.

5 Change 5 L to 5000 mL and 4 L to 4000 mL
Mean = (5000 + 450 + 4000 + 750 + 800) ÷ 5
= 11 000 ÷ 5
= 2200
The mean is 2200 mL or 2.2 L.

6 Change 96 cm to 0.96 m.
Mean = (1.41 + 1.16 + 1.07 + 0.96) ÷ 4
= 1.15
The mean is 1.15 m.

7 The sequence is counting forward by 54.
New number = 139 + 54
= 193
[Checking: 193 + 54 = 247]
The missing number is 193.

8 The rule is: 'bottom number = top number squared + 1'
Missing number $= 8^2 + 1$
$= 64 + 1$
$= 65$

9 The rule is: 'bottom number = 5 times top number + 2'
Missing number $= 5 \times 10 + 2$
$= 50 + 2$
$= 52$

10 The rule is: 'bottom number = 6 times top number + 1'
Missing number $= 6 \times 8 + 1$
$= 48 + 1$
$= 49$

11 Consider each of the choices:
2, 6: $2 \times 6 = 12$; $2 + 6 = 8 \neq 7$
6, 6: $6 \times 6 = 36 \neq 12$; $6 + 6 = 12 \neq 7$
1, 12: $1 \times 12 = 12$; $1 + 12 = 13 \neq 7$
3, 4: $3 \times 4 = 12$; $3 + 4 = 7$
This means the numbers are 3 and 4.

12 Start with Penelope's answer of 23 and work backwards using inverse operations:
23 – 5 is 18 and then halve it to get 9.
Penelope started with the number 9.

13 Third angle = 180 – (70 + 30)
= 180 – 100
= 80
The other angle is 80°.

14 Consider each of the choices:
Isosceles: possible with 70°, 70°, 40°
Scalene: possible with 70°, 60°, 50°
Right-angled: possible with 70°, 90°, 20°
Equilateral: impossible as each is 60°
The triangle cannot be equilateral.

15 Other angle = 180 – (90 + 40)
= 180 – 130
= 50
The other angle is 50°.

NUMBER AND ALGEBRA/MEASUREMENT AND GEOMETRY/STATISTICS AND PROBABILITY (Real Test)
Calculator allowed   **Page 108**

1 A 2 C 3 A 4 A 5 D 6 A 7 A, D 8 C 9 C 10 B
11 B 12 17 13 B 14 300 15 75 16 8

EXPLANATIONS

1 Change 200 g to 0.2 kg, 750 g to 0.75 kg
$$\text{Average} = \frac{2.3 + 1.6 + 0.2 + 0.75 + 1.09}{5}$$
$= (2.3 + 1.6 + 0.2 + 0.75 + 1.09) \div 5$
$= 5.94 \div 5$
$= 1.188$
The average mass is 1.188 kg.

2 Change 2.6 m to 260 cm and 3.3 m to 330 cm
$$\text{Average} = \frac{260 + 98 + 330 + 72}{4}$$
$= (260 + 98 + 330 + 72) \div 4$
$= 760 \div 4$
$= 190$
The average length is 190 cm.

3 There were 80 students surveyed.
Total of students in table = 61
Difference = 80 – 61 = 19
19 females read one book.

4 From table, 2 males read more than 2 books.
$$\text{Probability} = \frac{2}{80} = \frac{1}{40}$$

5 $x = 180 - 37$
$= 143$

6 $y = 180 - (102 + 53)$
$= 180 - 155$
$= 25$

7 If two angles were 20° and 40° then the third angle is 180° – (20° + 40°) = 120°. If the two angles were 10° and 20° then the third angle is 180° – (10° + 20°) = 150°. The third angle could be 120° or 150°.

8 The numbers are counting forward by 13.
Next number = 63 + 13
= 76
The next number is 76.

9 The numbers are counting backwards by 4. The pattern is 113, 109, 105, 101, 97, 93, ... This means the sixth number is 93.

10 The rule is: 'bottom number = 4 times the top number'
Missing number = 4 × 12
= 48
The missing number is 48.

11 Using the rule: 'bottom number = 4 times the top number'
Bottom number = 4 × 20
= 80
The bottom number is 80.

12 Continuing the pattern: 1, 5, 9, 13, 17 [adding 4] The missing value is 17.

13 1, 5, 9, 13, 17, 21
The 6th diagram would have 21 squares.

14 Length of road = 30 × 10 km
= 300 km
The road would be 300 km.

15 Write the pattern: 100, 95, 90, 85, 80, 75, ...
The sixth number is 75.

16 As 1640 ÷ ? = 205,   then ? = 1640 ÷ 205
= 8
The missing number is 8.

SPELLING (Real Test)
Common misspellings   Pages 110–111

1 typist

2 troupe

3 technique

4 refugee

5 shoeing

6 shield

7 enjoyable

8 plasticine

9 stare

10 levelling

11 withholding

12 monotonous

13 chronological

14 murmuring

15 whining

16 twelfth

17 wherever

18 responsible

19 thieves

20 reign

21 equipment

22 volume

23 strict

24 issuing

25 fashionable

GRAMMAR AND PUNCTUATION (Real Test)
Pronouns, prepositions and punctuation   Pages 113–115

1 A **2** verb: coiled, adverb: quickly, preposition: around, adjective: surprised **3** C **4** A **5** D **6** C **7** B **8** A **9** D **10** that **11** C **12** B **13** C **14** A **15** B **16** D **17** C **18** A **19** D **20** A, B **21** C **22** won't **23** B **24** If, Wattle, Grove **25** C

EXPLANATIONS

1 This is a grammar question. The correct word is *enters*.
Tip: Singular subjects (nouns) need singular verbs; plural subjects (nouns) need plural verbs. In this case *enters* must be used because there is a *fleet* (one) of ships.

2 This is a grammar question. Simply put, verbs are action or doing words, adverbs modify verbs, prepositions show position and adjectives describe nouns.

3 This is a grammar question. The correct word is the verb *has done*.
Tip: With the verb *done* you need a 'helper' —another verb to 'help' it. *Have*, *has* and *had* can be helping verbs: *The extra paint has done ...* The helping verb is always close to the verb it is helping. Because there is

only one lot of extra paint (single noun) the correct single verb is *has done*. *Did* is the simple past tense form of *do*. It does not need any helping or auxiliary verb, such as *had*.

4 This is a grammar question. The correct word is the noun *advice*.
Tip: *Advice* is an uncountable noun (Remember: it ends with *ice*, which is also a noun). Such nouns only have a singular form —*had (enough) advice*. The 'ise' ending is a verb.

5 This is a grammar question. The correct word is the verb *was*.
Tip: Singular subjects (nouns) need singular verbs; plural subjects (nouns) need plural verbs. Many pronouns act as singular nouns. In this case, *was* must be used because it refers to a single group (of *nobody*).

6 This is a grammar question. The correct word is the conjunction *but also*.
Tip: In English *not only* and *but also* make a pair (as do *either* and *or*). *Not only* joins two parts of a sentence adding additional information relating to Wesley's photography.

7 This is a punctuation question. The correct sentence is: *Jason's team's two wins were a shock to the supporters.*
Tip: *Jason* is a singular proper noun and team is a singular collective noun; both only require an 's. *Wins* does not take an apostrophe.

8 This is a grammar question. The correct sentence is: *His intentions are good, but his rough manner tends to intimidate.*
Tip: Singular subjects (nouns) need singular verbs; plural subjects (nouns) need plural verbs. In this case, *are* must be used for *intentions* because there is more than one intention. His (*rough*) *manner* takes a singular verb (*tends*). *Manner* is an uncountable noun. Such nouns only have a singular form of the verb—*tends*.

9 This is a grammar question. The correct word is the verb *equipped*.

Tip: 'Equipt' is incorrect. It is not an irregular verb. In words with *qu*, the *qu* tends to act as a single sound and the following vowels often act as a single vowel (e.g. *quizzed*, *squatted*).

10 This is a grammar question. *That* is used to single out something that is distinctive—the frog's endangered condition. It refers to a specific creature. *Who* is used to refer to people. *Which* is often used to refer to animals or things, but to be used correctly it is generally accepted a comma would be required after *frog*.

11 This is a grammar question. The correct sentence is: *"I know you two used the computer after I had left!" accused Georgia.*
Tip: The correct spelling for the past tense of *use* is *used*. *Had left* is the correct verb. In this case, the verb *left* needs a 'helper'— another verb to 'help' it. *Have*, *has* and *had* can be helping verbs: *had left* ... The helping verb is always close to the verb it is helping.

12 This is a grammar question. The correct sentence is: *Peter said to stop work so we put our pens down.*
Tip: This is an example of reported or indirect speech. The actual words spoken are not recorded so quotation marks are not required.

13 This is a grammar question. The correct sentence is: *If anybody thinks dogs are worse than cats then they are right!*
Tip: When adjectives are used to compare we usually add *er* or *est* (*cleaner*, *cleanest*). Some adjectives are irregular. The correct form for *worse* starts with *bad*, *worse* and *worst*. 'More worse' and 'worser' are incorrect.

14 This is a punctuation question. *They departed on Thursday 22 January.*
Tip: When writing the date, the article *the* and preposition *of* are omitted.

15 This is a grammar question. The correct word is the verb *lay*.
Tip: *Lied* means telling an untruth. *Laid* is the past tense of *lay*. (It is also how hens produce eggs). The past tense of *lie* is *lay*.

16 This is a punctuation question. The correct sentence is: *The reins are not yours, they belong to the stable and its owner's family.*
Tip: *Reins* is a plural noun referring to the straps used to control horses. *Yours* and *its* are possessive pronouns and do not require an apostrophe. As it is the owner's family, the apostrophe goes before the *s*.

17 This is a punctuation question. The correct sentence is: *Joseph asked, "Which position do you play?"*
Tip: Only the actual words spoken and the question mark are enclosed in the inverted commas (quotation marks). The question asked starts with a capital letter.

18 This is a grammar question. The correct word is the preposition *against*.
Tip: Prepositions put events in position in time or place. In English it is common usage to use some prepositions in particular situations: *the shovel would be leant against the wall.*

19 This is a punctuation question. The correct sentence is: *John has requested a full report, hasn't he?*
Tip: The sentence has two parts. It begins with a statement (*John has requested a full report*), and concludes with a question tag (*hasn't he?*). The two parts are separated by a comma. Question tags have the opposite verb to the introductory statement (*has, hasn't*).

20 This is a punctuation question. The correct sentence is: *The chair, made of wood, belongs to my aunt who is living in Adelaide.*
Tip: The words *made of wood* provide information about the chair but do not change the meaning of the sentence. Commas are used to separate parts of the sentence and to make the meaning clear.

21 This is a grammar question. The correct word is the adverb *carefully*.
Tip: *Carefully* is an adverb. Many adverbs end with *ly*. *Carefully* tells the reader how Lyn *wrote* (verb). *Careful* is an adjective. 'Carefuller' is not a word.

22 This is a punctuation question. The correct word is *won't*.
Tip: *Won't* is an unusual contraction, as it is short for *will not*.

23 This is a grammar question. The correct word is the verb *is*.
Tip: *Stationery* is an uncountable noun and only has a singular form. It must take a singular verb (*is*). The sentence is in the present tense.

24 This is a grammar question. In this sentence capital letters are required for the first word (If) and the two parts of the proper noun (Wattle Grove).

25 This is a grammar question. The correct choice is the term *an envelope*.
Tip: In a series, if one of the items is preceded by an article (*a* or *an*) all the items must follow the same pattern. *An* is the correct article as it starts with a consonant sound even though the initial letter is a vowel.

READING (Real Test)
Understanding explanations **Pages 118–119**

What is a phobia?

1 A 2 B 3 D 4 1C, 2D, 3A, 4B 5 D 6 A 7 B, F 8 C

EXPLANATIONS

1 This is a straight fact-finding question. You have to know how to apply the meaning of words in the text to the question. A phobia is a distressing anxiety. It is described in the passage as an abnormal and absurd, even morbid, fear that may be close to uncontrolled panic.

2 The writer describes most phobias as absurd because there is often no logical reason for the fear.

3 A child's fear of the dark often disappears when the child matures (gets older).

4 This is a matter of reading the list of phobias carefully and matching each phobia with the associated fear: arachnophobia/spiders, agoraphobia/crowded spaces, hydrophobia/water, haemophobia/blood.

5 Claustrophobia is the fear of small or confined spaces—such as in a car. It is not likely to be experienced on a hike, which is in the open air.

6 People with phobias often go to extreme measures to avoid confronting their fear.

7 A person with haemophobia has a fear of blood. Most people, whatever their occupation, experience the sight of blood. It would be most difficult if an ambulance driver or veterinarian (surgeon) had haemophobia.

8 A symptom of a phobia is a cold sweat. Cold sweats are often associated with the onset of a panic attack.

READING (Real Test)
Understanding explanations   Pages 120–121

Lava Tubes

1 C **2** B **3** A **4** D **5** B **6** They are blind. **7** A **8** D **9** 20 metres

EXPLANATIONS

1 All lava tubes are the result of past volcanic activity. The Undara Lava Tubes are significant because they are the longest (160 km), and most accessible, in the world.

2 Read the text carefully. A lava tube forms under a lava crust. The crust solidifies but the lava underneath keeps flowing. When the lava stops flowing, the tunnels remains.

3 Sections of the lava tube have collapsed. Over centuries the roofs of the tubes, in places, collapsed.

4 Patches of rainforest follow the line of the lava tube. It is evident in places where the roof of the tube has collapsed.

5 The pungent (strong) smell in the lava tube comes from decomposing animal and vegetable matter—especially bat droppings.

6 The animals (all living creatures) living in the lava tubes have adapted and evolved away from sunlight, many of which are blind having no use for eyesight.

7 Basalt is a black volcanic rock. The basalt tunnels are black.

8 The floor of the tunnel was once curved—part of a circular tube. Over thousands of years silt and dust along with masses of organic matter have covered the floor—making a flat surface—a false floor. In some places it is over 6 m thick.

9 This is a straight fact-finding question. The tubes have a diameter of 20 m. Diameter refers to the greatest distance across a circle.

READING (Real Test)
Understanding explanations   Pages 122–123

Jigsaws

1 2 **2** C **3** written response **4** D **5** A **6** B **7** D **8** C

EXPLANATIONS

1 The word jigsaw has two meanings. It is a type of saw for cutting sharp curves. The word also applies to the tiling puzzle originally made using a jigsaw.

2 Although the modern jigsaw is a power tool, its special feature is the width of the blade. It is narrow and can cut neat, tight curves.

3 The earliest jigsaws were designed as educational aids: 'The first jigsaw puzzles were designed as geography teaching devices'. They were map puzzles.

4 The significant advance in jigsaw puzzles was the introduction of interlocking pieces.

5 This is a straight fact-finding question. The answer is directly in the text: 'The first of these had a picture of a dairymaid offering a young man some fresh milk'.

6 There is an element of logic to this question: 'Jigsaws for children come in a variety of sizes, rated by the number of pieces to suit various age groups'. Obviously a very young child would not cope with many small pieces.

7 Without a picture there would be no clue where each piece went except by its shape. As all shapes are similar, a blank jigsaw would be the most difficult.

8 This is a straight fact-finding question. The question asks for the largest commercial jigsaw—a jigsaw that would be sold in a shop. The largest commercial puzzle has 24 000 pieces. It is not the largest jigsaw.

WRITING (Real Test)
Explanation 1   Page 125

Tick each correct point.
Read the student's work through once to get an overall view of their response.

Focus on general points
☐ Did it make sense?
☐ Did it flow?
☐ Did the writing and subject arouse your interest?
☐ Did you want to read on?
☐ Was the handwriting readable?

Now focus on the detail. Read the following points and find out whether the student's work has these features.

Focus on content
☐ Has the subject been clearly identified?
☐ Do the introductory sentences clearly identify (and define) the subject?
☐ Are the features of the subject precisely described (e.g. colour, size, shape)?
☐ Does the information sound factual and informed?
☐ Are the uses of the subject explained?
☐ Is there any information explaining specific or unusual instances of use? (optional)
☐ Does the writer suggest who would use the object?
☐ Does the writer give a concluding comment, opinion or personal judgement of the subject?

Focus on structure, vocabulary, grammar, spelling, punctuation
☐ Was there variation in sentence length and beginnings?

☐ Have 'longer' sentences been used (sentences with clauses beginning with words such as *so, because, when, if*)?
☐ Are the sections broken up into clear paragraphs?
☐ Are the paragraphs based on single topics (e.g. shape, use, how to operate)?
☐ Have subheadings been used? (optional)
☐ Have technical or scientific words been used?
☐ Do some sentences begin with such words as *because, if* and *when*?
☐ Is the explanation in the present tense?
☐ Are adjectives used to enhance the writing (e.g. *strong cord*)?
☐ Were capital letters where they should have been?
☐ Was punctuation correct?
☐ Was the spelling of words correct?

Practical suggestion: ask yourself if this explanation provides enough information for you to use the object.

Marker's suggestions (optional)

WRITING (Real Test)
Explanation 2   Page 126

Tick each correct point.
Read the student's work through once to get an overall view of their response.

Focus on general points
☐ Did it make sense?
☐ Did it flow?
☐ Did the writing and subject arouse your interest?
☐ Did you want to read on?
☐ Was the handwriting readable?

Now focus on the detail. Read the following points and find out whether the student's work has these features.

Focus on content

- ☐ Has the subject been clearly identified?
- ☐ Do the introductory sentences clearly identify (and define) the subject?
- ☐ Are the features of the subject precisely described (e.g. colour, size, shape)?
- ☐ Does the information sound factual and informed?
- ☐ Are the uses of the subject explained?
- ☐ Is there any information explaining specific or unusual instances of use? (optional)
- ☐ Does the writer suggest who would use the object?
- ☐ Does the writer give a concluding comment, opinion or personal judgement of the subject?

Focus on structure, vocabulary, grammar, spelling, punctuation

- ☐ Was there variation in sentence length and beginnings?
- ☐ Have 'longer' sentences been used (sentences with clauses beginning with words such as *so, because, when, if*)?
- ☐ Are the sections broken up into clear paragraphs?
- ☐ Are the paragraphs based on single topics (e.g. shape, use, how to operate)?
- ☐ Have subheadings been used? (optional)
- ☐ Have technical or scientific words been used?
- ☐ Do some sentences begin with such words as *because, if* and *when*?
- ☐ Is the explanation in the present tense?
- ☐ Are adjectives used to enhance the writing (e.g. *strong cord*)?
- ☐ Were capital letters where they should have been?
- ☐ Was punctuation correct?
- ☐ Was the spelling of words correct?

Practical suggestion: ask yourself if this explanation provides enough information for you to use the object.

Marker's suggestions (optional)

WRITING (Real Test)
Report from an outline   Page 127

Tick each correct point.
Read the student's work through once to get an overall view of their response.

Focus on general points

- ☐ Did it make sense?
- ☐ Did it flow?
- ☐ Did the writing and subject arouse your interest?
- ☐ Did you want to read on?
- ☐ Was the handwriting readable?

Now focus on the detail. Read the following points and find out whether the student's work has these features.

Focus on content

- ☐ Has the title been stated and does it suggest the subject matter?
- ☐ Do the introductory sentences clearly identify time and place?
- ☐ Are the events in chronological (time) order?
- ☐ Does the information sound factual or informed?
- ☐ Is kayaking briefly explained? (optional)
- ☐ Have personal comments or responses been added (usually only a single or a few words, e.g. *foolishly*)?
- ☐ Does the writer give a concluding comment, opinion or personal judgment of the subject?

Focus on structure, vocabulary, grammar, spelling, punctuation

- ☐ Are the facts presented in full sentences?
- ☐ Was there a variation in sentence length and beginnings?
- ☐ Do some sentences begin with adverbs of time (e.g. *later, after a while*)?
- ☐ Are the sections broken up into clear paragraphs?
- ☐ Is some information expanded to make short paragraphs?
- ☐ Have some EXPLANATIONS of terms been used (e.g. flagged area, transported)?
- ☐ Do some sentences begin with such words as *because, if* and *when*?
- ☐ Is the explanation in the past tense?

☐ Are adjectives used to enhance the writing (e.g. *rough surf*)?
☐ Were capital letters where they should have been?
☐ Was punctuation correct?
☐ Was the spelling of words correct?

Marker's suggestions (optional)

WRITING (Real Test)
Response to a picture
Page 128

Tick each correct point.
Read the student's work through once to get an overall view of their response.

Focus on general points
☐ Did it make sense?
☐ Did it flow?
☐ Did the writing and subject arouse your interest?
☐ Did you want to read on?
☐ Was the handwriting readable?

Now focus on the detail. Read the following points and find out whether the student's work has these features.

Focus on content
☐ Do the introductory sentences clearly identify time and place?
☐ Is there a brief description of the picture and its possible origins?
☐ Does the response relate to a real or imagined event?
☐ Does the response sound informed?
☐ Has the writer included some personal feelings?
☐ Does the writer predict an outcome of the incident in the picture (e.g. what may have happened next)?
☐ Have personal comments or responses been added (usually only a single or a few words, e.g. *sorry*)?
☐ Does the writer give a concluding comment, opinion or personal judgement of the subject?

Focus on structure, vocabulary, grammar, spelling, punctuation
☐ Was there variation in sentence length and beginnings?
☐ Do some sentences begin with adverbs of time (e.g. later, after a while)?
☐ Does the writer include adjectives and adverbs as emotive words (e.g. <u>sad</u> eyes)?
☐ Do descriptive sentences make reference to several senses (e.g. <u>warm</u> fur, <u>soft</u> purring)?
☐ Are different aspects of the scene in different paragraphs?
☐ Is the explanation in the past tense?
☐ Were capital letters where they should have been?
☐ Was punctuation correct?
☐ Was the spelling of words correct?

Marker's suggestions (optional)

SAMPLE TEST PAPERS
SAMPLE TEST PAPER 1

LITERACY – WRITING
Page 130

Persuasive text

Tick each correct point.
Read the student's work through once to get an overall view of their response.

Focus on general points
☐ Did it make sense?
☐ Did it flow? Were the arguments logical and relevant?
☐ Did the opinions expressed arouse any feelings/reactions?
☐ Was the body of the writing mainly in the third person?
☐ Did you want to read on to understand/ appreciate the writer's point of view?
☐ Were the arguments convincing?
☐ Has the writer been assertive (e.g. the use of is rather than a less definite term)?

□ Was the handwriting readable?

□ Was the writing style suitable for a persuasive text (objective; not casual or dismissive)?

Now focus on the detail. Read each of the following points and find out whether the student's work has these features.

Focus on content

□ Did the opening sentence(s) focus on the topic?

□ Was the writer's point of view established early in the writing?

□ Did the writer include any evidence to support his or her opinion?

□ Did the writer include information relevant to his or her experiences?

□ Were the points/arguments raised by the writer easy to follow?

□ Did the writing follow the format with an introduction, the body of the text and a conclusion?

□ Were personal opinions included?

□ Was the concluding paragraph relevant to the topic?

Focus on structure, vocabulary, grammar, spelling, punctuation

□ Was there a variety of sentence lengths, types and beginnings?

□ Was a new paragraph started for each additional argument or point?

□ Has the writer used any similes (e.g. as clear as crystal) to stress a point raised?

□ Did the writer avoid approximations such as probably, perhaps and maybe?

□ Did the writer use such phrases as I know … and It is important to …?

□ Did the writer refer to the question in the points raised (A good way to do this is to use the key words from the question or the introduction.)?

□ Has the writer used any less common words correctly?

□ Was indirect speech used correctly?

□ Were adjectives used to improve descriptions (e.g. expensive buildings)?

□ Were adverbs used effectively (e.g. firstly)?

□ Were capital letters used correctly?

□ Was punctuation used correctly?

□ Was the spelling of words correct?

Marker's suggestions (optional)

LITERACY – READING　　Pages 131–144

How to Make Finger Puppets

1 C **2** cotton wool **3** A **4** B **5** C **6** A
7 puppet theatre

EXPLANATIONS

1 The clue is in the first line: make these for your younger brother or sister. They are not a means of recycling old clothes. The only clothing involved is an old glove or two.

2 This is a fact-finding question. It is suggested that the beard for a finger puppet could be cotton wool: 'Add a beard to one or two with small pieces of cotton wool'.

3 The marking pen is used to draw on clothing features.

4 To make a bald-headed puppet, simply select an old glove finger that has a hole in the end. The person's fingertip becomes the bald head.

5 You have to use your experience to help answer this question. Because finger puppets are small and fiddly to make, it could be a frustrating and difficult task for someone developing manipulative skills.

6 The way the information is set out suggests that it would be in a craft book. It is not likely to be in a holiday's activity book— more an activity for a wet day at home. The bits and pieces are not necessarily those taken on holidays. Holidays usually are directed towards active physical activities. As the puppets only require one old glove, this activity is unlikely to feature in a recycling guide.

7 The cereal box can be made into a small puppet theatre. This is stated in the text.

Check Your Answers

Rough Riding

8 A **9** B, F **10** written response **11** B **12** D
13 A **14** 3, 2, 4, 1

EXPLANATIONS

8 In paragraph two, the text states: 'Bull riding involves a rider getting onto a large bull and attempting to stay mounted for eight seconds'.

9 Rough riding events include three competitions, two of which are saddle bronc riding and bareback bronc riding. The other event is bull riding.

10 The 'bull fighters' are in the arena to encourage the bull to 'perform'—'to influence its movements and enhance the ride'. They do not rescue a fallen rider but protect the rider from being injured by the bull.

11 The last paragraph states that bull riders feel that the use of spurs is justified as there is no criticism of the use of spurs in equestrian (horse) events.

12 The most dangerous time is at the end of the ride, particularly if the rider has been thrown and is vulnerable from the antics of the bull.

13 The electric prod is only used to 'encourage' the bull to leave the chute so that the ride can start.

14 This is a sequencing question. The correct order is: **1** The enclosed bull is mounted by the rider; **2** The competitor nods his head; **3** The bull breaks clear of the chute; **4** A buzzer announces the completion of a successful ride.

Car Boot Sale

15 twice a year **16** C **17** D **18** A **19** C **20** A
21 B **22** *Rough Riding* B, C; *Car boot sale* A, D

EXPLANATIONS

15 A biannual event happens twice a year—'bi' indicating two. Biannual is not to be confused with 'biennial' meaning every two years. You will see in the heading the word next, which indicates that there has already been a sale in 2020.

16 The Cambulla School Car Boot Sale is being held at the Cambulla Community Hall, as advertised under the pictures of the cars.

17 A mini stall is a blanket-sized stall (possibly on the ground). This information is in the tear-off slip.

18 The pet show is a new activity. The word inaugural means the first of its kind. If it is the first, then it is a new feature of the sale.

19 The organisers are promoting the event as a social event. This is indicated by the nature of the event and the features provided (e.g. face painting) but also as a 'friendly place'.

20 Just above the tear-off slip, participants are advised to pay on Friday. This is the Friday before the event. Insurance is included in the fee. Anything can be sold at the Cambulla Car Boot Sale. Mini stalls are restricted to toys.

21 This is a question where you must interpret the text within the context of the poster but also use your knowledge and experience to answer the question. The word *junior* implies a younger person. As the sale is at a primary school it is also implied that it would be a junior from the school.

22 The *Rough Riding* text describes what rough riding is and explains what certain events are about. The *Car boot sale* is intended to persuade people to either join in or attend. It also advises what must be done to participate.

The Wild Colonial Boy

23 C **24** B **25** 2, 1, 4, 3 **26** A **27** 1 B; 2 C; 3 A; 4 D
28 C **29** B

EXPLANATIONS

23 When you read the poem through you will see that it tells a story, in a poetic format, of the colonial days. There is no indication that Jack Doolan was a respected hero (he was loved by his parents). A ballad is not just a song that has survived for a long time—it also tells a story. The clue is in the introductory paragraph.

㉔ You have to know the meanings of the words and how they apply to the ballad. Doolan was outside the law: He 'stuck up the Beechworth mail coach / And robbed Judge MacEvoy'. Doolan was also flamboyant, which means he was showy and dashing. When told to surrender Doolan 'drew his pistol from his belt / And waved it like a toy, / "I'll fight, but not surrender," cried / The Wild Colonial Boy'.

㉕ This is a sequencing question. The correct order is: 1 Doolan left Castlemaine for Australia; 2 Doolan robbed Judge MacEvoy of his gold; 3 Doolan was faced with a warrant for his arrest; 4 Doolan engaged in a gunfight with three troopers.

㉖ You have to make a judgement from the way Doolan reacted to events and people. The law had put Doolan in jail (robbing Doolan's mother of a son) and Doolan saw this as a far worse crime than taking a judge's gold.

㉗ This is a fact-finding question. Reading the text carefully you will see that: 1 Judge MacEvoy was robbed; 2 Trooper Davis brought down Doolan; 3 Jack Doolan held up a coach; 4 Trooper Kelly was shot by Doolan.

㉘ You have to make a judgement from the way Doolan reacted to events and people. He was a criminal but he did have the attributes of daring. He challenged authority brazenly and openly. Even in his death Doolan is portrayed as heroic—he lost a fight where he was outnumbered three to one.

㉙ This is an inference-type question. The Doolan family believed they had been done an injustice which motivated Jack to embark on a life of crime. However, his crimes were only directed at those who had caused him grief. *He'd never rob a needy man / Or one who acted square. Square* is colonial slang for being fair and honest. The authorities in Jack's experience were not this!

What is wildlife rehabilitation?

30 C **31** D **32** A **33** B **34** *Colonial Boy* A, D;
Wildlife rehabilitation B, C **35** C **36** A, F

EXPLANATIONS

㉚ Kindness is not enough. A wildlife career needs patience to nurse sick baby animals back to health. A carer also needs emotional stamina (strength) in that they often see sick, injured and dying animals. Their efforts may not always be successful.

㉛ Wildlife rehabilitation is mostly about returning sick or injured or orphaned animals back to their natural habitat. Attending to animals' needs is an early step in this process.

㉜ The passage is an information report on the difficulties of being a wildlife carer, and the skills, time and commitment required. It is not a call for volunteer carers. Finding suitable properties for wildlife release is a small part of the overall program.

㉝ To determine which statement is true, read through the whole passage. Test the statements against the facts provided. Wildlife carers often put animals in cages. Cages are required when capturing distressed animals. A clue to the answer lies in the fact that one of a carer's duties is to clean cages.

㉞ The *Colonial Boy* text entertains the reader with a poetic rendition of a historical event. The *Wildlife rehabilitation* text explains the function of wildlife rehabilitation and informs the reader of some requirements of people involved in the activity.

㉟ A wildlife carer might use their own home when caring for young orphaned animals. Some animals are so young they need feeding every hour. It is implied that the home is the most convenient place for such demanding attention.

㊱ This is a fact-finding question: 'In Victoria, wildlife rehabilitators require a permit to care for native wildlife' and they need to be trained.

Going Down Canal Locks

37 B, E **38** D **39** 4, 2, 1, 3 **40** A **41** D **42** B
43 mooring in the lock

EXPLANATIONS

37 Locks are most common along canals. The introductory paragraph states: 'A lock is a section of canal closed off by gates to control the water level'. As a reader you should realise that many large rivers are very similar to canals, in that they are narrow and have a small fall over a longish distance.

38 The style of writing could be described as informative. The writer is attempting to advise travellers using the locks what to do to have a successful and safe passage through the locks: 'Canals, once used for commercial transportation, are now part of the enjoyment of travelling with family and friends on a canal system.' The information needs to be precise and accessible for 'ordinary' people.

39 Before descending from a higher level to a lower level it is essential to close the bottom gate first (1), then adjust the paddles (2) and allow the lock to fill (3). Finally open the top gate (4).

40 Paddles are located above the gates and allow operators to control the flow of water into or out of the lock.

41 Logic makes it plain that travellers using the lock would not pass a boat going the other way while in the lock (one up and one down). Boats cannot leave the lock until the water levels either side of the gate are the same. The sill is a barrier under the gate that projects into the canal.

42 A descending boat is going down the waterway. The level of water on the other side of the gate would be lower than the water level on the top side of the top gate. The boat can only leave the lock when water levels inside the lock and the waterway are the same. The gates do not open until this happens.

43 You have to work out what would happen. An accident could occur in a lock if a boat was moored. As the water drops, the mooring rope may not be long enough to allow the boat to float correctly. The boat could either be capsized or the rope snapped by the weight of the boat 'dangling' above the water. It would be extremely difficult to release the boat from its mooring once the water level has dropped.

A Gift for You

44 D **45** C **46** B **47** A **48** B, F **49** D **50** C, E

EXPLANATIONS

44 Carrie was surprised by the unexpected gift: She expressed her surprise as she wasn't expecting anything like this (a beautiful basket of flowers and wine).

45 The reason the courier gave (which was not the real reason) was that children might take the wine. Carrie found this a logical reason.

46 The reason that the couriers couldn't leave the wine was to get access to John's or Carrie's credit card details. The reasons given were part of an elaborate scheme.

47 It is implied in the email that Carrie was so angry at being a victim of a $4000 scam that included what seemed like a wonderful present that she would be reminded of her disastrous encounter with the scammers.

48 Carrie was conned by the couriers because they were friendly and apparently reasonable. They had simple, 'logical' reasons for their actions and their responsibilities. The couriers didn't arouse Carrie's suspicions. They were not intimidating.

49 The tone of Carrie's email and her subsequent actions suggests that she felt the trick was contemptible. She states: 'We've all received gifts like this and would never dream that it could be such a despicable act.' She felt disillusioned.

50 Rather than hide her embarrassment, Carrie wants to expose the scam to her friends (and their friends). The scammer would be well aware that their ploy would quickly be discovered. They would not feel threatened if the email were intended as a warning. The tone of the letter suggests that Carrie felt angry.

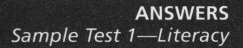
LITERACY – CONVENTIONS OF LANGUAGE
pages 145–148

1 A **2** D **3** A, D **4** C **5** D **6** B **7** B **8** A **9** soon, quickly, silently **10** verb: floated; adverb: brightly; preposition: in; adjective: coloured **11** C **12** D **13** B **14** D **15** C **16** B **17** A **18** A **19** D **20** A **21** B **22** C **23** D **24** A **25** B **26** championship **27** cautioned **28** ballooning **29** citizen **30** subdued **31** volcanoes **32** audience **33** exist **34** cricketing **35** mayor **36** correspondent **37** commission **38** countryside **39** prediction **40** incident **41** slightly **42** target **43** significant **44** charge **45** situation **46** source **47** responsible **48** threatened **49** criminals **50** hindrance

EXPLANATIONS

1 This is a grammar question. The correct word is the verb *had heard*.
Tip: With the irregular verb *heard* you need a 'helper'—another verb to 'help' it. *Have*, *has* and *had* can be helping verbs—(*Kelly*) *had heard* ... The helping verb is always close to the verb it is helping.

2 This is a grammar question. The correct word is the preposition *from*.
Tip: Prepositions put events in position in time or place. In everyday speech, certain prepositions regularly tend to go with certain words. We use *from* with *different* (*different from*) in order to show dissimilarity.

3 This is a punctuation question. The correct sentence is: *You don't understand, do you? The total is 'ten' but you said 'six'. Why is that so hard?*
Tip: This passage is made up of three parts: a question, a statement and a question. The locations of the capital letters are clues to where each sentence starts.

4 This is a grammar question. The correct word is the verb *knows*.
Tip: Singular subjects (nouns) need singular verbs; plural subjects (nouns) need plural verbs. In this case, the single verb *knows* goes with the single subject (*the whole*) *team*.

5 This is a grammar question. The correct word is the pronoun *which*.
Tip: Pronouns are used to refer to nouns. *Which* is a common pronoun used to refer to animals or things such as events. *Who* is used to refer to people. *What* is incorrect.

6 This is a grammar question. The correct word is the conjunction *so*.
Tip: Conjunctions join ideas in a sentence. The conjunction *so* indicates an action resulting from a previous situation (*the film was silly*).

7 This is a grammar question. The correct word is the verb *have*.
Tip: *Have* is part of the verb (past participle) *have been broken*. It is in the past tense. Singular subjects (nouns) need singular verbs; plural subjects (nouns) need plural verbs. In this case, the plural subject *nails* needs a plural verb *have*—not *has*.

8 This is a punctuation question. The correct sentence is: *Sandra, have you finished any of your reading or Maths?*
Tip: The comma is used after *Sandra* to separate the person spoken to from the rest of the sentence. Commas indicate pauses.

9 This is a grammar question. Adverbs are words that modify verbs, adjectives and other adverbs. They tell us how, when, where, to what extent and why.

10 This is a grammar question. Simply put, verbs are action or doing words, adverbs modify verbs, prepositions indicate position and adjectives describe nouns and pronouns.

11 This is a grammar question. The correct word is the preposition *on*.
Tip: Prepositions put events in position in time or place. In everyday speech, certain prepositions regularly tend to go with certain words. We use *on* with *time* (*on time*) in order to show punctuality.

12 This is a grammar question. The correct word is the conjunction *as*.
Tip: Some conjunctions operate as pairs, such as *either* and *or*. The term *as ... as* is another.

13 This is a writing strategy question. The correct sentence is: *In sentence 5 the exclamation mark is included to indicate that Kim is being told something that is all too obvious to her. Kim is feeling angry that she is being treated in such a way.*
Tip: Exclamation marks are used to show strong emotions.

14 This is a grammar question. The correct sentence is: *The police are calling for a regular check on underage drivers.*
Tip: Nouns are the names of people, places or things. Nouns are often the names of things that can be touched but they can also be the names of things that cannot be touched (like *a check*).

15 This is a grammar question. The correct word is the adjective *darker*.
Tip: Adjectives are compared in degrees. One bruise would be *dark*. When comparing two bruises, one is *darker.* When comparing three or more bruises, one of the bruises is the *darkest. More* (and *most*) are used with words of two or more syllables when it is inappropriate to add *er* or *est*.

16 This is a grammar question. The correct word is the verb *risen*.
Tip: *Risen* is part of the verb *had risen. Rise* is an irregular verb. Most verbs in English form their past tenses by adding *ed* (e.g. *he called*). There are a number of irregular verbs when this doesn't happen. We say *risen* instead of 'rised'. With the verb *risen* you need a 'helper'—another verb to 'help' it. *Have*, *has* and *had* can be helping verbs: *The sun had risen* ... The helping verb is always close to the verb it is helping.

17 This is a grammar question. The correct words are *adverb* and *adjective*.
Tip: Adverbs modify verbs. The adverb *lately* tells how often Mia was late. *Late* is an adjective. It describes Mia's state of being in conjunction with the 'being' verb *had been*.

18 This is a punctuation question. The correct word is *city's*.
Tip: The sentence is referring to just one of a number of cities (*each city*). As it is a singular noun. simply add 's.

19 This is a grammar question. The correct word is the verb *has*.
Tip: Singular subjects (nouns) need singular verbs; plural subjects (nouns) need plural verbs. *News* is an uncountable noun. Uncountable nouns have singular form so it takes the singular verb has. There is only one news—*the latest news*.

20 This is a grammar question. The correct word is the verb *cling*.
Tip: Singular subjects (nouns) need singular verbs; plural subjects (nouns) need plural verbs. In this case, *cling* must be used because there are *survivors. Clung* is incorrect as it is the wrong tense.

21 This is a grammar question. The correct word is the conjunction *Unless*.
Tip: *Unless* is a subordinating conjunction. It comes at the beginning and establishes the relationship between the dependent clause and the rest of the sentence. Most conjunctions are located within the sentence and join ideas together.

22 This is a grammar question. The correct sentence is: *A radio was playing inside the empty flat.*
Tip: An adverb adds to a verb. It describes, modifies or provides more information about a verb in a sentence. A radio was *playing* (verb) *inside* (adverb) the empty flat.

23 This is a grammar question. The adjectival clause is: *that she borrowed from the library.*
Tip: Complex sentences have a principal clause (independent clause) and a subordinate clause (dependent clause). An adjectival clause is a subordinate clause and does the work of an adjective. It describes or qualifies the noun *book*.

24 This is a grammar question. The correct word is the verb *mistaken*.
Tip: *Mistake* is an irregular verb. Most verbs in English form their past tenses by adding ed (e.g. *he called*). There are a number of irregular verbs when this doesn't happen.

We say *mistaken* instead of 'mistaked'. With the verb *mistaken* you need a 'helper'—another verb to 'help' it. *Have*, *has* and *had* can be helping verbs: *had mistaken* ... The helping verb is always close to the verb it is helping.

25 This is a grammar question. The brackets are required around *slow-witted person.* Tip: Sometimes the word used is a colloquialism or used in a sense that may not be familiar to the reader, so the writer may provide an explanation in brackets.

NUMERACY   **pages 150–154**

1 C **2** A **3** C **4** 8.1 **5** 4500 **6** 1961 **7** 14.40 **8** C
9 A **10** B **11** D **12** C **13** D **14** A, B, C **15** D **16** A
17 B **18** B **19** D **20** D **21** A **22** 200 000 **23** D
24 B **25** 2101 **26** C **27** 11 **28** 36 **29** 24 **30** D
31 B **32** D **33** C **34** D **35** B **36** 60 **37** C **38** C
39 D **40** A **41** D **42** 135 **43** C **44** A **45** 1.695
46 B, C and D **47** B **48** A

EXPLANATIONS

1 Number of times = 64×5
                = 320

$$\begin{array}{r} 64 \\ \times\ 5 \\ \hline 320 \end{array}$$

2 Money remaining = $7.80 − $6.90
        = $7.80 − $6.00 − $0.90
        = $1.80 − $0.80 − $0.10
        = $1.00 − $0.10
        = $0.90

$$\begin{array}{r} 7.8 \\ -6.9 \\ \hline 0.9 \end{array}$$

3 Estimates = $60 + $50 + $70 + $80
           = $110 + $150
           = $260

4 Multiply both numbers by 10 so that you are dividing by a whole number.
$3.24 \div 0.4 = 32.4 \div 4$
             = 8.1

5 Capacity when full = 6000×3
               = 18 000

$$4\overline{)18\,000} = 4500$$

Capacity when 25% full = 18 000 ÷ 4
                    = 4500
The tank will contain 4500 litres.

6 Darcy was born 25 years after 1903—he was born in 1928. Now from 1928 to 1994 is 66 years, which means Darcy was 66 when Jackson was born. Barry was half of 66, which is 33 years old and so was born in 1961.

7 Cost of 5 cappuccinos = $24
Cost of 1 cappuccino = $24 ÷ 5
                    = $4.80
Cost of 3 cappuccinos = $4.80 × 3
                    = $14.40

8 $3 + 5 \times (8 − 4 \div 2) = 3 + 5 \times (8 − 2)$
                      $= 3 + 5 \times 6$
                      $= 3 + 30$
                      $= 33$

9 Shape A: Per = 24 u;   Area = 20 u²
Shape B: Per = 24 u;   Area = 20 u²
Shape C: Per = 24 u;   Area = 20 u²
Shape D: Per = 24 u;   Area = 20 u²
All the shapes have the same perimeter and the same area.

10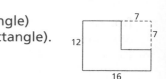

Sam   Peta   Greg   Emily
              26 days
     11 days   4 days

This means the third oldest is Greg.

11 (area of large rectangle)
  − (area of small rectangle).

12

13

14 The length of CB is 2 units, the length of RQ is 12 units. Consider each of the choices:
- As $2 \times 6 = 12$, the enlargement factor is 6.
- As lengths have been multiplied by 6, PQ is 6 times the length of AB.
- As lengths have been multiplied by 6, the perimeter is multiplied by 6.

- The areas of the triangles are 1 u² and 36 u². This means the area of II is 36 times the area of I.
The correct statements are A, B and C.

15 First night $= \frac{1}{6}$ of 120

$= 20$

There are still 100 pages in the book.

Second night $= \frac{1}{5}$ of 100

$= 20$

There are now 80 pages remaining.

16 Fraction $\frac{4}{30} = \frac{2}{15}$ which is closest to

$\frac{2}{16}$ which is $\frac{1}{8}$.

17 Consider each of the choices: 'The correct statement is 8 faces and 12 edges'.

18 Jerome leaves X and travels along Camber Street. He turns left into Drayton Street, and then right into Edith Street. Jerome will pass B on his left.

19 60 minutes in one hour so for 15 minutes:

$\frac{15}{60} = \frac{1}{4} = 0.25$

This means 4 hours 15 min = 4.25 hours.

20 As there are 3 even cards out of 5, the probability that the selected card is even

is $\frac{3}{5}$.

21 From the scale drawing, by measurement:
5 cm = 300 m
1 cm = 60 m   (by dividing by 5)

22 America $= 20\% = \frac{1}{5}$

Number of Americans $= \frac{1}{5} \times 1\,000\,000$

$= 200\,000$

200 000 travellers from America.

23 Total time $= 120 + 80 + 90 + 120$

$= 410$

Saasha spent 410 minutes, or 6 h 50 min.

24

25 Cost $= 1322 + 779$

$= 2101$

The cost is $2101.

26

		2	8
4	6	10	
	12		

27 Number of balls $= 12 \times 4 + 7$

$= 48 + 7$

$= 55$

Number to 5 friends $= 55 \div 5 = 11$
Each friend receives 11 balls.

28 The perimeter of each square is 24 cm. This means the length of each side is 6 cm. The length of the tile is 5 squares and 2 half-triangles. The two half-triangles together give the width of another square. This means 6×6 gives 36 cm length.

29 The perimeter is 24 cm and two sides add to 16 cm. This means the other side of the triangle is 8 cm. The area of the triangle is

$\frac{1}{2}$ of 8×6, which is 24 square centimetres.

30 Change 1200 g to 1.2 kg.
New mass $= 20.7 - 1.2$

$= 19.5$

The new mass is 19.5 kg.

31 From the divided bar graph,
2 units = 40
1 unit = 20
As AFL is 3.5 units long, and $3.5 \times 20 = 70$, then 70 students chose AFL.

32 The cost is $10 for each hour plus an extra

$15. Checking: $10 $(\frac{1}{2})$ + $15 = $20,

$10 (1) + $15 = $25, $10 $(1\frac{1}{2})$ + $15 = $30,

and so on.

33 Remember, 180° in a straight line.
Consider each of the choices:
The answer must be 135 as it is 3 times 45 and 135 + 45 = 180
This means $y = 135$.

34 Change 2.5 kg to 2500 grams.

$$\text{Mean} = \frac{680 + 800 + 2500 + 440}{4}$$

$$= (680 + 800 + 2500 + 400) \div 4$$
$$= 1105$$

The mean is 1105 grams, or 1.105 kg.

35

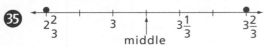

The middle is the middle of 3 and $3\frac{1}{3}$.

Now $3\frac{1}{3} = 3\frac{2}{6}$, so the middle of 3 and $3\frac{1}{3}$

is $3\frac{1}{6}$. [We could also have found the middle

by finding the average of the 2 fractions.]

36 On the plan the area for chickens:
Area = 5 × 2
= 10   10 squares
This means   10 squares = 40 m²
1 square = 4 m²
Now, for the vegetable patch on the plan:
Area = 5 × 3
= 15
Actual area = 15 × 4
= 60
The area is 60 m².

37 If the ratio of fruit to nuts is 3 to 5,
and 3 + 5 = 8,

then fraction of nuts = $\frac{5}{8}$

Mass in 480 g bag = $\frac{5}{8}$ × 480

= 5 $\boxed{a^{b}/_{c}}$ 8 × 480
= 300

There is a mass of 300 grams of nuts.

38 Fraction of kg bought $\frac{18}{24} = \frac{3}{4}$

John bought $\frac{3}{4}$ kg, or 750 grams.

39 Area of square = 4 × 4
= 16
Area of one triangle = $\frac{1}{2}$ × 4 × 3
= 6

Total area = 16 + 4 × 6   [4 triangles]
= 40
40 square units

40 Using 20% as $\frac{1}{5}$,

Cost of airline tickets = $\frac{1}{5}$ × 45 000

= 9000
The airline tickets cost $9000.

41 Speed = Distance ÷ Time
= 180 ÷ 2
= 90
Now, need to find the distance travelled in
3 hours at 90 km/h:
Distance = Speed × Time
= 90 × 3
= 270
Craig will travel 270 kilometres.

42

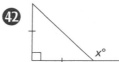

As the triangle is right angled and isosceles,
the angles are 90°, 45° and 45°.
x = 180 − 45
= 135

43 On the map, Hidden Waters to Outlook is
5 units.
5 units = 40 kilometres
1 unit = 8 kilometres   [dividing by 5]
On the map, distance from Highland County
to Sanctuary is 9.5 units
Distance = 9.5 × 8
= 76
The distance is 76 kilometres.

44 Volume of Solid A = 2 × 1 × 1
= 2   2 unit³
Volume of Solid B = 2 × 1 × 1
= 2   2 unit³
This means that A and B have the same
volume.
[Solid C has volume = 1 unit³ and Solid D
has volume = 4 units³]

45 There are 300 10 cent coins in $30.
Total mass = 300 × 5.65
= 1695
The total mass is 1695 grams, or 1.695 kg.

46 The correct statements are:
B: A cube has twice as many edges (12) as faces (6).
C: A triangular pyramid has 4 faces.
D. A triangular prism has the same number of faces (5) as a square pyramid (5).

47 Sarah's height is 3 cm less than Craig's height.

48 From (2, –1) Charlotte moves up to (2, 2) and then to the left to (–2, 2).

SAMPLE TEST PAPER 2

LITERACY – WRITING Page 156

Narrative text

Tick each correct point.
Read the student's work through once to get an overall view of their response.

Focus on general points
☐ Did it make sense?
☐ Did it flow?
☐ Did the story arouse any feeling?
☐ Did you want to read on? Did the story create any suspense?
☐ Was the handwriting readable?

Now focus on the detail. Read the following points and find out whether the student's work has these features.

Focus on content
☐ Did the opening sentence(s) 'grab' your interest?
☐ Was the setting established (i.e. when and where the action took place)?
☐ Was it apparent who the main character(s) is? (It can be the narrator, using *I*.)
☐ Was there a problem to be solved early in the writing?
☐ Was a complication or unusual event introduced?
☐ Did descriptions make reference to any of the senses (e.g. *pink sky, cool breeze*)?
☐ Was there a climax (a more exciting part near the end)?
☐ Was there a conclusion (resolution of the problem) and was it believable?

Focus on structure, vocabulary, grammar, spelling, punctuation
☐ Was there variation in sentence length and beginnings?
☐ Was a new paragraph started for changes in time, place or action?
☐ In conversations or speaking were there separate paragraphs for each change of speaker?
☐ Were adjectives used to improve descriptions (e.g. *hollow sound*)?
☐ Were adverbs used to make 'actions' more interesting (e.g. *listened carefully*)?
☐ Were capital letters where they should have been?
☐ Was punctuation correct?
☐ Was the spelling of words correct?

Marker's suggestions (optional)

LITERACY – READING Pages 157–170

'Tin Legs' Bader

1 A, F **2** C **3** written response **4** D **5** B **6** 1976 **7** B **8** A

EXPLANATIONS

1 You have to read the whole passage to understand the type of man Bader was. He was determined. He was determined to be a pilot regardless of the fact he had both legs amputated. He escaped from prisoner-of-war camps numerous times, even though he had 'tin legs'. He was also audacious— willing to take surprisingly bold risks.

2 Bader was rash. Rash means acting with impetuous behaviour. He was a member of the RAF aerobatic display team and was notorious for low-level aerobatics. In December 1931, he crashed during an unauthorised low-level stunt.

3 Officially Bader was not allowed to fly with artificial legs, but he did. The reason he became a fighter pilot again was because there was a shortage of pilots during the war. Official rules were overlooked in an emergency.

4 Many points indicate Bader was an exceptional pilot. He was a member of the aerobatics display team. Later in his career he shot down numerous German planes—even though he had artificial legs.

5 You have to read the whole passage to understand the intent of the reference. 'Tin legs' was not putting Bader down. Because of his exploits it was a term of respect.

6 This is a straight fact-finding question. He was knighted in 1976 for his work on behalf of the disabled—not his war exploits.

7 This is a straight fact-finding question. The Douglas Bader Foundation was set up to help those who had lost limbs.

8 The term 'friendly fire' is a euphemism (a neutral word or phrase used in place of one that might be considered harsh, offensive or too direct). It's the type of term used when an organization wants to downplay the actual situation. In this case it was fire coming from the victim's own allies (not the enemy).

Beagle Bay Church

9 B 10 the vessel (ship) *The Beagle* 11 *'Tin Legs' Bader* A, C; *Beagle Bay Church* A, B 12 A
13 C, E 14 B 15 B, F

EXPLANATIONS

9 This is a straightforward fact-finding question. The plans were drawn up prior to 1908. The monks settled at Beagle Bay mission around 1901. The Church was built between 1914 and 1918.

10 The answer is in the last paragraph: The community's name was derived from the vessel *The Beagle*, which moored at the bay when the priests were looking for a suitable mission place in 1889.

11 The *'Tin Legs' Bader* text is **inspirational**. Bader continued fighting against all odds. It is a short **biography**. The *Beagle Bay Church* text is also **inspirational**. Many would admire the effort made to build the church. The text also **describes** many features of the church as well as describing issues relating to its construction.

12 The Beagle Bay land was originally land belonging to the Aboriginal people of the area. This is recorded in the designs used on the altar: Some of the decoration designs form the tribal symbols of the Njul Njul, the Nimanborr and the Bardi people of the area.

13 The feature of the main altar is its 'stunning' decoration of shells, especially mother-of-pearl shells. In the second last paragraph is a description of the tribal and Christian symbols in the decoration designs.

14 Read the text and apply your knowledge of the words. Perseverance best describes the effort involved to construct the church: 'Day after day parties set off into the bush or to the coast to cut timber, cart sand, dig clay and gather tons of broken shells for lime'. There is no indication that the workforce found the task frustrating or that they particularly enjoyed the work. Labouring can hardly be described as uplifting—something that elevates somebody morally or spiritually.

15 The church was completed with materials from the Dampier Peninsula using the labour of the local tribal people.

The Glenn Miller story

16 Colorado 17 D, E 18 A 19 C 20 C
21 'In the Mood' 22 B

EXPLANATIONS

16 The answer is a fact located in the first paragraph: (In) *Colorado … Miller played in his high school band*.

17 The text is an example of a biography. A biography is an account of someone's life written by someone else. An autobiography is an account of a person's life written by that person. A biography is also a factual recount. It is a true record.

18 This is a language-type question. The saying *on the map* is an example of an idiom. The meaning is not directly obvious from the context. You have to interpret what is intended. It implies becoming famous or well known—making a mark.

19 You have to draw a conclusion after reading the whole text. Up until 1944 Miller's reputation as a musician and arranger was continuing to develop. His life was suddenly cut short in a plane crash on his way to entertain troops in Paris.

20 Miller will best be remembered as leader of a swing-jazz band. He *dominated the music charts with over 60 top hits* in the early 1940s. He had numerous hits and a film was made of his life story.

21 This is a language question. You have to understand the meaning of *signature song* in the context of the text. A signature song is one a musician is most remembered for.

22 This is a fact in the text. You read *It was his band's gig at the famed Glen Island Casino in New York (1939) that helped put Miller on the map*. His music after this gig received a lot of air play.

Sudoku

23 written response **24** nine or 9 **25** C **26** D
27 B **28** B **29** C, D

EXPLANATIONS

23 Sudoku is a game of elimination and logic. Using logic, the players eliminate numbers that do not fulfil the conditions of a particular place in the grid. Concentration is also required. Mathematical skills are not required.

24 Any number can appear only nine times in a Sudoku 9 x 9 grid. Any more than nine times and there must be two of that number in either a row, column or 3 x 3 square.

25 As Sudoku is a game of elimination, it is best to find a blank cell that has only one possible value (number). This then makes other blank cells easier to solve.

26 As solving skills improve, puzzle solvers will find that they don't have to write down all possibilities for each cell: 'Players with a bit of practice don't actually write down all possibilities for the unsolved cells. When starting to solve a puzzle, they often spot several cells where the value is obvious'.

27 You may make a decision based on logic, knowledge and experience. The answer is also in the text. Numbers are easier to recognise and remember than other sorts of symbols. The numbers are not required for calculations.

28 Advanced players will look at several cells at once to eliminate possibilities. They have developed the skill of spotting several cells where the value is obvious.

29 Read through the subsections carefully. In the *Standard Technique* in Point 3 you read 'Look for an empty cell that has just one possible value'. Now look at *Advanced Technique*s. You read (players) 'eliminate possibilities allowing them to continue solving using the standard technique'.

Escapees from the Garden

30 C **31** B **32** D **33** D **34** B **35** A
36 *Sudoku* B, D; *Escapees* C, D

EXPLANATIONS

30 This is a fact-finding question. The information is stated in the text: Once a plant has been declared noxious it is the landholder's responsibility to rid his or her property of the plant.

31 The foliage is poisonous to livestock. In fact, all parts of the plant are highly toxic but the roots are more toxic than other parts of the lily.

32 The meaning of the word naturalise, when applied to plants, means that a plant from another region has successfully established itself in a new region. There are clues in the passage to this meaning. The fact that it has spread successfully through large tracts of the Australian bush is an indication of how well it has 'naturalised'.

33 The Glory Lily has medicinal value but the reason it became a garden plant was due to its ornamental value. The picture shows how attractive the flower is.

34 Even though the Glory Lily is a smallish garden plant, its rapid spread through the bush has meant that it covers the ground smothering smaller and younger plants (taking nutrients, preventing sunlight reaching the ground).

35 The importance of the photographs is to help in the identification of a noxious plant. Gardeners are often influenced by the 'beauty' of a flower and do not appreciate its harmful effect. The Glory Lily is actually a 'declared' weed.

36 The *Sudoku* text explains the structure of the puzzle and advises how to solve the puzzle. The *Escapees* text describes a plant and advises on action if the plant is discovered on private property.

Types of Extinguishers
37 D **38** heat **39** C **40** A **41** D **42** A2, B3, C1 **43** A

EXPLANATIONS

37 You may have to read through the whole of the text to come to an answer. The fire symbol indicates that all three elements must be present at the same time to have fire. Each of the described extinguishers removes one of these elements.

38 The fire symbol and the text both show that, other than oxygen and fuel, for a fire to burn there must be heat.

39 The chemical extinguisher has a white band.

40 Water should only be used on flammable materials such as wood, clothing, etc. As water is relatively heavy compared to many liquid fuels, such fuels tend to float on the water. Water will spread the floating fuel rather than smothering the fire.

41 Water is a good conductor of electricity 'and there is a high risk that users may receive a severe electric shock if water is used on an electrical fire'. Once the power has been switched off there is no fear of water being a conductor.

42 You must read the information about each type of extinguisher carefully. For most house fires a water extinguisher is adequate. For electrical fires a dry chemical extinguisher (BE) will isolate the flame from its oxygen source. For laboratory liquids a carbon dioxide extinguisher is usually appropriate.

43 Find the section on Dry Chemical Extinguishers (2). These extinguishers inhibit fires by coating the fuel with 'a thin layer of powder', which prevents oxygen from feeding the fire. It separates the fuel from the oxygen supply.

How the Eye Works
44 written response **45** retina **46** A2, B1, C3
47 C **48** A **49** dogs cannot see colour **50** D

EXPLANATIONS

44 This is a fact-finding question. Go to the part headed *Rods*. You will see that rods are sensitive to light: 'Rods detect light and dark'. You may have expressed the correct answer in a variety of related ways.

45 This is a straightforward fact-finding question. Go to the section *Other important parts of the eye*. You will find that the retina changes the image into a message for the brain.

46 This is a straightforward fact-finding question. Go to the section *Other important parts of the eye*. The cornea is transparent, the sclera is white and the pupil is black.

47 This is a fact-finding question. Go to the part headed *Cones*. Without cones a person would be colour blind. They would only see shades of black and white.

48 This is a straightforward fact-finding question. Go to the section *Other important parts of the eye*. You will find that the iris controls the size of the pupil which regulates the amount of light entering the eye.

49 This is a fact-finding comparing answer. Read the section about rods and cones. Dogs' eyes do not have any cones. Dogs can only see shades of black and white (greys) whereas most humans can see colour.

50 This is a straightforward fact-finding question. Go to the section *Other important parts of the eye*. You have to apply the information you find. The pupil gets larger when the light is dim.

LITERACY—CONVENTIONS OF LANGUAGE
Pages 171–175

1 C 2 B 3 B 4 A 5 C 6 D 7 C 8 A 9 B 10 D 11 B 12 A, B 13 C 14 love, poetry, result, Gavin 15 A 16 D 17 C 18 B 19 B 20 C 21 B 22 A 23 D 24 verb: maintained; adjective: ancient; pronoun: his; conjunction: and 25 C 26 reply 27 nuisance 28 narrowed 29 poetry 30 plumber 31 carelessness 32 politician 33 admitted 34 propose 35 nineteenth 36 churches 37 southern 38 insist 39 league 40 structure 41 failure 42 reveller 43 stifling 44 recent 45 misspell 46 buggy 47 complete 48 videos 49 immediate 50 democratic

EXPLANATIONS

1 This is a punctuation question. The correct sentence is: *The inscription on the soldier's grave read: 'He completed his tour of duty with honour.'*
Tip: Colons are used to mark a pause and introduce a relevant quotation.

2 This is a grammar question. The first thing that happened was: *Raymond lost his pen.*
Tip: Reading the text carefully you will see that Raymond first loses his pen. He saw it again when stepping off the bus. Then his phone rang.

3 This is a grammar question. The correct words are *a lot.*
Tip: 'Alot' is not a word. *Allot* means 'share and give out'.

4 This is a grammar question. The correct word is the preposition *between.*
Tip: *Between* is used where just two people are involved (Sally and me). *Among* is used when there are more than three people (or things) involved.

5 This is a grammar question. The correct word is the verb *choose.*

Tip: *Choose* is present tense. *Chose* is past tense. It is an irregular verb. Most verbs in English form their past tenses by adding *ed* (e.g. *she waited*). There are a number of irregular verbs when this doesn't happen. We say *chose* instead of 'choosed. *I have made my choice—I chose red paper. Now you choose.*

6 This is a grammar question. The correct word is the adverb *well.*
Tip: *Well* adds meaning to the verbs, describing how she dives. Most adverbs end in *ly*—this is an exception. *Good* is incorrect. It is an adjective. *All right* suggests that everything was adequate and right. *Best* is incorrect as there is only a suggestion of comparing two things (swimming and diving).

7 This is a writing strategy question. The correct answer is: *This indicates that the narrator is attempting to distance herself from Sally and the project.*
Tip: When people start to get upset with associates they tend to depersonalise those people by using pronouns (such as *she*) rather than real names. It lets them disassociate themselves from any plans they don't like by being a little less friendly.

8 This is a grammar question. The correct sentence is: *I know Mathematics is difficult for you, but nothing else is available.*
Tip: Although *Mathematics* ends with an *s*, it is treated as a singular noun. *Nothing* is also treated as a singular noun.

9 This is a grammar question. The correct sentence is: *The agent inquired if we needed speakers for the band.*
Tip: This is an example of indirect speech. No quotation marks (speech marks) are required. As it includes the reporting of a question and not the actual question, no question mark is required.

10 This is a grammar question. The correct word is the adjective *thick.*
Tip: It is appropriate to describe people and animals as *plump*, *chubby* or *fat*, but not to describe trees as any of these.

11 This is a grammar question. The best sentence is: *Lance ordered a tub of fries and a beef burger, which he planned to eat before school*.
Tip: Joining several short sentences often makes text more fluid. It eliminates the repetition of certain words. Certain conjunctions improve the sequencing of events.

12 This is a punctuation question. The correct sentence is: *No, you shouldn't have done that Roger, old friend. You must save your money*.
Tip: A comma follows *No*, which is a short answer. *Old friend* is a noun phrase and is separated from the rest of the sentence. A full stop goes after *friend*. The next sentence begins with *You*, as it has a capital letter.

13 This is a punctuation question. The correct sentence is: *'Ingrid, I don't care,' she said, 'what you think about it.'*
Tip: The actual words spoken are *Ingrid, I don't care what you think about it*. It is all one statement and not a question. A comma follows *Ingrid* to separate her from the rest of the sentence.

14 This is a grammar question. Nouns are naming words. They can be classified as common, abstract, proper or collective.

15 This is a punctuation question. The correct sentence is: *Adelaide, South Australia, is often called 'The Garden City'*.
Tip: When both a city's name and that city's state (or country's name) are mentioned together, the state (or country's name) is separated from the rest of the sentence. Note: inverted commas are used for the title and capital letters for all words in the title: *'The Garden City'*.

16 This is a grammar question. The correct word is the adjective *prettiest*.
Tip: Adjectives are compared in degrees— *pretty*, *prettier* and *prettiest*. As there have been many birthday cakes, *prettiest* is the correct word. Longer words usually add *more* or *most* (*careful*, *more careful*, *most careful*).

17 This is a grammar question. The correct word is the verb *wrote*.
Tip: *Write* is an irregular verb. Most verbs in English form their past tenses by adding *ed* (e.g. *she waited*). There are a number of irregular verbs when this doesn't happen. We say *wrote* instead of 'writed' (or 'writ', which is a court order.) 'Wrid' is not a word.

18 This is a grammar question. The correct word is the verb *do*.
Tip: This is a common form of expression. The sentence begins with a statement and ends with a question tag. When the statement is in the affirmative the tag has a negative verb. When the statement is in the negative (*don't*) the tag has a positive verb.

19 This is a grammar question. The correct word is the conjunction *while*.
Tip: James is unlikely to be reading a book wherever his brother mows the lawn. *While* is the more appropriate conjunction in this instance.

20 This is a grammar question. The correct word is the term *will be*.
Tip: The report will be completed in the future—*on Tuesday*. Helping verbs or auxiliary verbs, such as *will be*, are used in conjunction with a main verb (*completed*) to express shades of time. The combination of helping verbs with main verbs creates verb phrases or verb strings.

21 This is a grammar question. The unnecessary words are *in a row*.
Tip: *Consecutive* means 'follow one another without a break'. The words *in a row* are superfluous. No meaning is lost by omitting *in a row*.

22 This is a grammar question. The correct sentence is: *Dad never invested foolishly, but only used the services of a wise advisor*.
Tip: *But* is a conjunction. It is used to connect two ideas with the meaning of 'with the exception of'. *Yet* suggests 'so far'.

23 This is a grammar question. The correct sentence is: *The walls were black with the soot from steam trains.*
Tip: Adjectives are used to describe people, places or things. *Black* in this sentence describes the colour of the walls.

24 This is a grammar question. Simply put, verbs are action or doing words, adjectives describe nouns, pronouns stand in the place of nouns and conjunctions join words or ideas.

25 This is a grammar question. An adverbial phrase is simply two or more words that can act as an adverb. They can modify a verb or adjective and tell how, when, why or where: *down the road*.

NUMERACY   Pages 176–182

1 E 2 D 3 A 4 73.7 5 B, D 6 D 7 14 8 450 9 B
10 C 11 D 12 B 13 1.75 14 C 15 C 16 D, C, B, A
17 C 18 B 19 A 20 79 000 21 32 22 A 23 C
24 A 25 8 26 240 27 A, B and D 28 D 29 C
30 C 31 D 32 A 33 36.8 34 C 35 4.39 36 C
37 A, C and D 38 C 39 27 40 30.50 41 A 42 C
43 15 44 19 45 400 46 2475 47 C 48 768

EXPLANATIONS

1 Height = 9.8 + 6.7
    = 9.8 + 6 + 0.7
    = 15.8 + 0.7
    = 15.8 + 0.2 + 0.5
    = 16.0 + 0.5
    = 16.5

$$\begin{array}{r} 9.8 \\ + 6.7 \\ \hline 16.5 \end{array}$$

The tree is 16.5 metres.

2 Amount = \$3.60 × 5
    = \$18.00

$$\begin{array}{r} 3.6 \\ \times 5 \\ \hline 18.0 \end{array}$$

Jordan spends a total of \$18.

3 Number of students = 836 ÷ 4
    = 209

$$\begin{array}{r} 209 \\ 4\overline{)836} \end{array}$$

There are 209 in Mulgabirra.

4 Difference = 50.7 − (−23)
    = 50.7 + 23
    = 73.7

The difference is 73.7 degrees.

5 32 − 10 − 2 = 22 − 2
        = 20

$$\frac{32}{2 + 2} \times 3 = \frac{32}{4} \times 3$$
$$= 8 \times 3$$
$$= 24$$

8 + 4 × 2 = 8 + 8
        = 16

50 ÷ 5 × 2 + 2² = 20 + 4
            = 24

$$\frac{16 + 16}{2} = \frac{32}{2}$$
$$= 16$$

This means $\frac{32}{2 + 2} \times 3$ and $50 ÷ 5 × 2 + 2^2$ equal 24.

6 The 3 is in the hundredths place in 14.9**3**1.

7   Total of all 6 numbers = 8 × 6
                = 48
      Total of first 4 numbers = 5 × 4
                = 20
      Total of last 2 numbers = 48 − 20
                = 28
Average of the last 2 numbers = 28 ÷ 2
                = 14

8 As $1 - \frac{3}{5} = \frac{2}{5}$, then two-fifths of the juice equals 360 mL.
One-fifth of jug = 360 ÷ 2
        = 180
Five-fifths of jug = 180 × 5
        = 900
The jug holds 900 mL, so there is 450 mL in the jug when half-full.

9 12 + 6 + 4 + 8 = 30.

$$P(\text{Green}) = \frac{6}{30}$$
$$= \frac{1}{5}$$

10 Quantity needed = 2 − 1.4
           = 2.0 − 1.4
           = 0.6
Need 0.6 L = 600 mL

11 Z is in the middle of $\frac{1}{4}$ and $\frac{1}{2}$.

Now $\frac{1}{4} = \frac{2}{8}$, and $\frac{1}{2} = \frac{4}{8}$, then the middle

of $\frac{2}{8}$ and $\frac{4}{8}$ is $\frac{3}{8}$.

12 Consider from 4.85 to 5: each unit is 0.05.
X = 4.85 − 4 × 0.05
   = 4.85 − 0.2
   = 4.65

13 Difference
    = highest high tide − lowest low tide
    = 1.93 − 0.18
    = 1.75

The difference is 1.75 m.

14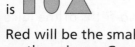

This means from lightest to heaviest it

is

15 Red will be the smallest area on the spinner. Green will be twice the size of red, and blue will be three times the size of red (or half of the circle).

16 A: 60 mL, B: 50 mL, C: 45 mL, D: 35 mL.
The order is D, C, B, A.

17 Relate the number of triangles to the number of sticks:
Rule is:
Double the triangles + 1 = sticks
Double the triangles + 1 = 37
     Double the triangles = 37 − 1
     Double the triangles = 36
          Triangles = half of 36
                  = 18

18 Averages:
Jamie: 18 ÷ 8 = 2.25
Luke: 16 ÷ 5 = 3.2
Jesse: 21 ÷ 7 = 3
Brodie: 20 ÷ 10 = 2
The player with the highest average is Luke.

19 Start 55 minutes before 10:15.
Start = 10:15 minus 55 min
       = 10:15 minus 1 hour plus 5 minutes
       = 9:15 plus 5 minutes
       = 9:20
Bianca started at 9:20.

20 Difference = 224 462 − 145 916
            = 78 546
            = 79 000 (nearest thousand)
The difference is 79 000.

21 Area: length × 6 = 60
          length = 60 ÷ 6
               = 10
Perimeter = 10 + 10 + 6 + 6
            = 32
The perimeter is 32 cm.

22 Top view: 4 by 3
Side view: 4 by 2
This means that front is 3 by 2.

The view could be:

23 As 20% = $\frac{1}{5}$, then

Replied emails = $\frac{1}{5}$ of 50
               = 10
Deleted emails = 50 − 10
              = 40
Kevin deleted 40 emails.

24 ⊡

25 The cube has 12 edges.
Length of the edge = 24 ÷ 12
                  = 2
Each length is 2 cm
Volume = 2 × 2 × 2
        = 8
The volume is 8 cm^3.

 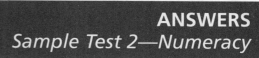

26 The angle represents 8 hours out of 12

Fraction of 360° = $\frac{8}{12}$ = $\frac{2}{3}$

Size of angle = $\frac{2}{3}$ × 360

= 240

The angle is 240°.

27 The pairs of shapes in A, B and D can join to form cubes.

28 Consider each of the choices:

$18 ÷ \frac{2}{3} = 27$ $18 ÷ \frac{1}{3} = 36$

$18 ÷ \frac{3}{4} = 24$ $18 ÷ \frac{3}{2} = 12$

The missing number is $\frac{3}{2}$.

(OR, 18 divided by a number gives 12, which is a smaller number—this means the number is bigger than 1.)

29 ☐ = 3   ◯ + 3 = 7

This means ◯ = 4

◯ + ◯ + ☐ = 4 + 4 + 3 = 11.

30 2 wraps + water = $4.40
2 wraps + $1.00 = $4.40
2 wraps = $3.40
1 wrap = $3.40 ÷ 2
= $1.70
A wrap costs $1.70
A wrap and 2 bottles of water costs $3.70.

31 First, 2.5 kg = 2500 grams.
Difference = 2500 − 150
= 2350
The difference is 2350 g, or 2.35 kg.

32 Travel time = 2.5 hours
Speed = Distance ÷ Time
= 180 ÷ 2.5
= 72
The speed is 72 km/h.

33 Distance = 4.6 × 8
= 36.8
The places are 36.8 km apart.

34 Try each of the choices: 3 × number of squares + 1 works because 3 × 1 squares + 1 gives 4 matches, 3 × 2 squares + 1 gives 7 matches, and so on.

35 Height of Emily = 59.24 + 32 × 2.90
= 152.04
Height of Ryan = 75.79 + 32 × 2.52
= 156.43
Difference in heights = 156.43 − 152.04
= 4.39
The difference is 4.39 cm.

36 From the output number of 7 we use the inverse operations and work back to the input number. 7 add 3 is 10 which is not odd, then subtract 4 gives 6. Also, 7 subtract 2 gives 5 which is odd, then subtract 4 gives 1. This means the input number could be 1 or 6.

37 $a + b + e + f$ = 180 because they are the angles in a triangle.
$a + d + f$ = 180 because they are the angles in a triangle.
$c + d + g + h$ = 360 because they are angles around a point.

38 There are 24 balls. From 3 out of 8 balls, we multiply by 3 and find that 9 out of 24 balls are red. This means that 15 of the balls are blue. The difference in the number of blue (15) and red (9) balls is 6.

39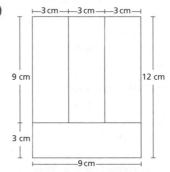

The dimension of each plank is 9 cm by 3 cm.
Area = 9 × 3 = 27

40 Using guess and check method, as 84 + 16 gives 100, then Jack can buy 7 packets of 12 rolls and 2 packets of 8 rolls.
As $3.50 × 7 + $3.00 × 2 is $30.50, then Jack bought exactly 100 toilet rolls and paid $30.50.

41 Three quarters of Pim's money $= \frac{3}{4} × \$560$
$= \$420$

Jack's earnings = $420 – $45
$= \$375$

42 Perimeter of the square is 26 cm
Side length of square = 26 ÷ 4
$= 6.5$
The square has a side length of 6.5 cm
Grant's new shape has 8 equal sides
Perimeter of new shape = 6.5 × 8
$= 52$
The perimeter is 52 cm.

43 Total students = 6 + 11 + 8 + 7 + 5 + 3
$= 40$
Fraction of group who had watched
2 movies $= \frac{8}{40} = \frac{1}{5}$

One-fifth of new group = 75 ÷ 5
$= 15$
The prediction is 15.

44 Number of 100-km distances = 245 ÷ 100
$= 2.45$

Number of litres = 2.45 × 7.8
$= 19.11$
$= 19$ (nearest litre)
Gordon would use 19 litres.

45 Differences in percentages = 80 – 65
$= 15$
15% of novel = 60
1% of novel = 60 ÷ 15
$= 4$
100% of novel = 4 × 100
$= 400$
There are 400 pages in the book.

46 Cost = 2 × 8 × 5 × $60 + $1650
$= \$6450$
Profit = $11 400 – $6450
$= \$4950$
Leno's payment = $4950 ÷ 2
$= \$2475$
Leno receives $2475.

47 A: Discount = 15% of $200
$= 0.15 × \$200$
$= \$30$ Price = $170
B: Discount = $30   Price = $165

C: Discount $= \frac{1}{3}$ of $240

$= \$240 ÷ 3$
$= \$80$ Price = $160
D: Discount = 10% of $180
$= 0.1 × \$180$
$= \$18$ Price = $162

The lowest sale price is $160 at Shop C.

48 Volume of original cube = 12^3
Volume of removed prism = $12^3 – 80 × 12$
$= 768$

The volume is 768 cm³.

SPELLING WORDS FOR REAL TESTS

To the teacher or parent

Read the word clearly to the student. Then read the sentence with the word in it to the student. Then read the word again.

Give the student time to write an answer. If the student is not sure of the spelling tell them to make their best attempt but that it is okay to skip a word if they cannot attempt a guess.

Spelling words for Real Test Week 1

Word	Example
1. leisure	Time at the leisure centre is time well spent!
2. symptoms	With those symptoms you should see a doctor.
3. afford	I can't afford tickets to the rock concert.
4. particular	Jo is quite particular about what she drinks.
5. stretching	If stretching your leg is difficult then let me help.
6. burglar	The burglar came in through a window.
7. shining	Mandy was shining her shoes when the storm struck.
8. separated	A low fence separated the crowd from the players.
9. ascend	We had to ascend four floors before finding the office.
10. changeable	How changeable has the weather been this week!
11. destroyed	The vandals destroyed the front garden.
12. propeller	The propeller was snagged in an old, discarded fishing net.
13. dyeing	The boys were dyeing their hair for the city's celebrations.
14. quarrelling	Shoppers were quarrelling over bargains at the opening sale.
15. whiteness	Does the whiteness of the sheets dazzle your eyes?

Spelling words for Real Test Week 2

Word	Example
1. umbrellas	The railways have hundreds of lost umbrellas!
2. truly	Morris truly believes in the benefits of hypnosis.
3. writing	Your writing in the test will have to be readable.
4. receipt	Ask the attendant for a receipt.
5. opposing	Any opposing team will have to play well!
6. marriage	My brother's marriage will be next weekend.
7. travelling	Aaron was travelling down a hill when he lost control.
8. becoming	Tina had a becoming smile and a soft voice.
9. similar	We had a similar experience in the caravan park.
10. doctored	The books had been doctored by a shady accountant!
11. anchored	The cruise ship anchored in the tranquil bay.
12. awful	There was an awful storm in the harbour.
13. business	What business does any official have for ringing me this early?
14. cotton	Cotton shirts were going at bargain prices at the sale.
15. ancestor	The letter was a fake and the gentleman was not an ancestor.

SPELLING WORDS FOR REAL TESTS

To the teacher or parent

Read the word clearly to the student. Then read the sentence with the word in it to the student. Then read the word again.

Give the student time to write an answer. If the student is not sure of the spelling tell them to make their best attempt but that it is okay to skip a word if they cannot attempt a guess.

Spelling words for Real Test Week 3

	Word	Example
1.	deceitful	Jude was as deceitful as any person I know!
2.	definite	Luke was definite in his decision to drop out of the team.
3.	lightning	The lightning struck a tree near the shed.
4.	superstition	For every superstition there is a logical explanation.
5.	opportunity	Any opportunity would be appreciated.
6.	adhesive	This quick-setting adhesive was designed for hobbyists.
7.	immediate	Archie had an immediate reaction to the medicine.
8.	applicator	Before use, twist the yellow applicator to OPEN.
9.	familiar	The juice has a familiar taste. I just can't pick it.
10.	reviewing	After reviewing the film the critics made a quick decision.
11.	neighbourly	It was neighbourly of Mr Amos to repair your picket fence.
12.	fulfilled	I have fulfilled my obligations more than once!
13.	financially	Wayne was left friendless and financially ruined after the sale.
14.	fierce	Police warned property owners about keeping fierce dogs.
15.	illegal	The letter was forged and the agreement was illegal.

Spelling words for Real Test Week 4

	Word	Example
1.	typist	Jane was as fast a typist as any person in the office!
2.	troupe	The circus troupe was applauded at the end of the show.
3.	technique	Try this technique for making a knot.
4.	refugee	For every refugee there is a pile of forms to complete.
5.	shoeing	The blacksmith was shoeing horses for the rodeo.
6.	shield	Put the shield next to the sword.
7.	enjoyable	This film is no longer enjoyable! It is too silly for words.
8.	plasticine	They play with plasticine at my brother's preschool.
9.	stare	If you must stare at the tourists, try to be less obvious.
10.	levelling	After levelling out, the plane turned towards Darwin.
11.	Withholding	The financial institution is withholding credit.
12.	monotonous	The monotonous beating of rival tom-toms was a distraction.
13.	chronological	History is nothing more than a list of chronological facts.
14.	murmuring	From a distance we could hear the murmuring of the creek.
15.	whining	The gearbox was whining as we struggled up the steep hill.

SPELLING WORDS FOR SAMPLE TESTS

To the teacher or parent

Read the word clearly to the student. Then read the sentence with the word in it to the student. Then read the word again.

Give the student time to write an answer. If the student is not sure of the spelling tell them to make their best attempt but that it is okay to skip a word if they cannot attempt a guess.

Spelling words for Sample Test 1

Word	Example
26. championship	Judy was in championship events at the show.
27. cautioned	Were you ever cautioned for speeding on the journey?
28. ballooning	Their ballooning adventure was successful.
29. citizen	Dino became an Australian citizen on Monday.
30. subdued	Dad subdued the angry player with comforting words.
31. volcanoes	Two volcanoes erupted a week apart.
32. audience	In the audience was the governor general.
33. exist	Did dinosaurs exist a thousand years ago?
34. cricketing	Was Bradman our greatest cricketing hero?
35. mayor	The mayor was elected at a council meeting.
36. correspondent	As a foreign correspondent I spent many years in Japan.
37. commission	The agent's commission was too much for most buyers.
38. countryside	The Browns bought a home in the countryside.
39. prediction	Len's prediction is for windy weather.
40. incident	An incident at the fete ruined the day!

Spelling words for Sample Test 2

Word	Example
26. reply	I forgot to reply to your invitation.
27. nuisance	The flies are a nuisance during the hot months.
28. narrowed	As the road narrowed Dad drove more carefully.
29. poetry	We listened to her poetry for half an hour!
30. plumber	He said he was a plumber but he didn't fix our tap.
31. carelessness	My carelessness resulted in a minor accident.
32. politician	Uncle is a politician in state parliament.
33. admitted	When asked a direct question the accused admitted to knowing the man.
34. propose	I propose we go over to Jane's place immediately.
35. nineteenth	The nineteenth hole in golf is the club house!
36. churches	There are two temples and two churches in town.
37. southern	Looking towards the southern sky we saw a flashing light.
38. insist	Our parents insist we have cereal for breakfast.
39. league	The soldiers joined a league going to islands in the Pacific.
40. structure	The incomplete structure collapsed during the cyclone.

Notes

Notes

Notes